NUCLEAR-WEAPON-FREE ZONE

About the Author

P. Moorthy, an M.Sc. (Peace-Making) from Madurai Kamaraj University and Ph.D from Jawaharlal Nehru University, New Delhi, has been teaching arms control, national security, peace, disarmament, human resource management, conflict resolution and international relations in Pondicherry University since 1988.

Dr. Moorthy is also associated with National Movement for Counselling the Youth and Mission Develop India Network. He has published two books and edits a quarterly Knowledge Society Journal. He was selected as a visiting Peace Fellow of Shanti Peace Foundation, Coimbatore; and is now nominated as International Educator of the Year 2005 by International Biographical Centre, Cambridge, England.

Nuclear-Weapon-Free Zone

P. Moorthy
Director
Centre for Gandhian Studies, School for Social Science and International Studies, Pondicherry Central University, Pondicherry

CONCEPT PUBLISHING COMPANY, NEW DELHI-110059

Cataloging in Publication Data—DK
Courtesy: D.K. Agencies (P) Ltd. <docinfo@dkagencies.com>

Moorthy, P., 1956-
Nuclear-weapon-free zone / P. Moorthy.
p. cm.
Includes bibliographical references (p.)
Includes index.
ISBN 8180692795

1. Nuclear-weapon-free zones. I. Title.

DDC 327.174 22

ISBN 81-8069-279-5

First Published 2006

Published and Printed by
Ashok Kumar Mittal
Concept Publishing Company
A/15-16, Commercial Block, Mohan Garden
New Delhi-110059 (INDIA)

Phones : 25351460, 25351794
Fax : 091-11-25357103
Email : publishing@conceptpub.com

Preface

The United Nations (UN) has decided to commemorate the 60th anniversary of 'Hiroshima day' in a fitting manner throughout the year 2005. Twenty million people of Japan fell victim to the American atomic bomb, code named 'little boy' on 6 August, 1945 followed by yet another bomb, named 'fat man' on Nagasaki on 9 August killing a few millions more. The human holocaust unprecedented in the history of warfare has been since then commemorated every year. The year 2005, being the 'International Year of Physics', is unique as the scientific community could explore applying of nuclear technology for peace, prosperity and human development by appropriate innovation in fission and fusion technology. However, there are 27,000 nuclear weapons in the stockpile of the nuclear weapon countries today. Most of these weapons are deployed by the United States (US) and Russia at the sea and land. The US has deployed in 1994 a military system, which can use nuclear weapons from the space. Such military plan of the US is known as 'Star Wars'. The European countries have their own space programme called 'Eureka'. Russia is not far behind in this plan, which had the first breakthrough in space technology by sending a rocket named Sputnik in 1957. As a result, the whole universe is encircled by the nuclear weapons. The efforts for stopping these nuclear forces by the UN along with the support of the developing countries have been thwarted time and again by the nuclear weapon countries since 1945. Instead, the nuclear weapon countries have been proposing various arms control measures.

Sixty years ago, immediately after using atom bomb on Hiroshima and Nagasaki on 6 and 9 August, 1945, the US representative, Baruch had proposed a plan to regulate the nuclear arms through an international mechanism under the umbrella of the International Atomic Energy Agency (IAEA). Russia had opposed the American initiative and her representative, Gromyko proposed a yet another arms control plan for curtailing the nuclear tests and for destroying all the existing nuclear weapons. The US did not agree to it. In consequence, Russia had exploded its nuclear device on 29 August, 1949. After the Soviet test, the United Kingdom (UK) exploded its nuclear device on 3 October, 1952.

Therefore, the question of nuclear test had become an important agenda in the UN. The developing countries had protested against continuous nuclear tests by requesting the UN to formulate an arms control mechanism that would curtail the nuclear test itself. Even after the request of the UN, the US, Russia and UK went ahead with their test plans claiming that such tests were needed for promoting science and technology for human prosperity. In this connection, the US had declared its 'atom for peace' plan in 1953. Not satisfied with the American plan that had aimed at spreading nuclear technology to like minded countries in the world; the developing countries had forced the UN to take strong measures for stopping such initiatives of nuclear weapon countries, especially the US. In 1959, the UN could succeed to certain extent in pursuing the nuclear weapon countries for signing an agreement for controlling their atmospheric tests.

As a result, for the first time in the history of nuclear arms control, the Antarctica Treaty was signed by them for keeping Antarctica free from nuclear tests. However, such initiative of the UN had set back as France had exploded its device on 3 December, 1960. Followed by France, China—one of the developing countries pleading for strong arms control measure in the UN, had also exploded its atomic device on 16 October, 1964. Continuing its arms control effort, the UN had introduced general guidelines for signing up regional as well as international arms control agreements in 1965 and requested all the countries to abide by it with the sole aim of contributing to general and complete Disarmament. India had played an important role for such an initiative in the UN. It should be mentioned that India was one of the leading countries that had promoted the concept of general and complete Disarmament under the leadership of the then Prime Minister Jawaharlal Nehru. In fact, Nehru had initiated steps for Partial Test Ban Treaty (PTBT) in the early 1960s, which helped the world nations formulate the Comprehensive Test Ban Treaty (CTBT) latter. During that period, both the US and the former Soviet Union had deployed a variety of nuclear weapons in Europe with the objectives of strengthening their military alliances, North Atlantic Treaty Organization (NATO) and the Warsaw Pact respectively. Irrespective of the setback that the UN had faced with the burgeoning weapon systems of these countries, it could succeed once again to make them sign the Outer Space Treaty in 1967.

Based on the UN principles, the Latin American countries had reached an agreement in February 1967 to establish Nuclear-Weapon-Free Zone (NWFZ) in their region. Followed by it, an international Nuclear Non-proliferation Treaty (NPT) was signed in July 1968 that came into force in 1970. Many developing countries had signed the NPT expecting a genuine arms control initiatives from the nuclear weapon countries. Although Article VI of the NPT says that each of the parties to the treaty undertakes to pursue negotiations in "good faith on effective measures relating to cessation of the nuclear arms race at an early date", the nuclear weapon countries did not follow it. Instead of disarming them, as expected by the treaty, they had produced and deployed further a number of nuclear weapons. Moreover, they had also established various infrastructures for successful launch of their nuclear weapons in different regions of the world. Since 1970s, the US and former Soviet Union had been actively involved in the guise of 'second cold war' deploying modernized nuclear weapons not only in Europe but also in Middle East, South East Asia, Africa, Latin America and in Pacific as well as Indian Ocean.

The unabated arms race reached its peak in 1980s during the period when the US and the former Soviet Union had signed a treaty for curtailing forward based Intermediate Nuclear Forces (INF) deployed in Europe. From 1987—the year when the INF treaty was signed—to the year 1991 when the demise of Soviet Union took place giving way for the collapse of Berlin wall and the fading away of cold war, the American nuclear forces in the name of nuclear doctrines, called Mutual Assured Destruction (MAD) and Mutual Assured Survival (MAS) had been dominating over the economically weak and politically inconstant Soviet nuclear forces in all aspects. Although such period of domination gave way for the 'economic globalization' of the present world under the guise of World Trade Organization

(WTO), it had spread nuclear technologies in a flexible way to many developing countries.

As a result, today more than fifty countries are connected with the nuclear war plans of the nuclear weapon countries directly. Indirectly, there are about hundred countries in the world linked with their 'war-games' based on the approaches of deterrence. For example, the US has established its links with South Africa, Israel and Pakistan and it has its nuclear infrastructures in developing countries like Guam, Philippines, South Korea etc. Russia has its nuclear connection with Cuba and certain Latin American countries. It is to be noted here that China acquired nuclear technology with the help of the former Soviet Union. Like the US and Russia, France and the UK involve many countries in their nuclear war plans. At present, the UK has proposed an ambitious plan for exploring into 'fusion technology' by inviting various expertise from world nations including India. In the case of China, Pakistan has become its strange supporter especially through the mutual exchange of human resources in the fields of both the nuclear as well as missile technology. Recently, it has also joined Australia to sign a nuclear agreement. Thus, all the nuclear weapon countries have been violating not only the global agreements but also the regional arms control treaties such as Antarctic, Outer Space, Seabed, Tlatelolco and Rarotonga. For instance, a technically well-equipped nuclear missile called MX (missile experimental) of the US can reach any part of the world in less than 20 minutes and destroy 140 well-developed cities like Tokyo, Washington, Moscow and London.

Moreover, there are also weapons such as air-launched cruise missiles (ALCMs) and submarine launched ballistic missiles (SLBMs) capable of reaching any target in the world. In addition, the US by virtue of implementation of its 1994 space programme, known as National Missile Defense (NMD) and Theatre Missile Defense (TMD) in order to defend their nation and their friendly countries in case of missile attack launched by any country, has become capable of hitting or blocking satellite-based communication systems of any nation in the world. There are about thirty countries in the world interested to develop such space technology similar to the US. According to Americans, the developing countries like North Korea may plan for hitting the

US by their missiles and therefore, it is essential to arm the outer space with effective nuclear forces.

Arms control at Sea is also having similar problems since the Sea is encircled by both the nuclear weapons and their infrastructures. Besides, huge amount of money is being spent on exploring into the new nuclear weapon systems by the nuclear weapon countries. For example, the US Department of Energy (DOE) has launched an extravagant nuclear missile programme with the help of supercomputer. Russia, Ukraine, Belarus and Kazakhstan are also planning to improve their nuclear weapon capability especially relating to the infrastructure to carry out effective war in this new millennium. The UK, France, China, India and Pakistan have been advancing their nuclear weapon systems including the thermonuclear fusion weapons, which are usually fuelled by the isotopes of hydrogen.

As of these reasons, nuclear weapons are posing greatest danger today to the entire world. Although they were the products of 1940s, still the world nations fascinate producing new types of weapons. Before dealing with the danger of nuclear weapons, some preliminary comments should be made in relation to the manufacture of nuclear weapons, as they are related with the nuclear-free zone concept. Generally weapons grade fissile material is the crucial ingredient for producing nuclear weapons. Production of plutonium-239 through neutron bombardment of uranium-238 in a reactor and enrichment of uranium to produce highly enriched uranium-235 (HEU) are the two most common methods of producing fissile material for bombs. (A third method is reactor irradiation of thorium to produce fissile uranium-233). Production of plutonium requires a reactor—a purpose-built reactor, a power reactor, or a research reactor—plus reprocessing facilities for extracting the plutonium from spent fuel. Reprocessing facilities can also be used to extract HEU or uranium-233 from irradiated material. Uranium enrichment facilities are generally complex and expensive. In nearly all countries pursuing nuclear weapons programmes, efforts have been made to domestically produce plutonium and to enrich uranium. It is also possible to acquire weapons-grade fissile material by gift, theft or purchase (including diversion of material acquired for civil purposes). In addition to fissile material, components such as high explosives, firing triggers and handling devices are also required. Developing these components requires considerable technical skill. Some delivery systems, such as aircraft modified for delivery of nuclear weapons, pose no great obstacle, but advanced missile systems are far more complex and expensive. Irrespective of their cost and the magnitude of danger in establishing them, these technologies are fast spreading among the developing countries.

The spread of such technologies is yet another problem chasing the world community today. Israel has clandestinely developed between fifty and hundred nuclear weapons, and acquired nuclear-capable ballistic missiles by the support of France and the US. Its nuclear weapons programme was launched in 1956, a year after the Chinese programme, which was started in 1957. Iran has been very seriously working for developing nuclear weapons since 1987. It is to be noted that in 1987, Iran's two research reactors were damaged by Iraqi air strikes. Since then, it has been reportedly involving in acquiring fabricated weapons for which it is faced with a lot of diplomatic hurdles including an American led war in the near future. Its programme has been supported by Russia, China and North Korea periodically. Iraq had obtained nuclear materials from former West Germany, Portugal, Nigeria, Brazil, Italy, France, Britain and Russia. The US had bombed the nuclear facilities of Iraq during the Gulf War in 1991 and it had also yet another war against Iraq in 2003 that changed the political map of the Middle East region in general and Iraq in particular. Libya's nuclear ambition is supported by China, former Soviet Union countries, France, India, and Pakistan. Algeria is pursuing its nuclear plan assisted by Argentina and China. Some more countries, which are ambitious in the region, if not weapon capability, are Egypt, Syria, and Saudi Arabia.

North Korea is another potential country that has been involving in the nuclear field for quite some time. Former Soviet Union and China have supported its nuclear programme. Although North Korea singed the NPT in 1985, it did not allow IAEA to inspect its nuclear facilities. Moreover, it has developed ICBM capability with the material support of Egypt and Iran. It is reported that North Korea has plan of selling long-range missiles to Iran and Libya. On the other hand, South Korea is supported by the US from the very beginning in this region in order to encounter the communist North Korea. Taiwan also has substantial nuclear weapon programme like South Korea. In Africa, South Africa is reported to have pursued nuclear weapons programme and abandoned it latter. Although South Africa has signed the NPT in 1991, it is involving in related nuclear activities. In fact, France had helped South Africa in the initial period.

In the case of Latin American region, Argentina had pursued a covert nuclear weapons programme for many years and therefore, refused to accede to the NPT. It also did not sign the Treaty for the Prohibition of Nuclear Weapons in Latin America in the beginning. Its nuclear programme was supported by Canada, West Germany, Switzerland and the Former Soviet Union. Brazil, a yet another potential country in the region, has pursued a covert nuclear weapons programme in response to Argentina's nuclear programme, which was supported by West Germany, France and the US. However, both Argentina and Brazil have ratified the Tlatelolco Treaty and agreed to IAEA inspections latter. In Europe, Romania, after ratifying the NPT in 1970, has covertly involved in producing nuclear weapons. Sweden and former Yugoslavia have registered their interest for developing nuclear technology by being very close to prominent nuclear states in this region. Apart from these countries, Australia, Austria, Belgium, Bulgaria, Canada, Chile, the Czech Republic, Denmark, Finland, Germany, Hungary, Indonesia, Ireland, Italy, Japan, Mexico, the Netherlands, Norway, Poland, Slovakia, Slovenia, and Spain are some of the countries in different regions of the world well connected in the nuclear war game of the nuclear weapon countries, which are also showing keen interest in the development of nuclear weapons. Due to the spread of nuclear technology, tensions prevail all over the world apart from spreading rumours and suspicions among nations.

Although there had been no war involving nuclear weapons since 1945, many conventional wars were fought due to suspicion. The American war against Iraq in 2003 may be noted as example in this case. All such wars had killed twenty seven million people. It is estimated that civilians represent eighty five per cent of the casualties, with a majority being children and the elderly. In the last decade alone, there occurred more than hundred wars in different regions of the world especially based on the religious differences. Fearing to religious conflicts, majority of the people seek political asylum in different countries. According to a recent report, more than four million people seek asylum every year in Europe due to fear of conflicts in their respective nations based on religious and ethnic differences. Since 1930s, during the period when the "exodus of scientists" took place from Europe to United States in which Albert Einstein was one of the leading members, the refugee problem has been very much bothering the world nations. In addition, the problem relating to the misuse of refugees by the recipient countries are yet another problem that questions the very credibility of scientists. In this context, Einstein had lamented immediately after listening to the news of American bombing on Hiroshima on 6 August, 1945 as follows: "Had I known what disaster the bomb could do, I would have chosen to be single shoemaker of Switzerland rather than play any part in its (atom bomb) creation".

With this backdrop, this book is written with the objective of reinforcing the human cause for freeing world from nuclear weapons and for facilitating the process of civilized human development in this 21st Century. For the purpose, it is divided into six chapters. The first chapter consists of three major sections, which deal with the general background of nuclear arms control, the concept and history of nuclear-free zones respectively. The second chapter focuses on the treaties of Antarctica, Outer Space, and Sea-bed. A comparative study of these proposals and a political analysis are also presented in this chapter. Latin America nuclear-free zone established by the Tlatelolco treaty is extensively analyzed in the third chapter and the fourth chapter is devoted for studying about the South Pacific nuclear-free zone established by the Rarotonga treaty. The fifth chapter extensively evaluates the political implications of nuclear-free zones and their connections.

The last chapter, being a conclusive one, evaluates the possibilities for attaining nuclear-free world based on non-violent approaches of Mahatma Gandhi.

Author

Acknowledgements

I express my gratitude to Prof. T.T. Poulose, former Chairman of the Centre for International Politics, Organizations and Disarmament (CIPOD), Jawaharlal Nehru University (JNU), who has supervised my Ph.D thesis on the basis of what the present book is developed. I am thankful to Professors George Rathjane, William Arkin, Alfonso Garcia Roble, Michael Mandelbaum, Leonard Spector, Stephen Flanagan, Aftab Kazi and Josef Nye for their help during my visit to the United States. I am also thankful to the Library staff members of Johns Hopkins University, Washington; Center for Defense Information, Washington; International Institute of Strategic Studies, London; Institute for Policy Studies, Washington DC; Centre for Defense Information, Washington DC; Arms Control Association, Washington DC; Carnegie Foundation for International Peace, Washington DC; Stanford University, Sans Francisco; Centre for Science and International Studies, Washington; Harvard University, Institute for Defense Studies and Analysis and Jawaharlal Nehru University, New Delhi.

My special thanks are due to my wife and kids who have helped me accomplish this task on time.

Author

Acknowledgement

Contents

1

Introduction

Since the dawn of nuclear age on 2 December, 1942 when Enrico Fermi made a chain reaction in a pile of uranium in the University of Chicago, the nations of the world have been utilizing nuclear energy for both destructive and constructive purposes. In fact, the history of nuclear energy began with the history of nuclear weapon test on 16 July, 1945 when the United States exploded the first nuclear bomb, code named 'Trinity' at Alamogordo, New Mexico. The former Soviet Union was the next country to explode a nuclear device on 29 August, 1949. After the Soviet test, other countries followed in the field were Britain on 3 October, 1952; France on 3 December, 1960; China on 16 October, 1964. In continuation of its exploration into the field of nuclear energy, the US had exploded a yet another thermonuclear bomb—code named 'Mike'—at Eniwetok Atoll in the Pacific on 1 November 1952, which was 500 times more powerful than the Trinity test. Similar tests were also conducted by the former Soviet Union on 22 November, 1955; the UK on 8 March, 1957; China on 17 June, 1967 and by France on 24 August, 1968.

Thus, thousands of nuclear test were conducted worldwide. It is estimated that the US had conducted more than thousand tests, Russia more than seven hundred, France more than two hundred, the UK and China more than forty respectively. With these experiences, the world nations have acquired thousands of nuclear weapons. At present there are 27,000 nuclear weapons in the stockpile of the nuclear weapon countries. Since 1945, there have also been various bilateral as well as multilateral initiatives to curb all these weapons of mass destruction (WMD). One of such multilateral initiatives includes the regional arms control treaty signed for establishing nuclear-free zones in various parts of the world. The following section attempts to explain the concept of nuclear-free zone.

The Concept

The concept of Nuclear-Weapon-Free Zone (NWFZ) is a distinct one, which means denuclearization, non-nuclearization and nuclear free. Denuclearization is applicable to the zone wherein nuclear weapons are already deployed. For example, Europe, Middle East and Asia can be noted. Non-nuclearization is applicable to the zone wherein no nuclear weapons are deployed or produced. Antarctica, Outer Space and Seabed may be cited as example in this case. Nuclear free means only the absence of nuclear weapons. Such treaty is established in the South Pacific region. Thus, the concept of the NWFZ is very flexible one. Therefore, the criterion to establish NWFZ depend upon the group of countries interested for establishing such zone in their respective regions. Accordingly, the objectives of the zone can also be different from that of any one established already. However, a general objective for establishing a zone in any part of the world should consider the following criterion:[1] the security of states included in the zone; world security; non-proliferation of nuclear weapons; regional arms control consideration; and security treaties.

The interested group of countries can select any one of the above objectives and formulate treaty for establishing NWFZ in their respective zone or region. In addition to the UN principles, the countries in the respective zone can also develop new criteria for the purpose. If countries in the respective zone identify reasons for establishing such zone, they can draft a treaty without any outside interference. Nevertheless, the treaty has to consider the followings:[2] definition of fundamental terms; obligation of the contracting nations; system of verification and control; the undertakings of nuclear weapon states; and the undertaking of states, which have territories in the proposed zone.

Therefore, the concept of NWFZ consists of all measures, which may assist nuclear disarmament in general. According to the UN expert group, a NWFZ treaty should respect in all its parts the status of complete absence of nuclear weapons as defined in the treaty or convention, which forms the constituent instrument of the zone. Moreover, it should refrain from contributing any act that would violate the treaty. In addition, the treaty, as noted by the expert group, should refrain from using nuclear weapons or threatening to use such weapons against the states, which comprise the zone. Finally, the expert groups recommend that the treaty should be signed and ratified by all nuclear-weapon-states.[3] If any one of these measures is not adopted, the zone may not serve the interest of achieving nuclear disarmament.

History

Even before the end of the Second World War, efforts were made to eliminate nuclear weapons on 26 June, 1945, when the UN Charter was signed by the fifty-two nations in the city of San Francisco, the United States (US). It was, however, disappointed on 6th and 9th of August, 1945 as the US used atomic bombs on the Japanese cities of Hiroshima and Nagasaki respectively. After these incidents, it had submitted a report known as Acheson-Lillienthal report in the UN, for utilizing the atomic technology for peaceful purposes and controlling all nuclear facilities of the world—ranging from uranium mines to research and production plants—under the umbrella of an International Atomic Energy Authority (IAEA). In support of this report, on 24 January, 1946, a resolution was adopted unanimously in the UN General Assembly for establishing Atomic Energy Commission (AEC) for ensuring the peaceful use of atomic energy.[4] In the AEC meeting of June 1946, the US representative, Bernard M. Baruch had presented a plan known as Baruch Plan for controlling all the atomic activities by a systematic inspection of the IAEA. It was opposed by the former Soviet Union, as the Soviet delegate, Andrei Gromyko, had proposed a counter plan to destroy all weapons in existence and to cease all production in the future. The US did not agree to it. As a result, the Soviet Union had exploded an atomic device on 29 August, 1949, just twenty-three days after the bombardment of Hiroshima.

Followed by the Soviet test, the United Kingdom had exploded its device in 1952, which forced the US propose in December 1953 an "Atom for Peace" plan in the UN emphasizing the rights of using nuclear energy for peaceful purposes. On contrast, in March 1954, three months after "Atom for Peace" proposal, the US itself had detonated a hydrogen bomb at Bikini Atoll in the Pacific Ocean. Consequently, the problem of controlling the nuclear tests was seriously being considered by the UN as it had requested the weapon powers to find out means for curbing the atomic tests immediately.[5] As of this reason, the big four—the US, the former Soviet Union, the United Kingdom, and France had met in Geneva summit conference in July 1955 wherein the US had proposed an "Open skies" proposal. According to this proposal, both the US and the Soviet Union should exchange blueprints of military installations. It was opposed by the Soviet Union by appealing the leaders of the conference to find out a solution for banning the nuclear weapon tests altogether and destroying the existing weapons as such.

As a result, the Geneva conference could not reach an agreement on test ban. In May 1957, the first hydrogen bomb was tested by the UK resulting in protests by many countries including India insisting the UN to act on preventing the 'big four' from testing their devices further. In support of the protests by the world nations and the appeal of the UN, the Soviet Union had proposed a three-year moratorium on tests in June 1957.[6] The US did not agree for moratorium and it had declared rather a programme known as 'Plowshare' for carrying out an underground test. As a result a new dimension to the problem was added up since detecting the underground tests were far more difficult than tests in the atmosphere. The Soviet Union had also complicated the disarmament process by reportedly developing missile-launching capability. On October 4, 1957, it had placed into orbits the first earth satellite, Sputnik-I and followed by it the Sputnik-II on 3 November in the same year. The Soviet Sputniks were considered by the US as a long-range missile that could attack a target even beyond Europe.[7] It should be noted here that, in 1948 itself the US deployed short-range missiles, Jupiter and Thor, in West Europe.

However, on 1 July, 1958, the conference of experts to study the possibility of detecting violations of an agreement on suspension of nuclear tests was convened in Geneva. Experts from the US, the UK, France, Canada and the former Soviet Union had attended the conference.[8] The conference was concluded on 21 August, 1958 pointing out that it was technically feasible to set up, with certain capabilities and limitations, a workable and effective control system for the detection of violations of a possible agreement on the worldwide cessation of nuclear weapon tests. This control system, known as "the Geneva system" provided a way for the first time in the history of controlling nuclear tests in the atmosphere. By that time, the US had completed fifty-four tests, eight of which were underground; the former Soviet Union had completed fourteen tests. On 22 June, 1959, the technical working group of the Geneva conference had considered the problem of detecting explosions at high altitudes and after a discussion, the conference had recommended for installing large satellites in an earth orbit at an altitude of over 18000 miles.[9]

As the big powers were agreed upon a system to be followed for controlling the atmospheric tests, the UN, on the other hand, had proposed a system to be followed for controlling the weapons as such. Therefore, in 1959, it had requested the big powers to consider Antarctica as a common heritage of the world, a place wherein military installations including nuclear weapons and nuclear tests should be prevented. On 1 December, 1959, the Antarctic Treaty was signed. It is the first multilateral treaty, which established nuclear-weapon-free zone in uninhabited area of the world.[10] It should be noted here that in contrast to the UN effort France had carried out its nuclear tests in 1960. However, succeeding in its effort, the UN had introduced the concept of non-proliferation in its resolution in 1961 in order to establish a system for controlling the nuclear tests, both military and civil. After long debates over the concept of non-proliferation, it had formulated in 1965 a set of principles, which had provided freedom to the countries interested for signing up arms control treaty in their respective regions. They are:[11]

- The Treaty should be void of any loophole which might permit nuclear or non-nuclear powers to proliferate, directly or indirectly, nuclear weapons in any form;
- The Treaty should embody an acceptable balance of mutual responsibilities and obligations of the nuclear and non-nuclear powers;

- The Treaty should be a step towards the achievement of general and complete disarmament and more particularly, nuclear disarmament;
- There should be acceptable and workable provisions to ensure the effectiveness of the Treaty;
- Nothing in the Treaty should adversely affect the right of any group of states to conclude regional treaties in order to ensure the total absence of nuclear weapons in their respective territories.

Based on these principles, in January 1967, the Outer Space Treaty was signed by a multilateral treaty arrangement. In the same year, Latin American countries had reached an agreement for establishing NWFZ in their region through a regional treaty arrangement. It is the first NWFZ established in an inhabited area of the world. Followed by this in 1971 the Seabed Treaty was signed and in 1986 the South Pacific NWFZ was established through a regional treaty arrangement by the South Pacific countries.[12]

Central Europe

The first initiative for establishing NWFZ in Central Europe had come from the former Soviet Union on 27 March, 1956, when a plan for creating a zone in Central Europe was proposed by Andrei Gromyko in the UN. According to the plan, the zone in Europe would consist of East and West Germany as well as some of the neighbouring countries. With reference to it, in 1957, Adam Rapacki, the then Foreign Minister of Poland, had put forward a plan for NWFZ in Central Europe that considered the following obligations:[13]

- No nuclear weapon would be manufactured, stock piled, or installed on the territory of Poland, Czechoslovakia, and East and West Germany;
- The use of nuclear weapons against these countries would be banned;
- The United States, the Soviet Union, the United Kingdom, and France would undertake the nuclear free status of the zone;

- A system of ground and air control with inspection bases would be set up to verify the observance of the commitments undertaken;
- The zone could be established by binding unilateral declarations in order to avoid any complications in negotiating a formal treaty.

It was rejected by the US on the ground that the creation of the NWFZ in Central Europe would involve the withdrawal of Western nuclear bases and would thus give some military and political advantages to the East. Further, it argued that major countries in the area of such zone should not upset the existing military balance. More importantly, according to US, the NWFZ should be subject to verification, and it should be established only in a balanced region, where there was no direct involvement of the US and the Soviet Union. As of these reasons, Rapacki had submitted a revised plan, which aimed at freezing the nuclear armaments in the first stage and reducing conventional forces in the second stage.[14] West European countries did not accept arguing that it would jeopardize the political interest of the West. However, in 1962, a third version of Rapacki plan was submitted. It was also to be implemented in two stages: freezing nuclear weapons and rockets and prohibiting the establishment of new bases in the area of the zone; in the second eliminating the armed forces and conventional forces. It was opposed by the West European countries on the ground that it would allow the conventional superiority of the former Soviet Union in Europe.[15]

In 1964, Poland Prime Minister, Gomulka, had put forward a new proposal known as the "Gomulka Plan" that was approved by the British Labour Party. According to it, all nuclear weapons, irrespective of the means of their employment and delivery should be frozen. It should be noted that the Gomulka Plan did not find any solution for the reduction of existing nuclear arms. On the other hand, a ban on any increase in their number was recommended by it. Although it was opposed by the West, in the mid 1970s, they themselves had found an alternative political step for establishing NWFZ in Europe. As a result, the NATO countries, excluding United States and Canada, had come to an understanding in the beginning of 1980s on the following principles:[16]

- A formal renunciation of the first use of nuclear weapons should be immediately signed with the Warsaw Pact countries;
- Simultaneously, an agreement should be negotiated to prohibit short-range, 'battlefield' nuclear weapons from a zone. According to the principles, the zone should be extended further to the northern and southern flanks of the central front. Finally, as noted, establishment of a European nuclear-free zone should follow this from Poland to Portugal.

On the basis of these principles, the report of the independent commission on Disarmament and Security issues under the Chairmanship of Olof Palme had suggested a Battlefield-Nuclear-Weapon-Free Zone (BNWFZ) in Europe covering from Central Europe to the northern and the southern flanks of the two alliances. BNWFZ had to cover the following type of weapons:[17] ADMs (atomic demolition mines); Nuclear artillery, ranging up to 100 kms; Lance (NATO); Pluton (France); SS-21 (WTO); and Hades (France) ranging from 300 to 1000 kms. Unfortunately, the Intermediate Nuclear Forces (INF) treaty signed by the US and the Soviet Union in 1987 did not support the ideas of BNWFZ, as the INF had only covered the nuclear missiles ranging from 500 to 5000 kms. It is to be mentioned that ADM, nuclear artillery, the missiles having the range of 100 kms, Lance (NATO), SS-21 (WTO), Scud and A (WTO), Scud and B (WTO), the missiles having the range of 200 to 300 kms and some of the corps support weapon system were not included in the INF treaty. Further, the proposal for NWFZ in Central Europe had faced yet another problem since 'Cheeky Sparrow' agreement for developing a European deterrence was signed up by West Germany and France.[18]

According to Cheeky Sparrow, the independent nuclear forces would serve the purpose of counterbalancing the conventional superiority of Warsaw Pact countries. In addition, Cheeky Sparrow would give France the right of developing nuclear missiles for the forward defense of Europe in order to fill the strategic gap after the withdrawal of US nuclear missiles from Europe. It should be noted that the withdrawal of American INF missiles, the Pershing-II in particular, would leave West Germany without a nuclear deterrent that could strike Soviet territory. Therefore, Cheeky Sparrow had allowed Germany maintain

French nuclear forces, as the conventional weapons especially to counter the Soviets tanks were thought to be too costly. France was thus planning to deploy its S-4 missile in the late 1990s.

Although there was political pressure because of the increasing public opinion against the Cheeky Sparrow in general and S-4 in particular, West Germany was going ahead. If the Cheeky Sparrow had been succeeded in West Germany, there would have been many European NATO members interested to have the European forward defense. For, the seven countries' agreement to jointly produce MSOW (Medium standoff weapons) could have paved the way for converting MSOW, the conventional missiles into nuclear missiles. Moreover, a number of nuclear infrastructures were with West Germany as well as with East European countries during that period.[19] Because of these reasons, the proposal for establishing NWFZ in Central Europe could not be put into practice. After the unification, countries in the region have not been seriously considering the concept of nuclear-free zone.

Northern Europe

The interest for establishing NWFZ in Northern Europe consisting of Scandinavian Peninsula and the Baltic area was first expressed by the former Soviet Union in the late 1950s. However, in 1963, Finland had initiated by submitting a detailed draft proposal for NWFZ in Northern Europe. According to it, Norway, Sweden, Denmark and Finland should be included in the zone. Since then, all Nordic States had been negotiating themselves and together with the nuclear weapon countries for arms regulation in the region. Nonetheless, a clear-cut line of opposition was drawn in 1978 when majority of the countries in this region and France had opposed the idea of Finland. The opposition to the zone proposal had come in the form of active defense preparedness by Sweden.[20] As of the reason, the proponent of the zone, Finland itself had started accumulating various military infrastructures. The air defense and surveillance capabilities were, therefore, increased in this region. Both Sweden and Finland were arguing that NATO missiles could be used over neutral countries in case of war and therefore, their capabilities were necessary.[21] Consequently, on December 23, 1987 the US had rejected the idea of NWFZ and campaigned against it among respective countries advocating that such concept would undermine the type of unity with the Atlantic alliance. Thus, the NWFZ proposal for Northern Europe could not be implemented.

The Balkans

In September 1957, a 'Peace Zone' proposal was put forward by the Romanian Prime Minister that included Bulgaria, Romania, Yugoslavia, Albania, Greece and Turkey.[22] The former Soviet Union had supported Romanian initiative and called for negotiations among NATO (North Atlantic Treaty Organisation) and the Warsaw Pact countries in order to cut off new missile deployments and to scrap the proposals of deploying multilateral forces as well as modernization of already existing forces in this region. It was rejected by the United States on the ground that cutting down these forces would lead for Soviet domination in the region. However, in 1979, the proposal for a Balkan NWFZ was seriously being considered since the NATO had planned to deploy cruise and Pershing-II missiles in Europe. Especially Romania and Bulgaria were vehemently opposed to the NATO's plan and requested other nations to consider the proposal for Balkan NWFZ seriously. In October 1981, State Council President of Bulgaria, Zhukov, had emphasized:[23] "We warmly support the idea of turning the Balkans into a nuclear free zone. We propose that a meeting of the leaders of the Balkan states be held as early as next year to discuss this problem. The turning of the Balkans into a nuclear free zone would correspond to the interests of our people. It would be a substantial contribution to the improvement of the international climate, to the gradual transformation of Europe into a continent free of nuclear arms; it would be one more victory for peace."

Followed by the support of Bulgaria, Greece had expressed its interest for establishing nuclear-free Europe. It should be noted that in 1981 election, the only issue was that of removing nuclear weapons from Greece and it was the only country to vote in the UN General Assembly in November 1982 for a Mexican-Swedish resolution calling for an immediate global arms freeze. It has to be mentioned that the effort to denuclearize the Scandinavian Peninsula was made in order to strengthen the Balkan NWFZ. More importantly, Greece had joined with Argentina, India, Mexico, Sweden and Tanzania on 22 May, 1984 for calling on nuclear weapon states to halt all nuclear testing, production and deployment so as to enhance the security of the world. The 1984 initiative was popularly known as the 'Declaration of the Six'.[24]

The US was not comfortable with these new plans including the six nation's initiative, as they would, according to it, disregard the American nuclear forces in Heraklion base in Greece and the joint-installation agreement signed with Turkey in 1980 that recognized the presence of the US in this region for the cause of defending Europe. Secondly, the US alleged that the military doctrine of 'flexible response' must retain the military forces installed in Greece, Turkey, Romania, Bulgaria, and Yugoslavia. It is important to note here that in Greece the US had deployed the following forces: F-4 fighter-bomber, F-100G fighter-bomber, 155mm howitzer, Honest John (surface to surface); in Turkey, F-4, F-104s, 155 mm howitzer, 8 inches howitzer, Honest John, and Nike-Hercules. The US also had deployed the forces like Frog SSM, SSM 155 mm howitzer and Frog-7 in Romania and Yugoslavia. However, the INF treaty signed in 1987 had cut off all the forces ranging between 500 and 5000 kms.[25] Thus, conducive atmosphere for establishing NWFZ in Balkan was achieved in the early 1990s. Due to the change of world politics after the fall of Berlin wall and the demise of the former Soviet Union, the idea of NWFZ in this part of the world is not gaining ground these days.

Africa

The idea for establishing NWFZ in Africa was expressed by eight African countries in 1961 just one year after France had carried out nuclear test in the Sahara Desert in 1960. Fourteen African countries in the UN had formally joined in the UN and put forward a proposal that led for passing a resolution for a "denuclearized zone" in Africa approved by the General Assembly.[26] It had called upon all African states not to carry out nuclear tests in any form in Africa; to refrain from using Africa for storing or transporting nuclear weapons; and to respect the continent as a NWFZ. Therefore, in 1965, twenty-eight African states were gathered together in the UN in proposing further a detailed plan in this respect, which was supported by the former Soviet Union and criticized by France. The UN General Assembly had requested all nations to respect the continent of Africa as a NWFZ; to abide by the declaration; and not to use or threaten to use nuclear weapons in Africa or take, any action, which would compel African states to acquire such weapons. It had also requested all the nuclear states to refrain from transferring nuclear weapons or technological assistance to any state in the region of Africa.[27]

However, the reported preparation of South Africa to explode a nuclear device had added a new dimension to the proposal of African NWFZ in 1970s and forced the UN appoint a panel of experts to examine the issue of African nuclear weapon programme. According to the UN study submitted on August 9, 1977, Africa was preparing for carrying out nuclear weapon test that was photographed by the US reconnaissance satellites passing over the Kalahari Desert in South Africa.[28] It noted further that the United States Government had an indication suggesting the possibility of a low yield nuclear explosion occurred on September 22 in the area of the Indian Ocean and South Atlantic including portions of the Antarctic continent and the southern part of Africa. Thus, it was concluded that there was a light signal recorded by the American VELA satellite on September 22, 1979.

After clarifying the issues related with the reported South African nuclear test, the UN in 1981 had approved a resolutions calling upon all States of Africa, "To consider and respect the continent of Africa as a nuclear-weapon free zone".[29] On December 1982, yet another resolution was adopted by the UN General Assembly, which expressed "concern that South Africa's continued pursuit of a nuclear weapon capability seriously jeopardizes Africa and poses a grave danger not only to security of African States but also to international peace and security".[30] The proposal for establishing African NWFZ could not be positively pursued since South Africa was very much interested in pursuing nuclear path. The change of regime in South Africa in the 1990s and the overall developments in the region after the formation of new world under the guises of World Trade Organization, however, do not permit the concept go too far to achieve the objective so far effectively.

Mediterranean

The proposal for establishing NWFZ in Mediterranean was submitted by the former Soviet Union in 1963. It was considered up by the Eight Nations Disarmament Committee (ENDC) on 27 May, 1963 to study further about the possibility of establishing such zone in this region.[31] According to this proposal, Egypt, Lebanon, Algeria, Tunisia, Jordan and Syria were to be included in the zone. Warsaw Pact countries were interested in this proposal by assuring to eliminate nuclear weapons from the Mediterranean. Whereas Italy and France were opposed to the proposal arguing that it could not be separated from European security as a whole and therefore, the UN should consider the European zone first rather than the Mediterranean. It should be noted that the Mediterranean Sea connects three continents: Europe, Asia and Africa, and waterways from Atlantic to Black Sea and from Pacific Ocean to Indian Ocean. In connection with this proposal, in 1981 the former Soviet Union had requested the UN to conclude an international agreement on the following points:[32]

- Extension of the internationally tested and justified confidence measures;
- Agreed reduction of armed forces in this region;
- Withdrawal of nuclear weapons carrying ships from the Mediterranean sea;
- Non-deployment of nuclear weapons on the territory of non-nuclear Mediterranean countries;
- Non-use of nuclear weapons by the nuclear powers against Mediterranean countries, which do not deploy such weapons.

Based on the Soviet interest, a resolution entitled strengthening of security and cooperation in Mediterranean region was passed and adopted by the UN General Assembly unanimously. Although all countries in the region were in support of the proposal, the peaceful nuclear programme pursued by Egypt did not create an atmosphere of co-operation for this task.[33] It has to be noted that both the former Soviet Union and the US had supported Egypt for its peaceful nuclear programme since it was party to NPT since 1981. In the same year the US had signed with Egypt a nuclear co-operation agreement and helped establish two nuclear power plants. Egypt was also collaborating with Libya in nuclear field as it was reported that Abdul Jallond,

Vice-Chairman of the Revolutionary Command Council of Libya had gone along with Egyptian assistant to China for obtaining atomic weapons. Although it was denied by Egypt first, it was accepted, as noted by the report, that it had assistance in the field of nuclear research. Argentina was also reportedly co-operated with Egypt in E1 Dabaa nuclear power plant project in 1984. Because of these developments, by 1987 Egypt was in possession of three E-25 Hawkeye early warning aircrafts of the US which could also deliver nuclear weapons.[34]

Moreover, the activities of the neighbouring countries of Mediterranean especially Spain and Italy were also not encouraging the establishment of NWFZ in the region. For example, both Spain and Italy had obtained French Boeing E-3 AWACS aircrafts, which could be used in Mediterranean region. French Defense Minister, Andre Girard had pointed out that a possible threat from the Mediterranean zone could not be ruled out in the future. According to him, to counter such threat it was necessary to keep the French AWACS. Thus the Mediterranean zone was deliberately involved with the nuclear NATO by the big powers. However, in support of the zone proposal, on 17 March 1988, the former Soviet Union had proposed a freeze on US and Soviet warships. This was the first step towards a US-Soviet agreement to withdraw all their naval forces, including nuclear forces from the Mediterranean.[35] It should be realized that the US sixth fleet, with an average of about fifty ships, was permanently stationed in Mediterranean. Similarly, the former Soviet Union had stationed more than forty warships in the area. As of these reasons, Mediterranean countries could not achieve the goal of establishing NWFZ. Because of the present developments from the early 1990s to the recent years of American attacks on neighbouring countries like Afghanistan and Iraq in the early 2000s, the free zone idea is not being too attractive to many countries of this region.

Indian Ocean as a Zone of Peace

On 8 October, 1964, Sri Lanka had come out with the idea of establishing Peace Zone in the Indian Ocean at the second conference of Non-aligned Nations (NAN) held in Cairo. It was promoted in the third conference held in Lusaka in September 1970 as the conference had adopted a resolution calling upon all states:[36] "To consider and respect the Indian Ocean as a zone of peace from which great power rivalries and competition as well as bases conceived in the context of such rivalries and competition either army, navy or air force bases—are excluded. The area should also be free of nuclear weapons."

At the Commonwealth conference of 1971 in Singapore, Sri Lanka had once again proposed that the Indian Ocean be converted into a peace and a nuclear-free zone by submitting a memorandum, which opposed the presence of the Soviet and the American forces in the Indian Ocean region. It had also called upon a committee to be formed in order to study the implications of its proposal with special reference to the practical measures for achieving the objectives of the December 1971 declaration. As a result, both the US and the former Soviet Union had initiated bilateral talks in 1977 to pursue possible limitations on their military activities in the Indian Ocean area and the number of *ad hoc* committee members was increased up to forty-eight by 1984. In the year 1977, the Littoral and Hinterland States, the big powers and the major maritime users of the Indian Ocean were attending a meeting in New York that had proposed to place responsibility on the *ad hoc* committee on the Indian Ocean to undertake the preparatory work towards the objective of setting up appropriate arrangements for any international agreement that might ultimately be reached. But the *ad hoc* committee was unable to complete the preparatory work for the conference.

As of these reasons, the US, the former Soviet Union, the United Kingdom and France had activated their nuclear submarines' movements carrying more than 2000 nuclear warheads in the Indian Ocean area, especially in the northwestern Indian Ocean. These nations had also installed many supporting facilities, positioning of stocks, contingency arrangements, and sustainability for peacetime deployment at sea. The US had established such facilities in Australia, Diego Garciá, Oman and Seychelles whereas the former Soviet Union had done the same in Vietnam, South Yemen and Ethiopia. France had also established its facilities in Djibouti and Reunion of the Indian Ocean countries.[37] These countries had also motivated their supporters in this region. For example, the US had its supporting nations in the Ocean area such as Pakistan, Sri Lanka, the Comoro Islands, Maldives and Bangladesh (Chittagong) which had strategic aircrafts, B-52 stationed in Diego Garcia and Masira apart from its periodically modernized facilities dispersed in Somali (Barbara, Mogadishu and Hargeisa), Kenya (Mombassa), Saudi Arabia (Dhahran), Oman (Markaz-Thamarit) and the Bahrain (Manama). Moreover, the US has at present Rapid Deployment Forces (RDF), which is at operation in the western part of the Indian Ocean. It is to be mentioned that the Marine Corp's air-ground task force of the American component of RDF is equipped with nuclear capable F/A-18 Hornet and AV-8B Harrier V/STOL fighters. As of these reasons, Indian Ocean peace zone is not achieved till date. The recent developments in the zone especially in reference to both India and Pakistan are very disruptive as they had developed nuclear weapons through their respective nuclear tests carried out in 1998. The proceeding section is concerned with NWFZ proposal for South Asia.

South Asia

In the tenth Annual Session of the UN Atomic Energy Conference held in Mexico in September 1972, Pakistan had put forward a proposal for establishing nuclear-weapon-free zone in South Asia. It was reaffirmed by President Bhutto, as he expressed in the inaugural meeting of the Karachi Nuclear Power Plant (KANUPP), on 23 November, 1972:[38] "We would welcome if the entire subcontinent by the agreement of the countries concerned could be declared a nuclear-weapon-free zone and the introduction of nuclear weapons banned." It was in 1974 when India carried out an underground explosion, Pakistan had submitted in the 29th session of the UN General Assembly convened on 28 October, 1974 to consider its resolution, which sought to endorse in principle the concept of a nuclear weapon free zone in South Asia. India had expressed its view on Pakistani proposal by noting the following points:[39]

- Pakistan did not consult India before bringing the question to the UN;
- South Asia is a part of Asia and therefore NWFZ is not feasible;

- As South Asia is surrounded by nuclear weapon states, and the Pacific Ocean wherein nuclear forces of the nuclear states are patrolling it is not practical one;
- India will not accept any imposition from outside countries to change its nuclear policy;
- India's nuclear programme is only for peaceful purposes and not for weapon production.

The former Soviet Union did not vote for Pakistani resolution stating that the adoption of a substantive decision by the General Assembly on the question should be preceded by a common understanding among the states that may participate in the establishment of such a zone. However, it had voted for Indian resolution. The United States did not support either of these resolutions. China had voted for the Pakistani resolution. France and the UK were abstained from voting. Since 1974, the Pakistani resolution had been reaffirmed in the similar pattern in every year. In 1987, Bangladesh had joined Pakistan in support of NWFZ in South Asia, and both of them together sponsored a resolution in the UN to this effect. Bhutan and Mauritius were in support of the Indian position against the proposal. However, the UN General Assembly had approved the resolution sponsored by Pakistan and Bangladesh in November 1987, which received the support of 144 countries, with 36 abstaining. The abstaining states were the former Soviet Union, Yugoslavia, Brazil, Indonesia, Argentina and France. The resolution had appealed the UN General Assembly to promote consultations among the states "with a view to exploring the best possibilities of furthering the effort for the establishment of such a zone."[40] However, it is important to note some of the activities of the proponent of the zone, Pakistan and the opponent of the proposal, India, which are directly hitting the very idea of establishing such zone in South Asia.

Pakistan's nuclear programme was initiated by setting up Pakistan Atomic Energy Commission (PAEC) under the Chairmanship of Dr. Nazir Ahmed in the mid 1950s. PAEC had established its first nuclear research facility at Nilore, near Rawalpindi in 1965. The Institute of Science and Technology (PINSTECH) had provided research and technicians to this institute. The first research reactor—PARR, was supplied by the

US in the same year. Since then, it has been developing nuclear technology including power reactors (Kanup), uranium resources/active mining sites/uranium mills, uranium conversion facilities, heavy water, enrichment facility, uranium purification facility, fuel fabrication facility, reprocessing facility, and research reactor (PARR). The uranium enrichment plants at Kahuta (32kms. southeast of the capital) and at Golra (9 kms west of Islamabad) were also established by Pakistan. Apart from these facilities, Pakistan has select combat aircraft able to deliver nuclear bomb, F-16 Falcon, Mirage 5 PA3, Q-5 Fantan A and Mirage 3EP. More importantly, it had tested its nuclear device in 1998 and had developed substantial numbers of nuclear weapons.[41]

India's nuclear programme was started in the mid-1940s, as the Indian Institute of Science and the Tata Institute for Fundamental Research were the two major institutes that were involved in training scientists and engineers during that time. From 1956 to 1966, India had set-up and operated research as well as power reactors. As of these reasons, the research reactor, Apsara was obtained by India during that period and Atomic Energy Commission was established. Since then, India has been concentrating on various aspects of nuclear technology. As a result, today, India has power reactors, uranium resources, uranium purification facility, heavy water, fuel fabrication facility, reprocessing facility, and research reactors. Also, it has selected combat aircraft able to deliver nuclear bombs.[42] Of all these activities, the recent nuclear tests conducted in the year of 1998 by India, the known advocate for peace in the world, have brought in the end of NWFZ in South Asia.

Middle East

In 1974, Iran had requested the UN to consider the question of establishing a denuclearized zone in the Middle East. Egypt subsequently had co-sponsored the request. Most of the states in the region supported the initiative of Iran. Therefore, on 9 December, 1974, the UN General Assembly had adopted a resolution recommending the idea of establishing a NWFZ in the Middle East and requested all the countries in the region to refrain from producing, testing, obtaining and acquiring or in any other way possessing nuclear weapons. As Israel did not respond to this call, many countries in the region were doubtful about Israel's activities in the nuclear field requesting the UN General Assembly in 1979 to undertake a study on the issue. After the formal study completed on Israel activities, the Committee had submitted its report titled 'Israeli Nuclear Armament' in 1981, which concluded that:[43] "There was widespread agreement among technical experts, that given Israel's nuclear activities and level of expertise, it was capable of manufacturing nuclear explosive devices and possessed the means of delivery of such weapons to target in the area."

As a matter of fact in 1987 Israel had test fired its intermediate range nuclear missile, Jericho-II. By the help of the US it had also developed warhead and guidance system for Jericho-II, which was tested in Mediterranean near Crete and deployed in the Golan Heights. It should be noted that Jericho-II that has the range of 1500 kms. would reach most Arab capitals. Moreover, Iran and Iraq had been concentrating on nuclear technology since the late 1970s. As of now, they have missiles which could reach different countries in this region. Besides, the very challenge posed to the NWFZ in this region had come from the US Rapid Deployment Forces (RDF) installed in and around Middle East region.[44] Its recent involvement in the region, especially warring against terrorism and Weapons of Mass Destruction (WMD) that led to the ruin of Afghanistan and Iraq, it is unpredictable as to how the nuclear-free idea would be considered by the countries of the region in future. The following chapter focuses on Antarctica, Outer Space and Sea-Bed.

NOTES AND REFERENCES

1. Alfonso Garcia Robles who is known as the father of nuclear-free-zone had explained the meaning of the term, absence in 1968: give "I take the word absence from the definition which in November 1964, was incorporated in the first resolution adopted by the Preliminary Meeting on the Denuclearization of Latin America. Absence is a conception of lucid clarity, which does not land itself to false or subtle interpretations and can mean nothing else but non-existence in perpetuity of nuclear weapons in the territories of the contracting parties, whatever state may have such

weapons under its domain." See *Disarmament Commission's Official Records*, Supplement for January to December 1968, p. 49.

2. See the UN Special Report of the Conference of the Committee on Disarmament, *Comprehensive Study on the Question of Nuclear-Weapon-Free-Zone in all its Aspects* (New York: United Nations, 1976), pp. 31-35.
3. *Ibid.*
4. *United States Department of States' Documents on Disarmament*, Vol. II, 1957-58. Washington DC: US Printing Office 1960), pp. 1020-1023.
5. *United Nations General Assembly Official Records*, Eighth Session, 470th Plenary Meeting, 8 December, 1953, p. 450.
6. See for a detailed study on nuclear test ban, Glennt Seaborg, *Kennedy, Khrushchev and the Test Ban* (Berkeley: University of California Press, 1981), pp. 1-25.
7. See M.A. Ahmed, *The Neutrals and the Test Ban Negotiations* (New York, 1967), p. 8.
8. See Earl H. Voss, *Nuclear Ambush: The Test Bann Trap* (Chicago: Regency Company, 1963), p. 324.
9. See Glenn Seaborg, *Kennedy, Khrushchev and the Test Ban*, n. 6, pp. 12-13.
10. *Ibid.*, for more details in this respect, See T.T. Poulose, *United Nations and Nuclear Proliferation* (New Delhi, B.R. Publishing Corporation, 1988), pp. 25-49.
11. *Eight Nations Disarmament Conference* (ENDC) Official Records 1965, A 152, 192 and 193.
12. *Ibid.*
13. *Disarmament Commission, Official Records*, Supplement, January to December 1956, Document DC/83, Annex 5(DC/SC.1/410) pp. 41 and 178.
14. *Ibid.*
15. See M. Saeter, "Nuclear Disengagement Efforts 1955-80: Politics of *Status quo* or Political Change?" in S. Lodgard and Mark Thee, (ed.), *Nuclear Disengagement in Europe* (London: Taylor and Francis, 1983), pp. 58-60.
16. See Gwen Prins, *Defended to Death* (New York: Penguin Books, 1983), pp. 265-66.
17. The Report of the Independent Commission on Disarmament and Security Issues, *Common Security: A Programme for Disarmament* (London: Pan Books, 1982), p.147.
18. *Indian Express* (New Delhi), 20 January, 1988.
19. *Ibid.*
20. *Official Records of General Assembly*, Twenty-Ninth Session, Document A/8706, pp. 27-28.

21. *Jane's Defense Weekly* (London), December 13, 1987 and see also *International Herald Tribune* (Paris), 14 December, 1987.
22. *Comprehensive Study of the Question of NWFZ in all its Aspects*, No. 10, Para 52, 53 and 54, and see also Gregory Treverton, "*Nuclear Weapons in Europe*", Adelphi Papers, No. 168 London: Institute for International Strategic Studies (IISS), 1981, pp. 2-30.
23. T. Zhivkov, "Speech delivered at the Ceremonial Meeting Dedicated to the 1300th Anniversary of the Foundation of the Bulgarian State", *Sofia Press Agency Release* (Sofia), 20 October 1981, p. 27.
24. *Atlantic News* (Bonn), Vol. 16, No.1465, 5 November, 1982, p. 4 and see *The Times of India* (New Delhi), 23 May, 1984.
25. *The Economist* (London), 9 February 1985: also *The New York Times*, 23 May,1984; See "30000 U.S. Nuclear Weapons", *Defense Monitor*, February 1975; also, *U.S. Congress Congressional Budget Office*, "Planning U.S. General Purpose Forces: The Theatre Nuclear Forces", January 1977, pp. 176-78 and See also the Stockholm *International Peace Research Institute (SIPRI)* year book, 1984 World Armament and Disarmaments (London: Taylor and Francis, 1984), pp. 27-32.
26. *Official Records of the General Assembly*, Fifteenth Session, Annexes, agenda items 67, 68, 69 and 73, Document A/4680, Para 17.
27. *Disarmament Study Series* 2, South Africa's Plan and Capability in the Nuclear Field (New York: United Nations, 1981), pp. 29-30.
28. *Ibid.*
29. *Ibid.*
30. Cited in T.T. Poulose, *United Nations and Nuclear Proliferation*, n.10, p. 87. For more Detail, Leonard S. Spector, *The New Nuclear Nations* (New York: Vintage Books, 1985), pp. 226-28.
31. *Official Records of the Disarmament Commission*, Supplement for January to December 1963, document, Washington D.C., U.S. Government Printing Office, pp. 242-43.
32. *UN Disarmament Periodic Review* (New York), Vol. VIII, No. 3, Winter 1985, pp. 90-93.
33. See "The Trial to Crazy Island", *Wall Street Journal* (New York), March 1984.
34. Joseph V.R. Micallef, "A Nuclear Bomb for Libya", August-September, 1981, p. 14, also *Jane's Defense Weekly* (London), Nov. 7, 1987.
35. *Jane's Defense Weekly*, December 19, 1987 and see also *Hindustan Times* (New Delhi), 18 March, 1988.
36. The Indian Ocean is regarded as the world's third largest Ocean, after the Pacific and the Atlantic. It touches Parts of Africa, Australia, Antarctica and Asia, including Middle East...Indian Ocean region can be divided into five pivotal areas: (1) East Africa and the ocean to the east of it, including the Island countries of Mauritius, Seychelles and Madagascar; (2) the Horn of Africa and the Red Sea

countries; (3) South East Asia, including the Persian Gulf states and the Arabian Peninsula; (4) South Asia; and (5) South-East Asia and Australia. See Rasul B. Rais, *the Indian Ocean and the Super Powers* (London: Croom Helm, 1986), pp. 13-34.

37. Diego Garcia is a coral Atoll 13 miles long and 4 miles wide, with a land area of the tip of India and 10000 miles from the mainland of the US. Diego Garcia was selected because of its central location and its potential as a major naval base... Diego Garcia was leased out by the UK to USA as a military base after evicting 1200 citizens from the Islands group. See Rasul B. Rais, *The Indian Ocean and Super Powers* (London: Croom Helm, 1986), pp. 76-78 *United Nations, Department of Disarmament Affairs,* Report of the Secretary General, the Naval Arms Race (New York: United Nations, 1986), p. 61; UN Department for Disarmament Affairs, *The United Nations and Disarmament: 1945-1985* (New York: United Nations, 1985), pp. 104-05; William Arkin and Fieldhouse, *Nuclear Battlefields: Global Links in the Arms Race* (Cambridge, M.A.: Ballidger, 1985), p.66; and Christopher Paine, "On the Beach: The Rapid Development Force and the Nuclear Arms Race", *MERIP Report,* Vol. 13, No. 1, January 1983, pp. 3-11.
38. See *UN Documents* A/PV224 (4974); A/PV 2375/1975 and *Official Records of Arms Control and Disarmament Agency (ACDA)* (New York: US Printing Office, 1974), p. 668.
39. See *UN General Assembly Official Records,* Twenty-ninth Session, Annex, agenda item 107, Document A/9706; also UNGAOR, First Committee Report, Session 29, A/C.1/pv.2002, p.76.
40. See, *The United Nations and Disarmament,* 1945-1985 (New York: United Nations, 1985), pp. 102-03 and UNGAOR, n.39, p. 76.
41. *Tribune* (New Delhi), November 11, 1987 and *Patriot* (New Delhi), December 2, 1987.
42. For a detailed study on Pakistan's nuclear programme, Sinha and Subramanian, *Nuclear Pakistan* (New Delhi: Vision Books, 1980), pp. 49-50 and for India Birla Institute of Scientific Research, Economic Research Division, *India and the Atom* (New Delhi: Allied Publishers Pvt. Ltd., 1982), pp. 60-77.
43. The Middle East region may be loosely defined as the countries immediately bordering the Soviet Union, i.e., Turkey and Iran; the Arab countries including the confrontation states of the Arab-Israel; the Persian Gulf states, which again cover Iran and Iraq but also Saudi Arabia, Kuwait, Qatar, the Emirates and the Yemen. One might also include Libya, the Sudan and even Somalia as peripheral states of the region, the last two because of their relationship with the Red Sea (on which Ethiopia also borders). See, J.C. Hurewit (ed.), *Soviet American Rivalry in the Middle East* (New York: Academy of Political Science, 1969), pp. 104-20.

44. See *Official Records of the UN General Assembly*, Twenty-ninth Session, Annexes, Agenda items 24, 27, 28 ,29, 30, 31, 34, 35, 100, 101, 103 and 107, documents A/9693 Add. 1-3; *Official Records of UN General Assembly*, Israeli Nuclear Armaments, Document A/36/431, 36th Session, September 18, 1981, p. 15; *Defense and Foreign Affairs Weekly (New York)*, August 3, 1987.

2

Antarctic, Outer Space and Sea-Bed Treaties

Background

Based on the UN principles, as explained in the foregoing chapter, the Antarctic Treaty, the Outer Space Treaty, and the Sea-Bed Treaty were signed in 1959, 1967 and 1971 respectively. The aims of the treaties are not only to restrict the nuclear activities of the nuclear weapon countries but also to prevent any military related activities in these regions. Therefore, these treaties have wider scope and include the plan for total demilitarization. Moreover, there are certain provisions for helping the developing countries especially in the field of science and technology relating to their economic development. For example, India's scientific development in Antarctica, Space and Sea are greatly co-operated by advanced countries, especially by the former Soviet Union. Many other developing countries are also assisted by some of the advanced countries.

Antarctic Treaty

On 1 December, 1959, the Antarctic Treaty was signed by twelve countries: Argentina, Australia, Belgium, Chile, France, Japan, New Zealand, Norway, South Africa, the United Kingdom and Northern Ireland, the Union of Soviet Socialist Republics and the United States of America. Poland became a consultative party in 1977, West Germany in 1981, and Brazil and India in 1983. In addition, twelve acceding states Bulgaria, China, Czechoslovakia, Denmark, East Germany, Italy, the Netherlands, Papua New Guinea, Peru, Romania, Spain and Uruguay have signed the treaty.[1] This is the first internationally recognized NWFZ in uninhabited geographical area.[2] It was ratified by the signatory countries and became effective from 23 June, 1961. There are fourteen basic provisions in the Treaty. Article V is about establishing nuclear free Antarctica. It says "any nuclear explosion in Antarctica and the disposal thereof radioactive waste material shall be prohibited. In the event of the conclusion of international agreements concerning the use of nuclear energy, including nuclear, explosions and the disposal of radioactive waste material, to which all of the contracting parties whose representatives are entitled to participate in the meeting provided for under Article IX are parties, the rules established under such agreements shall apply in Antarctica."[3]

Nevertheless, it does not rule out the nuclear test for peaceful purposes. To this effect, the treaty includes provision for creating a control system for verification providing the right of aerial observation at any time over the regions of Antarctica. The observers of the treaty have access at any moment to any area or installation and to all ships and aero-planes at points of discharge and embarkation in the continent.[4] Its provisions apply to the area south of 60 degrees south latitude without prejudicing, or in any way affecting, the rights or the exercise of the rights of any state under international law with regard to any sea within that area.[5] It should be mentioned that the US in the initial period of Antarctica NWFZ was not ready to agree to it because of a nuclear reactor it operated at Momurdo station in the Ross dependence from 1969 until 1972. However, between 1972 and 1979, the reactor site at McMurdo was released for unrestricted use and the reactor and contaminated material were shipped to the US for disposal in South Carolina and California.[6] Thus, Antarctica treaty had been practically implemented in the beginning of the 1980s.

With regard to the 'Peaceful use of Antarctica', it says, "For nearly two and a half decades, Antarctica and its surrounding maritime areas have been free from militarizing of any kind, including nuclear weapons. No armed conflict has taken place in the area. Peace on the continent has been maintained to a large extent through the agreements embodied in the Antarctic Treaty." It continues "the Treaty has provided a framework for the parties to the Treaty to carry out peaceful activities related to scientific research, exploitation of marine resources and protection of environment".[7] For the demilitarized status, Article I says: "(1) Antarctica shall be used for peaceful purposes only. There shall be prohibited, *inter alia*, any measures of a military nature, such as the establishment of military maneuvers, as well as the testing of any type of weapons, (2) The present Treaty shall not prevent the use of military personnel of equipment for scientific research or for any other peaceful purpose."[8] It also restricts countries with territorial claims on the continent (Chile and Argentina, for instance) stating that they must undergo certain limitations, which involve only the scientific experiment in Antarctica not of any military related actions including any military maneuvers or bases.[9] The purpose of the treaty is fully achieved from a scientific standpoint of the treaty, as the objective of the treaty is maintained through the efforts of the Special Committee on Antarctic Research (SCAR). This committee has been functioning since 1961 when the treaty came into force. SCAR is an institution that represents the participating countries at the highest levels. All the signatories have permanent delegates and, representatives to SCAR.[10]

Argentina, Australia, Chile, France, New Zeeland, Norway, and the United Kingdom are claimant countries. Argentina has eleven Antarctic bases. It should be mentioned that the Falklands or Malvinas Islands is also one among them for which the United Kingdom had fought with Argentina. However, the claimant countries have their bases in Argentina. Australia has four Antarctic bases, France has four, New Zealand has three and the UK maintains seventeen bases.[11] And the non-claimant countries, South Africa, Belgium, Japan, the United States, the Soviet Union, Poland, Germany, India and Brazil also have bases in Antarctica. South Africa has one station on the continent on a permanent basis—yielded by Norway—in Queen Mand Land, east of the Waddell Sea since 1948. Belgium acquired a permanent place. Japan has been interested since 1911, as the expedition of Choku Shirase took place in the same year. Now, Japan has its scientific station, "Showa", in Antarctica. The United States maintains eight bases. It had started its mission towards Antarctica in 1924. It should be mentioned that the US has been opposing the plan of third world countries to have space exploration from Antarctica. Therefore, it has not ratified the Antarctica Treaty.[12]

The former Soviet Union sent an official communication on 27 January, 1939 to Norway protesting Norway's declaration of Sovereignty over Queen Mand Land. However, its expedition to Antarctica started in 1819–21. It maintains eleven Antarctic bases. Poland started its expedition in 1959 and established an Antarctic polar station with the help of the United Kingdom in February 1977. Germany began its expedition during 1873–74 and established its first permanent station on the Princess Matha Coast. It had become a consultative member in the Antarctica Committee.[13]

India started the expedition in the summer of 1981-82, and leased the Norwegian ship Polarsirkel and conducted a scientific expedition along the Coast of Queen Mand Land.[14] By 1983 it had become a consultative member. Brazil started its expedition in May 1975. Like India, Brazil also becomes a consultative member of the Antarctica Treaty in September 1983. In the same year it had sent a scientific mission to Antarctic to study climatic conditions, minerals and Antarctic marine species. China and Uruguay become consultative parties in October 1985, thereby increasing the number of consultative parties to eighteen. Other countries, which have recognized the Antarctica treaty, are as follows: Denmark, Holland, Romania, East Germany, Bulgaria, Peru, Italy, Spain, Czechoslovakia, and New Guinea. Sweden is the only country that after having conducted an Antarctic expedition has not become interested in the area and has not recognized the Treaty.[15]

Critical Views of the Members of Antarctic Treaty

German Democratic Republic (GDR), the Federal Republic of Germany (FRG), Romania and Uruguay criticized the Treaty. The GDR stated that in its view Article XIII, paragraph 1 of the Treaty was policies are guided by the purposes and principles of the United Nations Charter have a right to become parties to treaties, which affect the interest of all states.[16] The FRG stated that the Treaty applies also to Berlin (West). Romania stated that the provisions of Article XIII, paragraph 1 of the Treaty were not in accordance with the principle according to which multilateral treaties whose object and purposes concern the international community, as a whole, should be open for universal participation. And Uruguay proposed that the establishment of a general and definitive statute on Antarctica in which the interests of all states involved and of the international community as a whole would be considered equitably. It also declared that it reserved its rights in Antarctica in accordance with international law.[17]

However, Malaysia is the only country, which is very much critical about the Antarctic treaty. On 29 September, 1982, Malaysian representative, Mahathir expressed reservations about the Antarctic treaty in the UN General Assembly. "An agreement between select groups of countries does not reflect the true feelings of the members of the United Nations or their just claims. A new international agreement is required so that these historical episodes are not made into facts to substantiate claims."[18] He expressed further at the seventh Non-Aligned Summit Meeting held at New Delhi from 7 to 12 March, 1983, as follows: "...we may have a truly universal co-operation on Antarctica under the umbrella of the United Nations similar to the convention on the Law of the Sea. The United Nations must address itself to the issue and re-examine the potentials for a more universal framework of international co-operation on Antarctica."[19] Antigua issued a statement in June 1983, which reads as follows: "What is sad about this connivance (the treaty system) between eastern and western industrialized are active participants with them to exclude other third world countries".[20] However, their critical views were very much opposed by consultative parties of Antarctic treaty and they issued a note on 29 July, 1983, which states as follows: "The revision or replacement of the Treaty which Malaysia is now proposing would undermine this system of international law and order in Antarctica with very serious consequences for international peace and co-operation. The consultative parties to the Antarctic Treaty object unanimously to the Malaysian initiative, and to any attempt to revise or replace the Treaty."[21]

Although the consultative parties were opposed to the views expressed by some of the third world countries, especially the views of Malaysia, Antigua, and Barbuda, the third world's view was considered seriously by the UN, and therefore, the UN General Assembly took up the 'Question of Antarctica' and discussed at five sessions held in November 1983.[22] In that discussion, the third world countries requested the UN to consider for "democratization of decision-making on the

International scene". Also they pointed out that "the world of 1959, when the Antarctic Treaty was first formulated, is different from that of 1983".[23] As of these reasons, the UN carried out a study on Antarctica in 1984. Based on this study, a resolution was passed referring to the future course of action relating to the problem of the Antarctic treaty. It stated that "the draft resolution... is the best that we could come up with in the end... what the draft resolution has done, in essence, is to postpone such in-depth discussion..."[24] Many third world countries, including Malaysia, Bangladesh, Philippines, Sri Lanka, Antigua, and Barbuda expressed their dissatisfaction over the UN resolution. As of this reason, the problem is not settled so far. A critical view about the treaty provision of Antarctica relating to the NWFZ is discussed in the last section of this chapter. The following section considers about the Outer Space Treaty. (See the Map)

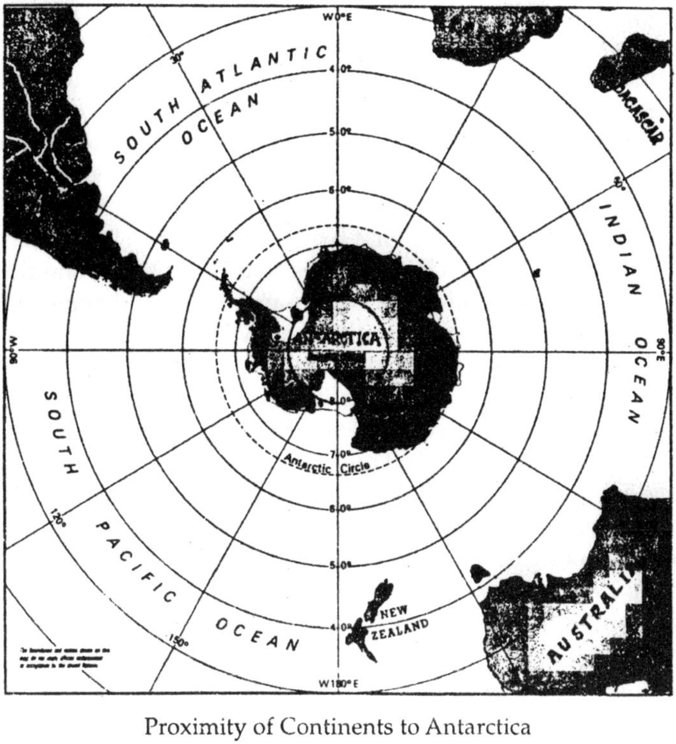

Proximity of Continents to Antarctica

Outer Space Treaty

As a second step towards the goal of preventing the spread of nuclear arms race by an arrangement of international treaty, the Outer Space Treaty was signed on 27 January, 1967. And it was entered into force on 10 October, 1967. This effort was made by the sub-committee on the Disarmament Commission and by the General Assembly in the late 1950s. For the first time in 1958, Soviet Union introduced a draft resolution providing in particular a ban on the use of cosmic space for military purposes and for an undertaking by the states to launch rockets into cosmic space only under an agreed international programme.[25] In 1960, five western powers submitted a plan for a ban on the placing of weapon of mass destruction in outer space. This plan was submitted to the Ten-Nation Disarmament Committee. In the same year, the United States have also proposed a programme for a ban on placing in orbit vehicles carrying weapons of mass destruction. In December 1961, the General Assembly recommended the guidelines regarding the outer space and celestial bodies. It claimed that outer space and celestial bodies are free for exploration. However, the parties intended to explore or use the outer space or celestial bodies should be in conformity with international law, and they are not subject to national appropriation. These principles were subsequently expanded by General Assembly resolution.[26] In December 1962, the US submitted its view to the First Committee of the UN. It reads:[27] "It is the view of the United States that outer space should be used only for peaceful—that is, non-aggressive and beneficial—purposes. The question of military activities in space cannot be divorced from the question of military activities on earth." And it continues: "To banish these activities in both environments we must continue our efforts for general and complete disarmament with adequate safeguards. Until this is achieved, the test of any space activity must not be whether it is military or non-military, but whether or not it is consistent with the United Nations Charter and other obligations of law."

In 1963, Mexico submitted to the conference of the Eighteen-Nation Committee on Disarmament the outline of a draft treaty on the prohibition of the orbiting or stationing in outer space of nuclear weapons and other weapons of mass destruction, including the prohibition of tests in outer space of these weapons.[28] This was the first time when the nuclear weapons had been considered to be a first one to be abolished in the outer space. The General Assembly, as it responded the Mexico's draft treaty, adopted resolution 1884 (XVIII) on 17 October, 1963. This resolution called upon all states to refrain from placing in orbit around the earth any object carrying nuclear weapons or any other kinds of weapons of mass destruction, installing such weapons on celestial bodies or stationing such weapons in outer space in any other manner.[29]

Followed by this effort, the Soviet Union and United States reached an agreement on a text entitled "Treaty on Principles Governing the Activities of States in the Exploration and Use of Outer Space, including the Moon and Outer Celestial Bodies". The principal provisions of the Treaty, relevant to the concept of NWFZ are:[30] (a) An undertaking by states parties not to place in orbit around the earth any object carrying nuclear weapons or any other kinds of weapons of mass destruction, install such weapons on celestial bodies, or station such weapons in outer space in any other manner; (b) A prohibition of all military activities on the Moon and other celestial bodies, including the establishment of military maneuvers, but excepting the use of military personnel in scientific research or peaceful exploration; (c) A provision that all stations, installations, equipment and space vehicles on the Moon and other celestial bodies would be open to representatives of states parties "on a basis of reciprocity".

Thus, outer space treaty was opened for signature in London, Moscow and Washington and it was signed on 27 January, 1967 and entered into force on 10 October, 1967. By 1 January, 1986, eighty-five states signed the treaty. The full text of the treaty is given in Appendix B. The treaty does not define the outer space. According to the UN study, there is no precise natural boundary between air space and outer space and no artificial demarcation has yet been agreed upon. And it says, however, in theory, the boundary is where terrestrial air space ends and in practice, the atmosphere becomes progressively thinner.[31] Therefore, many states view that a precise designation of the commencement of outer space would be unnecessary or inappropriate. And there are some other states favouring a more rigid definition of the parameters of outer space. In that regard one criteria has been in the forefront of interest: "the lower limits of the altitude where an object can perform a full orbit around the earth in uncontrolled, ballistic flight, namely, the lowest possible altitude of an object orbiting the earth in a circular orbit. About 100 kms. is low enough to allow a complete (circular) orbit".[32] And the treaty provisions which deal with nuclear and other weapons of mass destruction (Para I) and the provisions which deal with the peaceful uses of the moon and other celestial bodies (Para II) indicate that it does not prescribe conventional non-nuclear devices.[33] And therefore, the treaty has been termed as a clause of "partial disarmament". And Para I does not define standard by which it could be possible to make out as to what constitutes nuclear weapons or a weapon of mass destruction.

Also, it does not mention clearly about what it means by "orbit around the earth", and "orbit around the moon" or "orbit celestial bodies". The moon is considered to be celestial body in Para I. However, military use of other celestial bodies is not clear since these celestial bodies are yet to be utilized. And Para II does not specifically mention about the establishment of military bases, installations, fortification, the testing of any type of weapons and their military maneuvers on celestial bodies.[34] This can be interpreted as it has been permitting these installments in outer space. Also Para II does not define what it means by "peaceful purposes". Therefore, military activities of non-aggressive character are permissible even if they are conducted by the military with certain exception, for instance, those specifically forbidden by Article IV, that is, the establishment of military bases, installations and fortifications, the testing of any type of weapons and the conduct of military maneuvers on celestial bodies.[35]

Thus, Article IV of the treaty raises the question of whether or not space-based Ballistic Missiles Defense (BMD) lasers would fall into the category of "any other kinds of weapons of mass destruction" and thus be prohibited by the treaty. When this question was raised to US Secretary of Defense Cyrus Vance, he made the following characterization of such weapons. He said that the provision that weapon of mass destruction will not be placed in orbit around the earth undertaken to preserve man from yet another series of weapons which could threaten whole populations. When he was asked to describe, he continued: "I believe it would include such other weapon systems as chemical and biological weapons...or any weapon which might be developed in the future which would have the capability of mass destruction such as that created by nuclear weapons".[36]

The Soviet experts too had no definite view on the meaning of the weapons of mass destruction. However, the US-Soviet agreement, SALT II, defined this. In Article IX(c) of that proposed Treaty, each side "Undertakes not to develop test or deploy ...systems for placing into earth orbit nuclear weapons or any other kind of weapons of mass destruction including fractional orbital missiles".[37] These statements make equally clear that high-energy lasers are not among such weapons. However, it is worth noting the resolution adopted together by both the US and the Soviet Union in the Commission for Conventional Armaments, which was subsequently agreed by the UN. It states that:[38] "All armaments and armed forces, except atomic weapons and weapons of mass destruction, fall within its jurisdiction and that weapons of mass destruction should be defined to include atomic explosive weapons, radioactive material weapons, and lethal chemical and biological weapons...any weapons developed in the future which have characteristics comparable in destructive effect to those of the atomic bomb or other weapons mentioned above."

On the other hand, in 1976 and 1977, the Soviet proposed a draft agreement in which the weapons of mass destruction were explained again. Article I recognized the following types and systems of weapons as the weapons of mass destruction: radiological means of the non-explosive type acting with the aid of radioactive materials; technical means of inflicting radiation injury based on the use of charged or neutral particles to affect biological targets; infrasonic means using acoustic radiation to affect biological targets; and means using electromagnetic radiation affect biological targets. The most important definition according to the Soviet proposal is stated in the Article I and the Annex specifying that any types of weapons which are based on qualitatively new principles of action. According to Soviet Union, it includes the space based BMD system too. Thus the Soviet Union now argues that the US cannot proceed with Star Wars programme. The Soviet Union argued further that their proposed definition of "weapons of mass destruction were universal in character".[39] The US opposed that the definition of the weapons of the mass destruction stated in outer space treaty only confined to nuclear, radiological, chemical and biological weapons, and therefore the Soviet Union should abide by that. Moreover the United States argued that the Soviet Union should not go alone defining it. Thus, the US pointed out that it could deploy BMD lasers in the space for carrying out the Star Wars programme.[40] In brief, so long as the US adheres to its position, the outer space treaty would not be applicable to BMD system, the new military problem of American Star Wars programme, which is to be implemented, according to the US, by 1994. For the purpose of the study, it is important to understand the military use of outer space.

The military uses of outer space can be divided into two: (a) The use of satellites as integral part of military activities on earth and to enhance the performance of weapons based in terrestrial space and targeted to that environment (military support satellites); and (b) The use of outer space as environment for basing or employing devices for the destruction of satellites, missiles and nuclear warheads after they have been launched. The second category is referred to as space weapons. These weapons include weapons capable of destroying objects in outer space and weapons, which are space objects themselves. The first category is referred to as a system utilizing space.[41] Another distinction is explained in the outer space Treaty. According to that (a) "earth" weapons which enter outer space for part of their space to terrestrial space, and (b) all other weapons that could be used within, to or from space, including weapons utilizing new technologies. The second category is widely understood as space weapons. Thus, outer space treaty explains that the space weapons are the weapons, which are opposed to other weapons neither based in nor targeted to outer space.[42] These two categories explained above cannot be treated in isolation from each other. Therefore, the space weapons can be divided basically into two: space as environment where the destructive effect is produced (ground to space, sea to space, air to space, and space to space); space as the environment where the weapons are based (space to space, space to air, space to sea, and space to ground). It should be mentioned here that the recent controversy centered on 'star war' plan of United States is opposed because of the above mentioned calculation.

At the same time, the proponent of the star wars plan explains that the defensive activities in the space should not be calculated as offensive. Offensive weapons are the weapons, which can be used against military, economic, and other asserts of the adversary in their peacetime configuration. Defensive weapons are weapons, which can be used against the adversary's weapons, and even only after these (adversary's weapons) have been launched. Thus the proponents of star wars call the star wars as a defensive shield.[43] However, it is worth noting some of the existing satellites, which are important to carry out a military plan. These satellites are: meteorology and remote sensing satellites (photographic reconnaissance, electronic reconnaissance/electronic intelligence; ocean surveillance, early warning, navigation and global positioning satellites). They can help the command, control, and communications (c3) system of the military centers which serve the following military purposes: first, they may transmit data gathered by satellites to military control and command centers; second, they may transmit electronic signals between earth-based military command and control centers and military units.[44] They can thus provide military authorities with a worldwide command and control capability. In comparison with traditional earth-based communication network, they have large transmission capacities; third, they may provide communication links for mobile military forces such as air force, naval units and ground forces. High orbit communication satellites cover large geographical areas; fourth, they can be used for communication between national military authorities. High-orbit communication satellites may be less vulnerable than earth-based communication links in wartime.[45]

On the other hand, these satellites are also serving the arms control objectives. For example, reconnaissance and remote sensing satellites are used to confirm the absence of some military activities. This can relate to naval, air or troop movements in accordance with restraints, the non-deployment of certain classes of weapons, destruction or dismantling of weapons or the absence of testing of weapons. Thus one main task of satellites has been to provide the technical means whereby arms limitation treaties can be verified in order to give assurance that the provisions of those treaties are being observed. Observations from outer space by so called national technical means (NTMs) have been used for monitoring some of the bilateral agreements between the two major nuclear powers since 1972, most prominently the SALT and ABM treaties.[46] However, anti-satellite (ASAT) weapons, Anti-Ballistic Missile (ABM) or ballistic defense (BMD) weapons are deployed in the space.

ASAT and ABM/BMD weapons can be divided into two: Kinetic Energy Weapons (KEW) and directed energy weapons (DEW). The KEW, which can be propelled either by chemical rockets or by electromagnetic forces, derives their energy from the momentum of an object.[47] On the other hand, in DEW energy in the form of beams, propagated with the speed of light 3,00,000 km/sec is used for destruction of a target. Both the KEW and DEW can, in principle, be earth, air, or space-based. In the case of KEW, it is possible to deploy them on submarines while in the case of an earth-based laser weapon, for example, mirrors can be placed in orbit to reflect the energy to the target. The existing capabilities, both in the ASAT and in the ABM/BMD fields, all refer to KEW. It should be mentioned that the ABM treaty had permitted the ABM/BMD system.[48] Accordingly, the Soviet Union has an operational ABM system in accordance with the terms of the ABM Treaty. Although the first half of the 1960s, the US developed and deployed two nuclear-armed direct-ascent ASAT weapon systems, it was withdrawn from deployment in 1967 and 1975 respectively. Therefore, it should be stated that both the US and the Soviet Union are capable of producing and deploying ABM and ASAT weapon system at present.[49]

Also, the nuclear-powered spacecraft in the space which are deployed for the peaceful mission is dangerous in case an accident occurs in the space. The Russian Cosmos 954 and the American Skylab mishaps have proved that the accident in space is possible. Wreckage from the Soviet Cosmos 954 had hit a Japanese freighter in the sea in 1967. The Japanese raised this issue in the United Nations and got compensation from the Soviet Union.[50] In 1978, Cosmos 954, a five ton-nuclear powered Soviet Ocean surveillance satellite lost altitude and it crashed over sub-Arctic Canada. The debris was scattered over hundreds of square miles. Canada declined the Soviet offer to help clean up Cosmos 954's remains. However, Canada accepted the

American offer to clean up the sub-Arctic Canada. US-Canadian clean-up operation dubbed as "Operation Morning Light". And the Soviet Union paid the compensation to Canada.[51] In 1979, NASA's seventy-seven and a half ton Skylab re-entered Earth's atmosphere and its wreckage was scattered across the Indian Ocean and Australian outback. These mishaps were very much discussed in the UN Committee on the peaceful uses of outer space in the 1980s. And the UN Committee proposed that the countries which are having nuclear-powered spacecraft in the space should notify and assist the states which might face problems in case of accident to their spacecraft.[52] More details about the outer space controversy is given in the section, which deals with the politics of the treaty.

Sea-Bed Treaty

In 1968, the Soviet Union proposed in the conference of the Eighteen Nation Committee on Disarmament for initiating negotiations on an agreement that could prohibit the military use of the Sea-Bed and the ocean floor beyond the limits of national jurisdiction. On 18 March, 1969, a draft treaty was submitted by the Soviet Union, as the Committee initiated the negotiations on the subject. The Soviet draft treaty called for the complete demilitarization of the Sea-Bed, the ocean floor and its subsoil beyond a coastal zone of twelve miles. The US countered the Soviet draft with a draft treaty on 22 May, 1969. It prescribed the stationing of nuclear and other weapons of mass destruction in the same environment beyond a coastal limit of three miles.[53] On 7 October, 1969, both the Soviet Union and the US jointly submitted a draft treaty to the Eighteen Nation Committee. It was recommended by the UN on 7 December, 1970 by adopting a resolution (2660 XXXV) for signature and ratification of the treaty by the members of the UN. As a result, on February 11, 1971, the "Treaty on the prohibition of the Emplacement of Nuclear Weapons of Mass Destruction on the Sea-Bed and the Ocean Floor and in the Subsoil Thereof" commonly referred to as the Sea-Bed Treaty was signed. The treaty entered into force on May 18, 1972. Seventy-four countries have become parties to the treaty.[54] (See the Map).

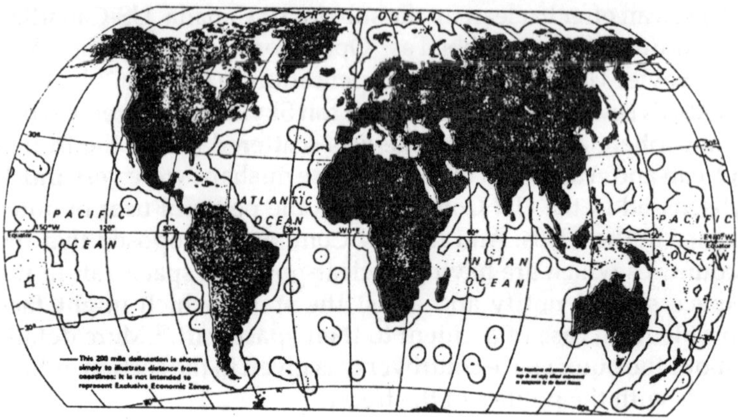

200-Miles Delineation

The former Soviet Union had maintained that there should be a comprehensive ban on military activities on the Sea-Bed and Ocean Floor and those parties to the treaty could apply the principle of free access "on a reciprocal basis to objects placed on the Sea-Bed in order to verify compliance". It had followed the UN principles used in the Antarctic Treaty and the Outer Space Treaty which states that "the system of control on the basis of free access" must be encouraged by the parties interested to sign a treaty. Nonetheless, the Soviet Union, did not accept for an international means of verification.[55] The US, on the other hand had submitted a draft treaty containing provisions to ensure the right of observation of activities on the Sea-Bed or otherwise infringe rights recognized under international law, including freedom of the high seas. Thus, it had rejected the principle of free access as a basis for verification. Also, it had argued that a right of access for the purpose of verification of a prohibition on the emplacement of nuclear weapons would be both impractical and unnecessary.[56]

Brazil was opposed to both the Soviet and American draft. And it maintained a well-grounded denunciation of a violation of a treaty, addressed to the Security Council, should then be followed by appropriate action by that Council aimed at the re-establishment of the previous conditions of security in the affected area. And it stated further that it was only proper that the Security Council should settle any dispute arising from the conflicting opinions presented by two or more states.[57] For verification, Brazil suggested that the area beyond the mileage adopted by the treaty, but still within the limits of the national jurisdiction over the Sea-Bed, the right of verification should be exercised with the participation of the state having sovereign rights for the exploitation of the area concerned.[58] Sweden also proposed the similar kind of verification procedure. It wished, however, to retain in principle the idea of free access contained in the Soviet draft treaty, although it repeated its criticism of the concept of reciprocity. It maintained that, in principle, the coastal state should be given the exclusive right "but also the obligation" to carry out verification in its maritime zone. Thus, it stated that in regard to the twelve-mile maritime zone, observation, if carried out in consistency with international law, would not be hampered by the exclusive rights of a coastal state.[59]

The United Arab Republic, Italy and Mexico had agreed for an international means of verification.[60] Especially Mexico stated referring to the US draft treaty which demanded a system of unconditional verification: that there were many claims of national jurisdiction over the Sea-Bed and ocean floor—unlike the Moon—and the growing scientific, industrial and commercial utilization of the Sea-Bed and ocean floor, besides the cost of the gigantic technical problems which that kind of unconditional inspection would raise in the hostile environment of the Sea-Bed and ocean floor. Mexico stated further that it could agree to the Soviet proposal rather than to American one. Nigeria also agreed to the Soviet proposal. It stated that the United States proposal did not more than confirm an existing right. And referring to the Soviet proposal it suggested that the Soviet proposal did not include an international arrangement for verification in its draft and therefore, it should be introduced.[61]

Although India was in support of the idea of international means of verification to ensure the strict observance of the provisions of the treaty, it was critical about both the United States and the Soviet draft treaty.[62] India's representative stated: "While my delegation fully appreciated the concern of the sponsors of the two drafts before us about the technical difficulties ... it is not clear to us why, if the existing technological "know-how" and capacity are adequate for emplacing structures and installations on the Sea-Bed, they should not also be adequate for verifying what is emplaced". He continued: "In the view of the delegation of India, the principle of verification through suitable international machinery or agency or arrangement is essentially sound and would go very far in the direction of removing suspicions, lessening tension and creating an international atmosphere of trust".[63] More importantly, India pointed out that any control provision, which did not ensure with necessary safeguards, a reasonable opportunity for access to the structures and installations placed on the Sea-Bed, would be illusory. "Unless such provisions were made, those states which have the capacity to make such emplacements on the Sea-Bed would be placed in a position of advantage and superiority as compared with all the technologically less-advanced states".[64]

Canada proposed that all installations and structures on the Sea-Bed and ocean floor beyond the twelve-mile coastal band would be open to observation and inspection by representatives of the other States parties to the treaty. Ethiopia was agreeing with the US draft treaty, as it appreciated Canadian demand for the right of every party to inspect the Sea-Bed deployment of any country beyond twelve-mile. Relating to the Ethiopian comment, Canada proposed three important aspects of the verification. According to that, first, there must be some mechanisms to ensure that disputes regarding verification could be resolved once a State has become concerned that the treaty was not being fully complied with. Second, there must be provisions, which would guarantee the ability of all signatories to share in the verification procedures, either independently or in co-operation with other parties, so that the signatories should not be at unfair disadvantages owing to the lack of technology or skill. And finally, there should be a clear restatement of the pertinent rights of coastal States under existing international law; so that these States may be assured that their rights are fully protected.[65]

Argentina, Czechoslovakia and Yugoslavia, the States who become members of the CCD in 1969 were agreed for an international means of verification.[66] Burma suggested that the treaty containes an affirmation in explicit and unambiguous language, that: "Verification procedure shall not be carried out on the continental shelf in a manner that could impair the rights of coastal States under the 1958 Geneva Convention on the continental shelf in a manner that could impair the rights of coastal States under the 1958 Geneva Convention on the Continental Shelf... and under existing international laws". And it added "additionally, the inclusion of a provision leaving the possibility open for coastal States to be associated with later-stage verification procedures on their continental shelf is clearly desirable".[67]

As these arguments came up from many States, the United States and the Soviet Union submitted a second revision of the joint draft treaty in April 1970. In that, they specified that all countries concerned could participate in mutual consultations and verification arrangements. Reacting to this revised draft of both the United States and the Soviet Union, the member countries argued together for the right of the coastal states, which was not clear, even in their revised draft. Therefore, they stated that the coastal States should be given categorically the right not only to be notified of the consultations and the measures of co-operation engaged in by the States situated in the region but also to participate in them: "For that reason specific mention ought to be made of the competence of the state concerned to act in such matters not as a mere possibility but as an authentic right, so that the interest of that State may be sufficiently guaranteed in the inspection procedure conducted only by other countries".[68] Also, they argued that the revised treaty relied too heavily on the Security Council, which might complicate the role of Security Council in the future.

Because of this, in September 1970, a third revision of the draft treaty was submitted by both the Soviet Union and the United States. The newly revised draft provided for the member states the right of international verification, especially it recognized that verification could be carried out by a State not only by its own means or with the full or partial assistance of other parties, but also "through appropriate international procedures within the framework of the United Nations and in accordance with its Charter".[69] Most of the member states agreed to this newly revised draft treaty. On 11 February, 1971, it was signed and entered into force on 18 May, 1972.

The main provisions of the treaty are as follows. Article I says: the parties undertake not to emplace nuclear and other weapons of mass destruction and facilities specifically designed for storing, testing or using such weapons beyond the outer limit of a zone of the Sea-Bed, defined in Article II as a zone conterminous with the 12-miles wide zone referred to in the 1958 Geneva Convention on the Territorial Sea and the Contiguous Zone. Article III deals with verification procedure. It grants each party the right to verify through observation the activities of other parties on the Sea-Bed beyond the zone defined by Articles I and II. Article IV states that nothing in the treaty shall be interpreted as supporting or prejudicing the position of any state party in relation to law of the sea. Article V says that the parties "undertake to continue negotiations in good faith concerning further measures in the field of disarmament for the prevention of an arms race on the Sea-Bed, the ocean floor and the subsoil thereof". Article VI specifies the procedure to be followed in amending the treaty. Article II states about the review procedure of the treaty. According to this, the treaty could be reviewed every five years since the date of its entry into force. And Article VIII deals with the States parties right to withdraw from the treaty in case the functioning of the treaty does not satisfy the member states. Article IX states about the states of the nuclear free sea and the obligation of the member states for establishing NWFZ in the sea.[70]

Although the treaty aimed for nuclear free sea, it did not prevent the nuclear arms at sea. For example, there are at present 15490 nuclear weapons at sea deployed by the nuclear weapon countries. These forces are deployed at the Norwegian Sea, the Bering Sea, the Sea of Japan, the Arabian Sea, the Mediterranean Sea, and underneath the Arctic. The first nuclear submarine, USS Nautilus, was commissioned by the US in 1954. Since then, the nuclear submarines have been playing a most formidable role in naval warfare.[71] The US has 9347 nuclear warheads deployed both in strategic submarines and in the non-strategic forces. They include Poseidon/c3 missiles, which carry ten warheads, and the Trident 1/c4 missile, which carries eight warheads, and the non-strategic forces: Tomahawk sea-launched cruise missiles, ASROC and SUBROC anti-submarine rockets, Terrier surface to air missiles, B-57 nuclear depth bombs, and two other types of bombs. Apart from these forces the US operates 168 nuclear reactors in 149 vessels, including ballistic missile submarines, attack submarines, aircraft carriers, cruisers, and a single deep-research vessel. Also, it operates eight land-based proto-type nuclear plants.[72] The Soviet Union has 5428 warheads deployed both in the strategic submarine forces and non-strategic forces. The UK has 64 nuclear warheads. France has 256 and China has 169 nuclear weapons at sea. These can reach any part of the sea. Their movements, therefore, undermine the very aim of the Sea-Bed treaty. Moreover, they play a link role for both the land and space-based forces. Most of the communication networks are connected through sea.

Thus, sea plays an important role in the nuclear strategy of nuclear weapon countries. For example, the US has deployed thirty-seven per cent of its nuclear forces at sea. Between one-quarter and one-third of all the nuclear weapons in the world are based at sea.[73] Politics of the Sea-Bed treaty is discussed in the last section of this chapter. The following section concentrates on a comparative study of Antarctic, Outer Space and Sea-Bed Treaty. (See the following Table)

Signatories of the Treaties

State	*Antarctic Treaty*	*Outer Space Treaty*	*Sea-Bed Treaty*
Afghanistan	–	–	1971
Argentina	1961	1969	1983
Australia	1961	1967	1973
Austria	–	1968	1972
Bahamas	–	1976	–
Barbados	–	1968	–
Belgium	1960	1973	1972
Botswana	–	–	1972
Brazil	1975	1969	–
Bulgaria	–	1967	1971
Burma	–	1970	–
Byelorussia	–	1967	1971
Canada	–	1967	1972
Cape Verde	–	–	1979
Central African Republic	–	–	1981
Chile	1961	1981	–
China	1983	1983	–
Congo	–	–	1978
Cuba	–	1977	1977

(Contd.)

(Contd.)

State	*Antarctic Treaty*	*Outer Space Treaty*	*Sea-Bed Treaty*
Cyprus	–	1972	1971
Czechoslovakia	1962	1967	1972
Denmark	1965	1967	1971
Dominican Republic	–	1968	1972
Ecuador	–	1969	–
Egypt	–	1967	–
El Salvador	–	1969	–
Ethiopia	–	–	1977
Fiji	–	1972	–
Finland	–	1967	1971
France	1960	1970	–
German Democratic Republic	1974	1967	1971
F.R. Germany	1979	1971	1975
Ghana	–	–	1972
Greece	–	1971	–
Guinea-Bissau	–	1976	1976
Hungary	–	1967	1971
Iceland	–	1968	1972
India	1983	1982	1973
Iran	–	–	1971
Iraq	–	1968	1972
Ireland	–	1968	1971
Israel	–	1977	–
Italy	1981	1972	–
Ivory Coast	–	–	1972
Jamaica	–	1970	–
Japan	1960	1967	1971
Jordan	–	–	1971
Korea, Republic of South	–	1967	–
Kuwait	–	1972	–
Law People's Dem. Republic	–	1972	1971
Lebanon	–	1969	–
Lesotho	–	–	1973
Libya	–	1968	–
Luxembourg	–	–	1982
Madagascar	–	1968	–
Malaysia	–	–	1972
Mali	–	1968	–
Malta	–	–	1971

(Contd.)

(Contd.)

State	*Antarctic Treaty*	*Outer Space Treaty*	*Sea-Bed Treaty*
Mauritius	–	1969	1971
Mexico	–	1968	–
Mongolia	–	–	1971
Morocco	–	1967	1971
Nepal	–	1967	1971
Netherlands	1967	1969	1976
New Zealand	1960	1968	1972
Nicaragua	–	–	1973
Niger	–	1967	1971
Nigeria	–	1967	–
Norway	1960	1969	1971
Pakistan	–	1968	–
Panama	–	–	1974
Papua New Guinea	1981	1980	–
Peru	1981	1980	–
Poland	1961	1968	1971
Portugal	–	–	1975
Qatar	–	–	1974
Romania	1971	1968	1972
Rwanda	–	–	1975
San Marino	–	1968	–
Sao Tome and Principle	–	–	1975
Saudi Arabia	–	1976	1972
Seychelles	–	1978	1976
Sierra Leone	–	1967	–
Singapore	–	1976	1976
Solomon Island	–	–	1981
South Africa	1960	1968	1973
Spain	1982	1968	–
Swaziland	–	–	1971
Sweden	–	1967	1972
Switzerland	–	1969	1976
Syria	–	1968	–
Taiwan	–	1970	1972
Thailand	–	1968	–
Togo	–	–	1971
Tonga	–	1971	–
Tunisia	–	1968	1971
Turkey	–	1968	1971

(Contd.)

(Contd.)

State	Antarctic Treaty	Outer Space Treaty	Sea-Bed Treaty
Uganda	–	1968	1972
U.K.	1960	1967	1972
Ukraine	–	1967	1971
Upper Volta	–	1968	–
Uruguay	1980	1970	–
USA	1960	1967	1972
USSR	1960	1967	1972
Venezuela	–	1970	–
Vietnam	–	1980	1980
Yemen, People's Dem. Republic of	–	1979	1979
Yugoslavia	–	–	1973
Zambia	–	1973	1972

Source: SIPRI, *World Armament and Disarmament* (London: Taylor and Francis, 1984), 654-667; For latest information, see SPRI Year Book series till 2005.

Comparison

Antarctic, Outer Space, and Sea-Bed treaties were signed in different times. For example, the Antarctic treaty was signed in a period when the world had just experienced the horror of atomic war, which resulted in the annihilation of twenty million people in Hiroshima and Nagasaki, Japan. Since the world community tried to find a way out for controlling the atomic weapons during the period of the late 1940s to the late 1950s, the UN established a set of principles, as seen in the first chapter, and it asked the world community to abide by these principles. On the basis of the UN principles, the Antarctic treaty was signed in 1959. This was the first treaty, which was concerned about establishing nuclear free Antarctica.[74] The Outer Space treaty was passing through a second stage of the effort in controlling the atomic weapons. In the same period, the Latin American NWFZ treaty and the treaty on the non-proliferation of nuclear weapons (NPT) were initiated and signed. However, the Outer Space treaty was signed first in January 1967, although the negotiations for this treaty started later than the above mentioned treaties. The negotiations for both Latin American NWFZ treaty and NPT were initiated in the early 1960s and they were signed in February 1967, and in July 1968 respectively.[75] And the third treaty concerning to establish NWFZ, the Sea-Bed treaty, was signed in a period when the world community witnessed a bilateral agreement between the US and the Soviet Union for the limitation of anti-ballistic missile systems (ABM Treaty). Although negotiation for ABM treaty started earlier than Sea-Bed treaty, Sea-Bed treaty was signed only in May 1972. However, these treaties were the result of the time when the world had been witnessing a variety of nuclear armaments.[76]

These treaties have both similarities and differences. All are aiming for demilitarized zone in uninhabited areas. For, each treaty has a separate provision to deal with this objective. Also, they include a provision for nuclear free status of Antarctica, Outer Space, and Sea-Bed. They have more members unlike any other multilateral agreements for establishing NWFZ in the world. The number of signatories for them is twenty-eight, eighty-five and seventy-four respectively, whereas the NWFZ treaties for Latin America and South Pacific have only twenty-three and ten respectively. They are not having additional protocols. Their verification system is established on the basis of an international understanding. Also, they are encouraging the scientific activities in Antarctica, Outer Space and Sea-Bed.[77] The differences of these treaties are as follows: The zone of application is different from each other Antarctica is the Ice Continent to which the treaty is fully forceful. Whereas Outer Space and Sea-Bed treaty, are very ambiguous in terms of application. The Sea-Bed treaty, and the Antarctic treaty permit peaceful nuclear activity, while the Outer Space treaty is not clear about that.[78]

Regarding the establishment of NWFZ, the Antarctic treaty prohibits military related nuclear activities in the whole region, whereas Sea-Bed treaty is concerned about only outer limit of a Sea-Bed zone (conterminous with the twelve miles outer limit of the zone referred in the 1958 Geneva Convention on the territorial sea, and the contiguous zone). Thus, the Sea-Bed treaty permits military related nuclear activities.[79] The Outer Space treaty is ambiguous about nuclear activities. Moreover, Sea-Bed treaty, and Outer Space treaty are related with the Partial Test Ban Treaty (PTBT) signed in 1963, and ABM treaty in 1972 respectively, whereas the Antarctic treaty is not related with any treaty. Also, the Sea-Bed treaty and the Outer Space treaty have been the center of controversy, as the increasing nuclear activities of nuclear weapon powers in the sea and in the space are going on.[80] Especially, the Outer Space treaty is critical as the American plan of Star Wars has been a point of discussion all over the world. But, the Antarctic treaty keeps itself in a low profile, although some of the third world countries, like Malaysia, Antigua and Barbuda, are not satisfied with the treaty system. It should be noted that the nuclear related controversy is much less in the case of Antarctica, unlike in the Sea-Bed and Outer Space.[81] For example, the proposed US plan for implementing the star wars programme would undermine the concept of NWFZ. In the case of Antarctica there are no such plans.

Politics

Antarctic treaty, which came into force in the early 1960s, has very fundamental problems relating to the treaty system and the formulation of the provisions for demilitarization.[82] Regarding to the treaty system, the third world countries, as seen in the foregoing section of this chapter, are critical and they want Antarctica to be a place of common heritage in a true sense. Therefore, many countries argued for creating effective treaty system than the available one.[83] Since 1983, the year when the UN initiated discussion for establishing nuclear free zone in Antarctica, the treaty system has not been seriously thought about, as pointed out by the third world countries, by the UN for effective implementation. Thus many third world countries demanded for a total change in the system of the Antarctic treaty.[84]

However, the consultative parties of the treaty argued that the system of the Antarctic treaty should be a flexible one not a rigid one. According to them, if any country interested in Antarctica for scientific activities can join the system of the treaty. For example, India and China joined the system in 1983 and in 1985 respectively although they had in the beginning a difference of opinion about the treaty. It should be noted that by 1959 twenty-eight members joined the treaty. Therefore, changing the system of the treaty, in their view, it is not necessary. Also, some of the members, such as Brazil and Chile, have a view that they have the right for claiming the Ice Continent as their property since they are having a continental connection. Noting this view, the consultative parties, especially Brazil and India, hold their views that the third world countries should deal carefully the question of Antarctica as they cannot expect a rapid change from the countries which had been enjoying the Ice Continent for hundred of years together.[85]

The second problem is related to the treaty's provisions. Articles V and I are concerned about demilitarized and nuclear free Antarctica. According to Article I military activity is not permitted in Antarctica. However, para second of the article suggests that the "present treaty shall not prevent the use of military personnel of equipment for scientific research or any other peaceful purpose".[86] This gives, however, a loophole for the consultative parties interested for military related activities. For example, the US communication system established in Antarctica can be used for war purpose. This operates as a link communication center for other communication facilities established in various parts of the world. Especially, the sea based nuclear systems are well connected with Antarctica. The sea-based nuclear installations both submarine based nuclear system and systems established only for sea-communicable through Antarctica. Apart from these sea based nuclear forces and their related activities connected with the Antarctica, the US also has a plan of connecting the space based military system with Antarctica. This example is applicable in the case of the Soviet Union too, as the Soviet Union has been concentrating underneath the Arctic since the late 1970s. Thus, the Antarctica based scientific installations of consultative parties, especially, the US and the Soviet Union, can contact satellites, surveillance stations, ships, and aircraft monitor enemy vessels, submarines and land support activities.[87] Thus, the chance of maintaining Antarctica as a demilitarized, and therefore, NWFZ is very bleak.

Politics of the Outer Space treaty can be analyzed on the basis of the existing reality today. There are military activities, as explained in the above sections, which are directly or indirectly related with nuclear controversy in the outer space. Of all, the Star Wars programme of the US is very important to be understood. According to the US, the Star Wars programme is allowed by the outer space treaty whereas the Soviet Union holds the view that the Outer Space treaty does not permit it. They, however, can hold these two differing views, basically because of the freedom that the outer space treaty gives to the contracting parties.[88] Most of the western countries, including the UK, France and West Germany argue that the treaty is nothing to do with research programme for establishing defense system in the outer space. Some of the Asian countries, such as Japan, also are concerned about this type of research. It should be mentioned here that most of the spare parts or essential equipments relating to the implementation of Star Wars programme of the US are being produced in Japanese Industries. And the European unity in this research is well known as Europeanized Star Wars Programme.[89]

The Soviet Union, although it is opposed to the way the US and its friendly countries interpret the outer Space treaty, it has the capability of doing things as the American do. In fact, the Soviet Union can be noted as the forerunner in the Outer Space, since the late 1950s and the early 1960s were the period of the Soviet superiority in the Outer Space technology, as the Outer Space activity was initiated by the Soviet Union as the Russian rockets only reached the Outer Space first (Sputnik) in 1957, launched in the moon in 1959, and carried man and woman to the Outer Space in 1961 and in 1963 respectively. Thus, the Soviet Union is capable of dealing the Star Wars programme accordingly.[90] And one more problem related with the Outer Space treaty is the problem of the interpretation of ABM treaty, which was signed in 1972. Basically, the ABM treaty came into existence for cutting down the unwanted anti-ballistic system, which was at that time possible to be established on earth. That capability was not coping with the deterrent game of both the US and the Soviet Union, as they followed, if not in the view of the Soviet Union fully, offensive game.[91] According to that, there had to be a mutual agreement to put their deterrent forces strait against each other.

The point, therefore, emphasized by the offensive game at that time was that the system of hitting or the system, which would overlook the existing technology of deterrent forces, was not permitted. In order to stop that development, as the Soviet Union had the capability first in the ABM technology, the ABM treaty was signed in 1972. ABM treaty is interpreted by the US differently today. According to them, the ABM treaty is not prohibiting the defensive technology with which an interested party can develop military related system in the space for its security. Therefore, the US argues that both the Outer Space treaty and the ABM treaty permit the defensive development in the Outer Space.[92] Thus, according to the US, the deterrent game would go like this in the years to come. However, to avoid nuclear deterrence, if not in the real sense, which had been opposed by the international community throughout the nuclear era from 1940s, the US proposed a plan of maintaining non-nuclear deterrence, i.e. 'dealing the enemy without nuclear weapons' principally the Soviet Union, being a partner so far for the game played, argue that existing nuclear deterrence and nuclear infrastructures are so complicated which cannot be easily ignored by following such a game in the future.[93] Although, the principle is not formed so far, the way things go between the US and the Soviet Union, it can be stated that the defensive game will start by the beginning of the 1990s.

Nonetheless, both offensive and defensive systems what the US talk about cannot be clearly defined. For the military, both are same. If the defensive game for maintaining balance of power is accepted, there is going to be a much more danger, as the laser beam weapons are no less than nuclear weapons. Moreover, existing nuclear weapons and their infrastructures based in the sea and land of the world will be connected with both the nuclear or non-nuclear threat from the Outer Space.[94] Thus, that would be a dangerous level of deterrent game because it camouflages the whole issue of disarmament. Even to maintain the game it is very difficult, as any partner can develop system, which will undermine this game. For example, if any one of them hit the communication satellites in the space, practically defensive system cannot be maintained. Therefore, it is like again playing the same game with different balls, which is more dangerous in the technologically well-developed modern world.[95] For these controversies, the Outer Space treaty has no solution. The following writing takes care of the Sea-Bed treaty.

According to Article I of the Sea-Bed treaty, the parties agree not to emplace nuclear and other weapons of mass destruction and related facilities beyond the limit of twelve miles. Thus, it allows nuclear activities in the territorial sea. As of this reason, today, there are nuclear forces deployed in the territorial water can reach distant part of the sea. For example, the US territorial bases having nuclear forces are operating from ten states: Alaska, California, Florida, Georgia, Hawaii, Maine, New Jersey, South Carolina, Virginia, and Washington and at three overseas locations (Guam, Italy and the UK).[96] These forces, therefore, undermine the very objective of the treaty stated in Article IX. According to Article IX, the member states should undertake the obligations of establishing NWFZ in the sea. Despite, member's states have been more and more interested in nuclear submarines. Argentina and India can be noted in this regard.

Also, there have been nuclear accidents in the sea. For example, British nuclear submarine was sunk in the sea in1982, during the Falkland War. In 1983, Soviet nuclear-powered submarine was sunk in the North Pacific. And the Soviet Yankee Class submarine was sunk with sixteen nuclear missiles, warheads and nuclear reactors in the Atlantic in October 1986.[97] The Sea-Bed treaty does not have any provision to deal with this problem. Moreover, the verification system that the Sea-Bed treaty establishes cannot be carried out, as the sea-based nuclear forces are capable to hide under the water. Of all, the systems established in the sea such as Ocean surveillance, command and control systems, and electronic warfare system are too dangerous that connect both the land and space based forces.[98] The next chapter focuses on Latin America nuclear-free zone, the first zone established in the inhabited area of the world.

NOTES AND REFERENCES

1. *United Nations General Assembly Record* (UNGAR), 39th Session, Study on the Question of Antarctica, A/39/583 (Part I), 31 October, 1984.
2. Geologically and geographically Antarctica is divided into two regions by the Trans-Antarctic mountains, which extend from the Ross Ice Shelf in the Pacific Sector to the Filcher Ice Shelf in the Pacific Sector to the Filcher Ice Shelf in the Atlantic Sector. To the east of the mountains lies East or Greater Antarctica, a Pre-Cambrian shield covered almost entirely by an ice sheet rising to about 42,000 meters above sea level and averaging circa 2,500 meters in height. This region includes Mount Erebus (33,794 meters), one of several volcanic landforms while west of the Tran Antarctic mountains lies west or

Lesser Antarctica, an area characterized by various mountain ranges, such as the Ellsworth Mountain, where in the Vinson Massif at 4,897 meters (formerly given as 5,140 meters) represents the highest point in the continent. About 95-98 per cent of the continent is covered by the ice sheet, even during the summer season, and the ice, which has an average thickness of 2,450 meters, exceeds 4,500 meters in places". See Peter J. Beck, *The International Politics of Antarctica* (London, 1980), pp. 8-9.

3. *UN Treaty Series,* Vol. 402, No. 5778, p. 72; also for the Text of the Treaty, See, Appendix A.
4. *Documents on Disarmament* 1945-1959, n.1, pp. 1020-23.
5. *United Nations Special Report of the Conference of the Committee on Disarmament* (UNSRCCD), Comprehensive Study of the Question of NWFZ in all its Aspects (New York: UN, 1986), pp. 10-11.
6. See Ramesh Thakur and Hyam Gold, "The Antarctic Treaty Regime: Exclusive Preserve or Common Heritage?", *Foreign Affairs Reports* (New York), Vol. XXXXII, Nos. 11 and 12, November-December 1983, pp. 169-86.
7. *UN, Treaty Series,* No.3, pp. 72-73.
8. *Ibid.*
9. See Ramesh Thakur and Hyam Gold, "*The Antarctic Treaty Regime: Exclusive* Preserve or Common Heritage", No. 6, pp. 169-86.
10. *UN General Assembly Record,* No. 1, Part I.
11. Ramesh Thakur and Hyam Gold, No. 6, pp. 180-85.
12. For more details in this regard, see Peter J. Beck, No. 2, 21-46.
13. *Ibid.*
14. For more details about India's expedition to Antarctica See, Sanjay Chaturvedi, "India and the Antarctica Treaty System: Realities and Prospects", *India Quarterly* (New Delhi), Vol. XLII, No. 4, October-December 1986, pp. 351-80.
15. For more critical views expressed by the third world countries, see Green Peace International, *The Future of the Antarctica: Background for a Second UN Debate* (Lewes: Greenpeace, 1984), pp. 11-14.
16. Jozef Goldblat, *Arms Control Agreements* (New York: Praeger, 1982), p. 282.
17. *Ibid.*
18. *UNGAR* A/37/PV 10, pp. 17-20, 29 September, 1982.
19. Mahathir, "On Antarctica", *Foreign Affairs Malaysia* (Kuala Lumpur), Vol. 16, No. 1, March, 1983, pp. 7-8.
20. *New York Times,* 22 June, 1983.
21. *International Herald Tribune* (Paris), 30 July, 1983.
22. *Ibid.*
23. *UNGAR A/C* 1/38 PV 42, pp.22, 28 November, 1983.
24. *UNGAR A/C* 1/39 PV 55, pp. 17, 30 November, 1984.

25. *Official Records of the General Assembly*, Thirteenth Session, Annexes, Agenda Item 60, document A/C. 1/L.
26. *Ibid.*
27. *UN Document A/C.* 1/PV. 1289, p. 13, 3 December, 1962; US also stated that there is "In any event, no workable dividing line between military and non-military uses of Space".
28. *Official Records of Disarmament Commission*, Supplement for January to December 1963, Document DC/208, Annex 1, SECT. N (ENDC/98).
29. *Ibid.*
30. *Ibid.*
31. United Nations, *Disarmament: Problems Related to Outer Space* (New York: United Nations Publication, 1987), p. 3.
32. *Ibid.*
33. The anti-satellite weapons are directed energy weapons capable of functioning in two distinct environments. It could be stationed on earth and directed towards Outer Space or placed somewhere in Outer Space or celestial body and directed towards the earth or other object located in space. See Robinson, "Soviet push for Beam Weapons", *Aviation Week and Space Technology* (New York), Vol. 106, May 2, 1977, p. 16.
34. See the Text of the Treaty in Appendix B; also for a critical view about the treaties' provision, see Rex J. Zedalis and Catherine L. Wadw, *Anti*-satellite Weapons and the Outer Space Treaty of 1967, *California Western International Law Journal* (San Francisco), Vol. 1, No. 8, 1978, p. 481.
35. *Arms Control and Disarmament Agency (ACDA)*, Arms Control and Disarmament Agreements (Washington, D.C: US Government Printing Office, 1982), p. 140.
36. See for example, the exchange between Senator Frank Carlson (R. Kansas) and UN Ambasador Arthur Goldberg, p. 34. Cited from Keith B. Payne, *Laser Weapons in Space Policy and Doctrine* (Boulder, Westview Press, 1983), pp. 74-75.
37. US Senate, *Hearings of the Committee on Foreign Relations*, 96th Congress, First Session, pp. 1611-1612.
38. *UN DOC.* A/C. 1/34/L.7.
39. U.S.S.R., "On definition of new types of weapons of mass destruction and new systems of such weapons" (CCD/514, August 10, 1976), in Report of the Conference of the Committee on Disarmament, *UN General Assembly Official Records*, 31st Session, Supplement No. 27 (A/31/27), Vol. II, pp. 276-79, quoted at pp. 276-77.
40. See Paul B. Stares, *Space and National Security* (Washington D.C.: The Brookings Institution, 1987), pp. 39-42, 66-71.
41. Bhupendra Jasani, "The Military Use of Outer Space", in World Armaments and Disarmament, *SIPRI Year Book* 1986 (London: Oxford University Press, 1986), pp. 131-57.

42. *Star Wars Delusions and Dangers* (Moscow Military Publishing House, 1985), pp. 8-10.
43. Bhupendra Jasani, n.41, p. 150.
44. Bhupendra Jasani, *Satellites for Arms Control and Crisis Monitoring* (Oxford: Oxford University Press, 1987), p. 41.
45. *Ibid.*
46. *Ibid.*
47. See Raymond L. Garthoff, "ASAT arms control; still possible", *Bulletin of Atomic Scientists* (BOAS) (Illinois), Vol. 40, No. 7, August/ September 1984, p. 30; also Thoms H. Karas, The New High Ground; Systems and Weapons of Space-Age War (New York: Simon and Schuster, 1983), pp. 148-49.
48. John Pike, "Anti-Satellite Weapons and Arms Control", Arms Control Today, December 1983, pp. 5-7.
49. For more detail, See United Nations Institute for Disarmament Research (UNIDIR), *Satellite Warfare*, A Challenge for the International Community (New York: UN, 1987).
50. For detailed discussion, see Carl Q. Christol, "International Liability for damage caused by Space Objects", *American Journal for International Law* (AJIL) (Washington), April 1980, Vol. 74 at 346-71; also Alexander F. Cohen, "Cosmos 954 and the International Law of Satellite Accidents", AJIL, Fall 1984, Vol. 10, No. 2, at 78-91.
51. *Ibid.*
52. *UN Press Release* (New York), A/AC. 105/L.162/Add. 3, 11 June, 1986.
53. *Eight Nations Disarmament Committee* (ENDC)/240, Union of Soviet Socialist Republics, Draft Treaty on the Prohibition of the Use for Military Purposes of the Sea-Bed and Ocean Floor and the Subsoil thereof, 18 March, 1969.
54. *Ibid.*; for more detail see the table which shows the names of the signatories to the multilateral treaties.
55. *ENDC/PV.* 400, 3 April, 1969; ENDC/PV. 409, 8 May, 1969, p. 15.
56. *ENDC/PV*. 414, 22 May, 1969, pp. 7-8; see also, *ENDC/PV*. 443, 16 October 1969, p. 20.
57. *ENDC/PV*. 413, 21 May, 1969, p. 7.
58. *Ibid.*, pp. 6-8.
59. *ENDC/PV* 422, 24 July 1969, pp. 17-19.
60. *ENDC/PV* 430, 21 August, 1969, pp. 20-21; ENDC/PV. 421, 22 July, 1969, pp. 33-35; *ENDC/PV* 410, 13 May, 1969, pp. 19-20; *ENDC/PV* 423, 29 July, 1969, pp. 14-15; and *CCD/PV* 441, 9 October, 1969, pp. 10-13.
61. *ENDC/PV* 426, 7 August, 1969, pp. 20-21.
62. *ENDC/PV* 421, July, 1969, Para 48.
63. *ENDC/PV* 428, August, 1969, pp. 12-13.
64. ENDC/PV. 428, 14 August, 1969, pp. 11-12.

65. *ENDC/PV* 428, 14 August, 1969, pp. 12-13. Conference of the Committee on Disarmament (CCD) 270, Canada, "Working Paper on Article III of Co-Chairman's Draft Treaty on the Prohibition of the Emplacement of Nuclear Weapons and Other Weapons of Mass Destruction on the Sea-Bed Ocean Floor and in the Subsoil Thereof" 8 October, 1969.
66. *CCD/PV* 445, 23 October, 1969, pp. 19-20; *CCD/PV* 443, 16 October, 1969, pp. 17-18; and *CCD/PV* 434, 4 September, 1969, pp. 27-29.
67. *CCD/PV* 445, 23 October, 1969, pp. 27-28.
68. *CCD/PV* 477, 7 July, 1970, pp. 15-16; CCD/PV.480, 21 July, 1970, pp. 20-21.
69. CCD/269/Rev. 3 Union of Soviet Socialist Republics and the United States of America, "*Draft Treaty on the Prohibition of the Emplacement of Nuclear 'Weapons and Other Weapons of Mass Destruction on the Sea-Bed and Ocean floor and in the subsoil thereof*", 1 September, 1970.
70. For the Text of the Treaty, see Appendix C.
71. *Ibid.*
72. See James Capable, "Is there a Naval Arms Race", *International Relations* (London), Vol. 8, No. 5, May, 1986, pp. 455-74.
73. For more detail see, John Pike, n.48, pp. 5-7.
74. For a good study on sea-based nuclear weapons, see, William M. Arkin, "The Nuclear Arms Race at Sea", *Neptune Papers* (Washington), Vol. 1, 1987, pp. 1-15.
75. For a good background of the nuclear free idea, see Gus Hall, "For a World Without Weapons", *Political Affairs* (New York), Vol. 65, No. 3, March, 1986, pp. 39-40.
76. For a detailed study on multilateral arms control, see Jozef Gold blat, "Arms Control Agreements", in SIPRI Year Book 1984, *World Armaments and Disarmament* (London: Taylor and Francis, 1984), pp. 671-94.
77. *Ibid.*
78. See the Texts of the Treaties in Appendices A, B and C.
79. For more detail, see Jozef Goldblat, "Arms Control in Outer Space", in SIPRI Year Book 1982, *World Armaments and Disarmament* (London: Taylor and Francis, 1982), pp. 441-45.
80. *Ibid.*
81. See Jozef Goldblat, "*Violation of Multilateral Arms Control Treaties: Possible Responses in Rene Hang (ed.), Verification of Arms Control Agreements: The Role of Third Countries* (Geneva: Programme for Strategic and International Security Studies, 1985"), pp. 83-95.
82. *Ibid.*
83. See Peter J. Beck, n. 2, p. 181.
84. *UNGAR*, n. 1, Part I.
85. *New York Times*, 22 June 1983.
86. See *Greenpeace International*, n. 15, pp. 11-14.

87. See Article I of the Antarctic Treaty.
88. For a good study carried out in this regard, see William M. Arkin, *"Nuclear-Weapon Command, Control and Communications"*, in SIPRI Year Book 1983, World *Armaments and Disarmament* (London: Taylor and Francis, 1983), pp. 69-86.
89. For a detail, see the *Text of the Treaty in Appendix* B. Bhupendra Jasani, n. 41, pp. 131-57.
90. For more detail on Soviet Star Wars programme, see, Rodney W. Jones and Steven A. Hildreth, *"Star Wars: Down to Earth, or Gleam in the Sky?"* The Washington Quarterly, Fall 1984, pp. 16-26.
91. For more detail, see United Nation, Department for Disarmament Affairs (UNDDA), *Study on Deterrence* (New York: UN, 1987), pp. 1-95.
92. See Jonathan B. Stein, "Anti-Tactical Ballistic Missiles—New Threat to the ABM Treaty", *Arms Control Today* (Washington), October, 1985, pp. 1-16.
93. Gus Hall, n. 74, pp. 39-40.
94. For more detail on nuclear connection of Outer Space, see Bhupendra Jasani, *"Nuclear Power Sources on Satellites"*, in SIPRI Year Book 1983, *World Armament and Disarmament* (London: Taylor and Francis, 1983), pp. 457-66.
95. *Ibid.*
96. William M. Arkin, n. 73, pp. 1-16.
97. *Ibid.*
98. William M. Arkin, n. 87, pp. 69-86.

3

Tlatelolco Treaty: Latin America Nuclear-Weapon-Free Zone

Introduction

Tlatelolco treaty is the first multilateral treaty signed for establishing nuclear-weapon-free zone (NWFZ) in Latin America.[1] It is in force for twenty countries in this region. It is significant as there are countries following different political systems such as democracy, military rule and communism and there are uprising political movements in many countries. Also, it is significant because big powers like the US, the Russia, France and the UK are involved both militarily and politically in this region. The US, the UK, France and the Netherlands are having territories lying within the limits of the zone. For example, the US territory in Latin American Zone is Puerto Rico. Also, the US has 28,000 acres at Guantanamo Bay, which was leased from Cuba in 1903. The UK fought a war with Argentina, which familiarized the British nuclear related activities in Latin America. France has its interest in the region as it has its colonial affiliation with many small countries. The Russia, being a latest partner in Latin America after Second World War, especially after Cuba became a communist country, plays an important role in balancing the power struggle in this region. It should be noted that because of the Soviet nuclear missiles in Cuba, which made a crisis in the continent in the early 1960s, the NWFZ was proposed by the Latin American Countries.

However, the treaty of Tlatelolco, which aims for nuclear-free Latin America, is the first treaty for establishing NWFZ in the inhabited area of the world and the Antarctic, Outer Space, and Sea-Bed treaties are for establishing NWFZ in the uninhabited areas of the world. Also, it is the first treaty which elaborately explains the objectives of the NWFZ and frames the scope of the treaty as follows: obligation of the contracting parties, zone of application, definition of nuclear weapons and use of nuclear energy for peaceful purposes. Conversely, the treaty is much criticized because of the nuclear weapon states' nuclear related activities in the zone and nuclear activities of Latin American Countries, especially, Argentina, Brazil and Mexico.

History

The idea of establishing NWFZ in Latin America came from Brazil in 1962, as it informed its interest to Mexican Government. Mexican Government considered this idea and its representative to the UN, Alfonso Garcia Robles, who is known as father of NWFZ, worked hard to put the idea into practice. As a result, on 21 March, 1963, the Mexican President, Lopez Mateas formally proposed the non-nuclearization of Latin America in a letter addressed to four heads of States of Bolivia, Brazil, Chile and Ecuador. In that letter, the President expressed his interest for nuclear free Latin America and asked them to co-operate for a multilateral agreement. On 29 April, 1963, the heads of States signed a joint declaration. It announced that their Governments are prepared to sign a multilateral agreement whereby countries would undertake not to manufacture, receive, store, or test nuclear weapons or nuclear launching devices.[2] It adds further, "to bring this declaration to the attention of the heads of States of other Latin American Republics, expressing the hope that these Governments will accede to it, through such procedures as they consider appropriate"; and "to co-operate with one another and with such other Latin American Republics as accede to this declaration".[3]

To this effort, the General Assembly of the United Nations adopted a resolution (1911 XVII) in support of the idea of Latin American Countries. It called upon the Latin American Countries to initiate studies concerning the measures that should be agreed upon with a view to achieve the aims of said declaration.[4] A Preparatory Commission for the Denuclearization of Latin America was established in November 1964 in Mexico city. The task of this Commission was to prepare a preliminary draft for a multilateral treaty without any outside interference. The Commission adopted two basic resolutions: The first defined the term, "Denuclearization", specifying that it should mean solely "the absence of nuclear weapons" and not the prohibition of the peaceful use of the atomic energy which, on the contrary, should be encouraged, especially for the benefit of the developing countries; the second established the Preparatory Commission for the Denuclearization of Latin America (COPREDAL) and instructed the Commission to prepare a draft treaty on the subject.[5] The Commission met four times in Mexico city. In this meeting, apart from the twenty-one members of the Latin American Countries, there were observers from Austria, Belgium, Canada, Republic of China, Denmark, Finland, Sweden, Yugoslavia, the United Arab Republic, the United Kingdom and the United States. There were a number of difficult and complex questions followed in the discussion. However, the progress made in 1965 and 1966 made it possible for the treaty to be signed on 14 February, 1967, at Tlatelolco.

Scope of the Treaty

The Tlatelolco treaty comprises a preamble, thirty-one articles, one transitional article and two Additional Protocols. The preamble defines the fundamental aims of the treaty. It says: "That military denuclearization of Latin America—being understood to mean the undertaking—to keep their territories for ever free from nuclear weapons—will constitute a measure which will spare their peoples from the squandering of their limited resources on nuclear armaments".[6] And it continues that it will protect them against possible nuclear attacks on their territories and will also constitute a significant contribution towards preventing the proliferation of nuclear weapons and a powerful factor for general and complete Disarmament. The articles of the treaty may be described briefly as follows: Article 1 defines the obligations of the parties. Articles 2 and 5 provide definitions of the terms:[7] contracting parties, territory, zone of application and nuclear weapons. Article 6 deals with the "meeting of all the signatories", while articles 7 to 11 establish the structure and procedures of OPANAL (the agency for the prohibition of Nuclear

Weapons in Latin America, known by its Spanish acronym OPANAL).[8] Also these articles state the functions and powers of its principal organs: The General Conference, the Council and the Secretariat. And articles 12 to 16 explain the functioning of the control system.

Article 17 contains general provisions on the peaceful use of nuclear energy and article 18 deals with peaceful nuclear explosions. Article 19 states about the relations of OPANAL with other international organizations, while article 20 outlines the measures against a serious violation of the treaty. Article 21 safeguards the rights and obligations of the parties under the charter of the United Nations and, in the case of state members of the organization of American States, under existing regional treaties. Article 23 makes it binding for the contracting parties to notify the Secretariat of OPANAL of any international agreement concluded by any of them on matters which the treaty is concerned. Article 24 explains the settlement of controversies concerning the interpretation or application of the treaty. And Articles 22, 25-27, and 29-31 contain "final clauses" which deal with questions such as privileges and immunities, signature, ratification and deposit, reservations, amendments, duration and denunciation, and authentic texts and registration.[9]

The transitional article says that "Denunciation of the declaration referred to in article 28, paragraph 2, and shall be subject to the same procedures as the denunciation of this Treaty, except that it will take effect on the date of delivery of the respective notification". It continues: "In witness whereof the undersigned Plenipotentiaries, having deposited their full powers, found in good and due form, sign this Treaty on behalf of their respective Governments".[10] Additional protocol I is created by the treaty for the States having territories within the limits of the geographical zone established by the Treaty: United States, United Kingdom, France, and the Netherlands. And additional protocol II is for the nuclear weapon states—United States, Soviet Union, United Kingdom, France and China. However, for the purpose of the study, it is worth examining some important provisions of the treaty: The provisions dealing with the obligations of the contracting parties, the zone of application, the definition of nuclear weapons, the system of verification and control, and the use of nuclear energy for peaceful purposes. Also, the two additional protocols of the treaty are explained.

Obligations of the contracting parties are explained in article 1 of the Treaty. According to article 1, the contracting parties undertake "to use exclusively for the peaceful purposes the nuclear material and facilities which are under their jurisdiction, and to prohibit and prevent in their respective territories: (a) The testing, use, manufacture, production or acquisition by any means whatsoever of any nuclear weapon ... and (b) The receipt, storage, installation, deployment and any form of possession of any nuclear weapons ", by the parties themselves, directly or indirectly, on behalf of any one else, by any one on their behalf or in any other way. It continues further: "The contracting parties also undertake to refrain from engaging in, encouraging or authorizing, directly or indirectly, or in any way participating in the testing, use, manufacture, production, possession or control of any nuclear weapon".[11] However, article 30 of the treaty provides a clause of denunciation, which contradicts the article 1 of the Treaty. It gives the contracting parties more freedom of action by which a party, if it wishes to get rid of the commitments acquired under article 1, can go against the very purpose of the Treaty. According to article 30, "Any party may denounce it ... if in the opinion of the denouncing state, there have arisen or may arise circumstances connected with the content of this Treaty or of the Additional Protocols I and II which affect its supreme interests or the peace and security of one or more Contracting Parties".[12] It is not explained in the provision at what circumstances a party can decide to denounce it. Therefore, a party is fully allowed to decide about the circumstances in which it thinks that it can denounce article 1 of the Treaty. Both the nuclear weapon states and the zone members having an advanced technology could, theoretically, escape from the treaty through the unexpected use of its right given by the article 30.[13] Zone of application is explained in the provision of article 4, which is related with the procedure adopted in article 28. Article 28 explains as to how the Treaty shall enter into force among the States (See the Map).

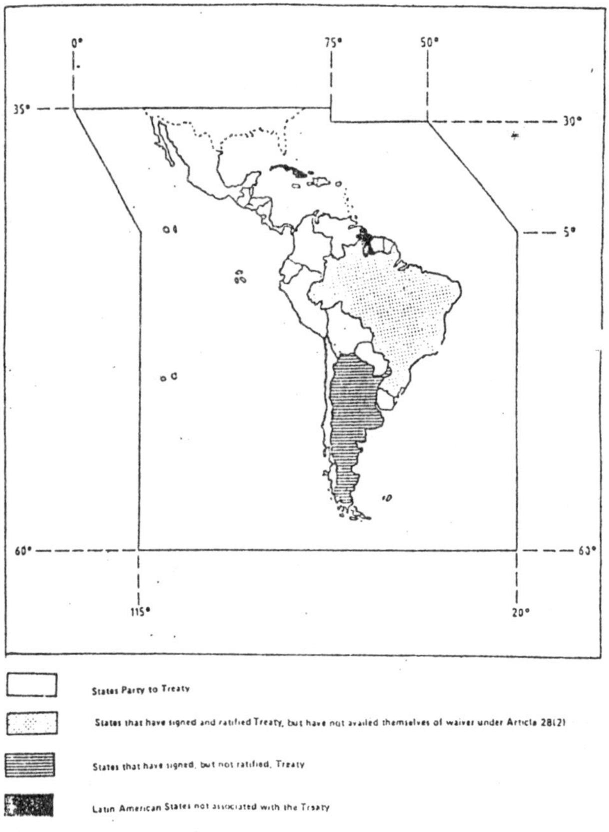

For, according to this, the following requirements have to be met: (a) Deposit of the instruments of ratification, (b) Signature and ratification of additional protocol I, (c) Signature and ratification of the additional Protocol I, (d) Conclusion of bilateral or multilateral agreements on the application of the safeguards system of the IAEA.[14] It has to be notified that according to article 28, government cannot be given admission as article 25 explains that the General Conference of the contracting parties shall not take any decision regarding the admission of any country whose territory is the subject of a dispute, between an extra-continental country and one or more Latin American Countries, so long as the dispute has not been settled by peaceful means.[15] The conclusion of bilateral agreements on the application of the safeguard system has to be in accordance with article 13 of the Treaty which says: "Each contracting party shall negotiate multilateral or bilateral agreements with the International Atomic Energy Agency... These agreements shall enter into force, for each party, not later than eighteen months after the date of the initiation of such negotiations except in case of unforeseen circumstances..." It is not clear as to what the provision means by the "unforeseen circumstances".[16]

Therefore, there are two interpretations of the term "zone of application": (a) Provisional/movable zone, and definitive/fixed zone. They are explained in paragraphs 1 and 2 of article 4. Paragraph 1 says: "The zone of application of this treaty is the territories for which the treaty is in force".[17] According to this definition the 'zone of application of the zone grows and the number of contracting states increase. Therefore, it is movable. And regarding a fixed definition, paragraph 2 says: "Upon fulfilment of the requirements of article 28, paragraph 1, the zone of application of this Treaty shall also be that which is situated in the Western hemisphere within the following limits (except the continental part of the territory of the United States of America and its territorial waters".[18] However, the treaty does not include the exclusive economic zone and it permits the freedom of navigation.

Moreover, the zone of application depends heavily on the assurances of nuclear weapon states. In case the nuclear weapon states are not following the assurance of "Not to contribute in any way to the performance of acts involving a violation of the obligations of article 1 of the Treaty", the zone of application is difficult to be achieved.[19] Furthermore, there is no provision in the treaty, which should get the guarantee of nuclear weapon states in a situation, which may lead, for a nuclear war. Peacetime guarantee cannot be practically feasible to be maintained in the wartime. Therefore, the United States, the United Kingdom and the Soviet Union argued that the guarantee would be unnecessary if it was only enforced during peacetime.[20] Also, the treaty does not have any provision, which may deal with the new nuclear weapon states in the future. The map (see page 63) shows the zone of application of the treaty of Tlatelolco. It indicates States party to the treaty, states that have signed and ratified the treaty, but have not waived the entry-into-force provision (article 28), states that have signed, but not ratified the treaty, and Latin American States not associated with the treaty.

Definition of the term nuclear weapon is included in article 5. It says: "For the purposes of this treaty, a nuclear weapon is any device which is capable of releasing nuclear energy in an uncontrolled manner and which has a group of characteristics that are appropriate for use for warlike purposes". In addition, the treaty provides that "An instrument that may be used for the transport or propulsion of the device is not included in this definition and it is separable from the device and not an indivisible party thereof".[21] It should be noted that, if any contracting party does not agree to this definition, it might jeopardize the effectiveness of the zone. Also, it is very difficult to differentiate between nuclear explosive devices usable for military and peaceful purposes.[22] Therefore, for the purpose of this study, both the military and peaceful nuclear activities are considered in the following section of the chapter.

System of verification and control is explained in articles 12-16 and article 18, paragraphs 2 and 3. Articles 12-16 include control system (article 12), IAEA safeguard (article 13), reports of the parties (article 14), special reports requested by the General Secretary (article 15), and special inspections (article 16), article 18, paragraphs 2 and 3, deal with the explosions for peaceful purposes and related items for verification as well as control. According to paragraph 2, article 18, the parties interested for peaceful nuclear explosion should give information about the nature of the nuclear device and the source, place and purpose of the explosion, the procedures, the expected force of the device and "information on any possible radioactive fall-out from the explosions and the measures which will be taken to avoid danger to the population, *flora, fauna* and territories of any other party or parties".[23] And paragraph 3 gives the right of observing all the preparations of explosion of the device to the General Secretary and the technical personnel of both the Councils (OPANAL) and IAEA in order to confirm with the information provided by the parties in accordance with paragraph 2.[24]

On the other hand, the control system shall be used specifically, according to article 12, for the purpose of verifying: That devices, services and facilities intended for peaceful uses of nuclear energy are not used in the testing or manufacture of nuclear weapons, that none of the activities prohibited in article 1 of this treaty are carried out, and that explosion for peaceful purposes are compatible with the article 18 of this treaty.[25] Moreover, for carrying out special inspections, article 16 gives the right to the OPANAL. These peaceful inspections will be carried out under certain circumstances. After carrying out the inspections, OPANAL is subject to transmit the reports on those inspections to the Security Council and General Assembly of the United Nations.[26] Thus, article 12 establishes two types of safeguards systems—applicable to all the installations and nuclear weapon states. The first one is to assure the absence of illicit use of nuclear energy for peaceful purposes. And the second is to make evident any secret introduction of nuclear weapons into the zone area by nuclear weapon states.[27]

Also, article 12 includes special safeguards to prevent the misuse of the peaceful nuclear explosions. The IAEA enforces the first kind of safeguards (Article 13). According to article 18, the IAEA shall share with the OPANAL. The second kind of safeguards has been assigned by OPANAL. (Article 16, paragraph 1, sub-paragraph (b) and from 2-B). However, it has to be noted that the first kind of the information submitted by the inspected state with the verification and observations carried out independently by the IAEA. Since it comprises full-scope safeguards over all nuclear activities of contracting parties as well as the territories of US, UK, France and Netherlands covered by the Additional Protocol I, it is very difficult to implement.[28] Also, there is nothing in the articles relating to verification and control to prevent the nuclear states: US, UK and France from using their territories for nuclear activities. In the case of the second safeguard system, the OPANAL might face technical problem as the activities of nuclear weapon states are interrelated. Moreover, technically it is impossible for OPANAL to carry out an effective inspection. And there is no mention in these articles so as to how the nuclear activities of nuclear weapon states, which are signatories to the Protocol II, should co-operate with these kinds of verifications.[29]

Therefore, Latin American Countries, Argentina and Brazil, argued against the verification and control system established by the treaty of Tlatelolco in various occasions. In the Tenth General Conference of the OPANAL, Brazil stated, "It is necessary to establish as a counterpoint adequate and reliable procedures to verify compliance with the obligations of the nuclear-weapon powers in regard to zone". And it argued further: "Only with the adoption of these procedures, which are today non-existent, can we assure the indispensable balance between the responsibilities and commitments of each of the groups of states involved. This measure is a demand of the security proposals of the zone of application of Tlatelolco which recent experience confirms."[30] The Brazilian argument for an effective verification should be seen in the light of recent development in the Atlantic Sea. More than 500 nuclear weapon states are patrolling in the sea. These forces are generally used for warlike purposes. The NWFZ of Latin America has no mechanism to carry out any measure against these activities.[31]

Use of nuclear energy for peaceful purposes [known as Peaceful Nuclear Energy (PNE)] is dealt in article 17. It says: "Nothing in the provisions of this Treaty shall prejudice the rights of the contracting Parties, in conformity with this Treaty, to use nuclear energy for peaceful purposes, in particular for their economic development and social progress." Article 17 was established because of the recommendation of the Preparatory Commission, which became one of the paragraphs in the preamble to the Treaty. It notes: "...together with the traditional peace-loving outlook of Latin America, give rise to an inescapable necessity that nuclear energy should be used in that region exclusively for peaceful purposes". And it continues: "... that the Latin American Countries should use their right to the greatest and most equitable possible access to this new source of energy in order to expedite the economic and social development of their peoples".[32] Therefore, for avoiding the misunderstanding concerning the scope of the treaty, the last session of the Preparatory Commission indicated that the treaty should intend not to prevent civil, but military activities of nuclear energy. In addition, the last session, therefore, changed the original name of the instrument from "Treaty for the Denuclearization of Latin America" to "Treaty for the Prohibition of Nuclear Weapons in Latin America". However, article 17 is inter-related with article 1, article 5 and article 18.

Article 1 explains the primary objective: To refrain from engaging in, encouraging or authorizing, directly or indirectly, or in any way participating in the testing, use, manufacture, production, possession or control of any nuclear weapon. To answer as to what does article 1 mean by nuclear weapon, for the first time in the nuclear history, article 5 of the Treaty of Tlatelolco defines nuclear weapon as "any device which is capable of releasing nuclear energy in an uncontrolled manner and which has a group of characteristics that are appropriate for use for war like purposes". Contracting parties interested for PNE should follow these two articles. Following these two, the party which prepares for PNE should provide all types of information about the nuclear devices, as stated in article 18, to follow the measures of observation, verification and control by the General Secretary and the Council of OPANAL and by IAEA.[33] However, article 18 contradicts itself, as paragraph 1 of this article reads: "The Contracting Parties may carry out explosions of nuclear devices for peaceful purposes—including explosions which involves devices similar to those used in nuclear weapons—or collaborate with third parties for the same purpose".[34] Therefore, there are different interpretations by different countries.

The United States, Great Britain, the Soviet Union and Mexico pointed out that articles 1 and 5 exclude, for the present, the implementation of article 18 given that today's technology does not differentiate, *de facto*, between nuclear devices for military or civilian purposes.[35] Argentina and Brazil consider that article 18 does not ignore that similarity but rather underlines it. However, the basic question is: How far article 18 is subordinated to Articles 1 and 5. In principle, article 18 establishes the right to carry out civil nuclear explosions including explosions similar to those used in nuclear weapons. It recognizes two important points:[36] A nuclear explosive device different from nuclear weapons is possible to carry out and a nuclear explosion with peaceful aims, even in the case of using similar devices to a nuclear bomb, does not necessarily involve a violation of articles 1 and 5. Thus, article 18 does not exclude the eventual use of a nuclear device different from a nuclear weapon; neither does it forbid the use of a device, technically speaking, equivalent to such a weapon of mass destruction.[37] However, the point emphasized between article 18 and articles 1 and 5 is that the contracting parties have greater freedom of interpreting these articles without bothering about technicalities. Therefore, it can be stated that the party interested for PNE can go for any type of explosion. Because of these reasons, there is no guarantee that nuclear explosions with potential military use will never happen in Latin America.

The two Additional Protocols to the treaty are created for the extra-continental States: US, UK, France, and Netherlands and nuclear weapon powers: US, Soviet Union, UK, France and China. Also, it is important to note that these additional protocols serve the interest of the United Nations, as their texts recall the UN resolution 1911 (XVIII) of 27 November; 1963 and say that the Tlatelolco Treaty "represents an important step towards ensuring the non-proliferation of nuclear weapons". Further, it states that the non-proliferation of nuclear weapons", is not an end in itself but, rather, a means of achieving general and complete disarmament at a later stages', and expresses finally the desire to contribute "towards ending the armaments race".[38]

Additional Protocol 1 has three articles. Under article 1, those extra-continental States which are internationally responsible for territories lying within the limits of the geographical zone established by the Treaty would agree "To undertake to apply the statute of denuclearization in respect of warlike purposes as defined in Articles 1, 3, 5 and 13 of the Treaty" to their territories. It should be mentioned that Protocol 1 does not give the states the right to participate in the General Conference or in the Council of OPANAL. Also, it is not imposing on them any of the obligations relating to the system of control established in Article 14 of the Treaty (providing for semi-annual reports), Article 15 (providing for special inspections). And the Treaty's article 27 is not applicable to the Protocol. Additional Protocol II has five articles.[39]

According to articles 1, 2 and 3, the nuclear powers—US, Soviet Union, UK, France and China would undertake: To respect the zone in all its express aims and provision (article 1); not to contribute in any way to the performance of acts involving a violation of the obligations of article 1 of the Treaty (article 2): not to use or threaten to use the entry-into-force provision, article 28.[40] Cuba has neither signed nor ratified list of Latin American States that have signed or ratified the treaty of Tlatelolco, dates of signature or ratification of the treaty by nuclear weapon States, and status of IREA safeguards agreements for parties to the treaty, is given in the following tables. The next section focuses on the attitude of nuclear weapon states: US, Soviet Union, UK, France and China. (See the Tables).

Latin American States that have signed/ratified the Treaty of Tlatelolco

	States Party to Treaty		
Country	*Signature*	*Ratification*	*Waiver*
Antigua and Barbuda	Oct. 11, 1983	Oct. 11, 1983	Oct. 11, 1983
Bahamas	Nov. 29, 1976	Apr. 26, 1977	Apr. 26, 1977
Barbados	Oct. 18, 1968	Apr. 25, 1969	Apr. 25, 1969
Bolivia	Feb. 14, 1967	Feb. 18, 1969	Feb. 18, 1969
Colombia	Feb. 14, 1967	Aug. 4, 1972	Sep. 6, 1972
Costa Rica	Feb. 14, 1967	Aug. 25, 1969	Aug. 25, 1969
Ecuador	Feb. 14, 1967	Feb. 11, 1969	Feb. 11, 1969
El Salvador	Feb. 14, 1967	Apr. 22, 1968	Apr. 22, 1968
Grenada	Apr. 29, 1967	Jun. 20, 1975	June 20, 1975
Guatemala	Feb. 14, 1975	Feb. 6, 1970	Feb. 6, 1970
Haiti	Feb. 14, 1967	May 23, 1969	May 23, 1969
Honduras	Feb. 14, 1967	Sep. 23, 1968	Sep. 23, 1968
Jamaica	Oct. 26, 1967	Jan. 26, 1969	Jun. 26, 1969
Mexico	Feb. 14, 1967	Sep. 20, 1967	Sep. 20, 1967
Nicaragua	Feb. 15, 1967	Oct. 24, 1968	Oct. 24, 1968
Panama	Feb. 14, 1967	Jun. 11, 1971	Jun. 11, 1971
Paraguay	Apr. 26, 1967	Mar. 19, 1969	Mar. 19, 1969
Peru	Feb. 14, 1967	Mar. 4, 1969	Mar. 4, 1969
Dominican Republic	Feb. 28, 1967	Jun. 14, 1968	Jun. 14, 1968
Surinam	Feb. 13, 1976	Jun. 10, 1977	Jun. 10, 1977
Trinidad and Tobago	Jun. 27, 1967	Dec. 3, 1970	Jun. 27, 1975
Uruguay	Feb. 14, 1967	Aug. 20, 1968	Aug. 20, 1968
Venezuela	Feb. 14, 1967	Mar. 23, 1970	Mar. 23, 1970
States that have signed, but not ratified Treaty			
Argentina	Sep. 27, 1967		
States that have signed and ratified Treaty, but have not availed themselves of waiver under article 28(2)			
Brazil	May 9, 1967	Jan. 29, 1968	
Chile	Feb. 14, 1967	Oct. 9, 1974	

(Contd.)

(Contd.)

Country	*States Party to Treaty*		
	Signature	*Ratification*	*Waiver*
Latin American States not associated with the Treaty			
Belize	St. Vincent and the Grenadines		
Cuba	St. Lucia		
Dominica	St. Christopher and Nevis		
Guyana	St. Christopher and Nevis		

Status of IAEA safeguarded agreements

	Treaty of Tlatelolco	
Country	*Signed but not in force*	*In force*
Antigua and Barbuda	x	
Bahamas	x	
Barbados	x	
Bolivia	x	
Colombia		x
Costa Rica		x
Ecuador		x
El Salvador		x
Grenada		x
Guatemala		x
Haiti	x	
Honduras		x
Jamaica		x
Mexico		x
Nicaragua		x
Panama		
Paraguay	–	x
Peru		x
Dominican Republic		x
Surinam		x
Trinidad and Tobago		
Uruguay	–	x
Venezuela	–	x

Source: *International Atomic Energy Agency*—Annual Report, 1985 (Vienna: The International Atomic Energy Agency, 1986), for latest information, *see* SPRI Year Book series till 2005.

Dates of signature/ratification of the Treaty of Tlatelolco

Country	*Signature*	*Ratification*
Additional Protocol I		
France	Mar. 2, 1979	—
Netherlands	Mar.15, 1968	Jul. 20, 1971
United States	May 26, 1977	Nov. 23, 1981
Additional Protocol II		
China, People's Republic of	Aug. 21, 1973	Jan. 12, 1974
France	Jul. 18, 1973	Mar. 22, 1974
United Kingdom	Dec. 20, 1967	Dec. 11, 1969
United States	Apr. 1, 1968	May 12, 1971
USSR	May 18, 1978	Jan. 8, 1979

Source: *International Atomic Energy Agency*–Annual Report, 1985 (Vienna: The International Atomic Energy Agency, 1986), for latest information, *see* for latest information, *see* SPRI Year Book series till 2005.

Attitude of Nuclear Weapon States

The United States signed the Additional Protocol I of the treaty in 1977, and ratified it in 1981. It signed the Additional Protocol II in 1968 and ratified it in 1971. According to Additional Protocol I, the US should not test, use, manufacture, produce or acquire by any means whatsoever of any nuclear weapons in its territory— Puerto Rico— which is included in the zone.[41] Also, the Protocol I prohibits "the receipt, storage, installation, deployment, and any form of possession of any nuclear weapons directly or indirectly" in Puerto Rico.[42] In the beginning, the US did not agree to the Protocol I. And it argued that the Protocol I did not prevent the usages of nuclear weapons that could possibly be used against the Contracting Parties of the Treaty (Article 3). Article 4 explains that the duration of the protocol is the same as that of the Treaty. According to article 4, "the definitions of territory and nuclear weapons set forth in Articles 3 and 5 of the Treaty shall be applicable to this Protocol, as well as the provisions regarding ratification, reservations, denunciation, authentic text and registration contained in Articles 26, 27, 30 and 31 of the Treaty".

Finally, article 5 notes that "this Protocol I of the treaty is signed and ratified by Netherlands, the United Kingdom and the United States. France signed the Protocol I, but not ratified it. Protocol II of the treaty is signed and ratified by Netherlands, the United Kingdom and the United States. Protocol II of the treaty is signed and ratified. Protocol II of the treaty is signed and ratified by China, France, the Soviet Union, the United Kingdom and the United States. The Tlatelolco treaty is currently completely in force in twenty-three Latin American countries including Mexico, Colombia and Peru. Argentina, Brazil, Chile and Cuba are not full parties to the agreement. Argentina has signed the treaty, but not ratified it. Brazil and Chile have signed and ratified, but both of them have not waived. However, the Latin American Countries, especially with the initiation of Mexico, suggested that the US could be given transport privilege. As of this reason, in 1977, the US decided to sign Protocol I. On signing protocol I, the US stated that it would take its own time to consider the ratification of Protocol I. Although the signature of the US to Protocol I was appreciated by many Latin American Countries, the Soviet Union was not satisfied and it stated in May 1978, that "permission for transit rights of nuclear weapons in any form would contradict the goals of the Treaty — and would be incompatible with the non-nuclear status of the contracting parties"[43] especially, the Soviet Union showed its dissatisfaction over the special consideration given by the Latin American Countries to the US. The US argued against the Soviet interpretation of Protocol I and stated that the main responsibility lies on the zone countries, and therefore, a strict measure against the States party to the additional protocols would go against the interest of NWFZ in Latin America.[44]

The failure of the US to ratify Protocol I had allowed down the treaty's momentum. Therefore, the Latin American States raised questions regarding the US commitment to non-proliferation in the region. In February 1980, OPANAL Secretary-General, Gros Espiell, informed the US State Department indicating that "the failure of the US to ratify Additional Protocol I, almost three years after its signature deeply preoccupies the Latin American Parties to the Tlatelolco Treaty. This lack of ratification appears to demonstrate little interest in the question of the military denuclearization of Latin America.

Such an action by the US — Clearly incompatible with the repeated declarations of President Carter and Secretary of State Vance of full and total support for the Tlatelolco Treaty — (affects) negatively the negotiations to obtain the signatures and ratifications of those which are still not full parties to the Tlatelolco Treaty, Cuba, Guyana, Argentina, Brazil, and Chile".[45] And he stated further: "All the credibility of the US policies on the matter relating to nuclear proliferation in Latin America will be compromised, in actuality, if it does not proceed quickly with ratification of Additional Protocol I".[46] In 1981, the US, however, ratified Protocol I. After ratifying it, the US pointed out its understanding with which it signed Protocol I. According to that, the Protocol I of the treaty does not affect the exclusive power and legal competence under international law of a state adhering to Protocol I to grant or deny transit and transport privileges to its own or any other vessels or aircraft irrespective of cargo or armaments.[47] Also, Protocol I, according to the US, does not affect rights under international law of a state party to Protocol I "regarding the exercise of the freedom of the seas, or regarding passage through or over waters subject to the sovereignty of a state".[48]

It is important to note the military activity which is against the Protocol I of the treaty. The US military activity in Puerto Rico is carried out in four areas:[49] (1) Preparations and planning for the command and control of nuclear missile carrying submarines from the Naval Station, Roosevelt Roads; (2) Plans to activate a base for nuclear anti-submarines warfare (ASW) Weapons at Roosevelt Roads (and at key West, Florida) to carry out nuclear ASW operations I the zone; (3) Training with and testing of nuclear weapon systems within Puerto Rico and elsewhere in the zone; and (4) Command of and communications for nuclear weapons from facilities in Puerto Rico and the zone. Roosevelt Road is designated as an "alternate command" headquarters for strategic missile-carrying submarines in the Atlantic Ocean. More than thirty submarines are based in the Atlantic Ocean. It should be noted that the US has thirty four strategic submarines in total. However, the submarines based in the Atlantic Ocean are at Kings Bay, Georgia, Charleston, South Carolina, and Holy Loch, Scotland. The US has a plan to move the headquarters of those submarines to Puerto Rico.[50] Moreover; the US has the high frequency (HF) radio transmitter at Isabella. This is the important communication center in Puerto Rico to communicate with submarines and ships. The US military maintains three important long-range communication stations in Puerto Rico. They are: the low frequency transmitter at Aguada, the high frequency transmitter at Isabella, and a high frequency receiver at Sabana Sea. Also, Puerto Rico has Anti Satellite nuclear weapons and related installations.[51]

More importantly, there are nuclear infrastructures which can be used in a crisis period. They are: command headquarters, communications, training and testing facilities. Thus, thirty-two nuclear depth bombs to Roosevelt Roads for wartime ASW operations and thirteen nuclear related facilities of the US are deployed in Puerto Rico *in toto*. Also, in US Virgin Island the US has three testing installations which support strategic submarine and missile research and training. More detail is added in the Appendix F. The US signed and ratified Protocol II with declaration that in connection with Article 3 of the Treaty, which defines the term "territory" as including the territorial sea, airspace and any other space over which the state exercises sovereignty in accordance with its own legislation, "the US ratification of the Protocol could not be regarded as implying recognition of any legislation which did not, in its view, comply with the relevant rules of international law. Each of the parties retains exclusive power and legal competence, unaffected by the terms of the Treaty, to grant or deny non-parties transit and transport privileges".[52] In connection with this, the US stated that it would consider that an armed attack by a party which was assisted by nuclear weapon state would be incompatible with the party's obligations under Article 1 of the Treaty. Regarding Articles 1, 5 and 18, it noted that the definition contained the Article 5 of the Treaty is understood as encompassing all nuclear explosive devices; Articles 1 and 5 of the Treaty restrict accordingly the activities of the contracting parties under paragraph 1 of Article 18. And it continued: "Article 18 paragraph 4 permits, and US adherence to Protocol II will not prevent, collaboration by the USA with the parties to the Treaty for the purpose of carrying out explosions of nuclear devices for peaceful purposes in a manner consistent with the policy of not contributing to the proliferation of nuclear weapon capabilities".[53] Thus, the United States keeps the option open for its nuclear activities in a crisis period. It has installed the nuclear infrastructures in many zones countries. For example, the US nuclear infrastructures are with Antiqua, Argentina, Bahamas, Barbados and Panama. The following would focus on the United Kingdom and its attitude towards the Tlatelolco Treaty.

The United Kingdom was the first country to sign the additional protocol of the treaty. It signed and ratified both the protocols in 1967 and in 1969 respectively. After doing so, the UK expressed its view about the treaty that it did not regard its signing and ratification of the Protocols as implying recognition of any legislation which does not, in its view, comply with the relevant rules of international law.[54] Thus, the UK, like the US, did not agree with the Article 3 of the Treaty which defines the territory. Also the UK stated that "the treaty does not permit the parties to carry out explosions of nuclear devices for peaceful purposes unless and until advances in technology have made possible the development of devices for such explosions which are not capable of being used for weapon purposes".[55] However, it is important to note the activities of the UK in Latin American Zone. British nuclear activities in the zone are three-fold: the use of nuclear powered submarines; the presence of nuclear weapons in the British Naval Task Force; and the stationing of a nuclear armed submarine within range of Argentina.[56] The UK had used five nuclear powered submarines in the Falkland war: Spartan, Splendid, Valiant, Courageous and Conqueror. It should be mentioned that the conqueror submarine was responsible for sinking the Argentine cruises General Belgrano. Argentina opposed this attack and stated that the UK violated the Tlatelolco treaty. However, the UK viewed that the nuclear powered submarines were not prohibited by the treaty. It argued that its nuclear powered submarine did not fall within the definition of a nuclear weapon contained in the treaty as a "device which is capable of releasing nuclear energy in an uncontrolled manner" (Article 5).[57]

Furthermore, in the Falkland conflict, British ships were reported to have carried on the board the nuclear weapons. These forces were equipped with ANS helicopters. They were: Aircraft Carriers, Type 82, County Class, Type 42, Type 22, Type 21,

Leander, and Rothsay.[58] However, it should be noted that the UK did not agree to the report of Argentina. Thirdly, the UK was also reported to have carried in the ships the Polaris nuclear missiles. This was not accepted by the UK. However, it should be noted that Argentina is not adhered to the treaty as it has not ratified the treaty. Therefore it would not be legal violation of the treaty. However, the UK activities in the Falkland war gave a set back to the non-proliferation regime in Latin America, as it did not abide by the Protocol II which the UK undertook not to use or threaten to use nuclear weapons against the zone. France is signatory of both the Protocols. However, it has not ratified protocol I. According to France, the treaty of Tlatelolco will not affect the right of self-defense. For, self-defense, therefore, it reserves the right of transiting across the territories of French Republic situated in the zone of the treaty, the nuclear weapons and related materials. Thus, France expressed its interest of maintaining its defense policy, 'force de frappe', even in connection to some other regions. Also, France stated that "it was prepared to consider its obligations under Protocol II as applying not only to the signatories for which the statute of denuclearization was in force in conformity with Article 1 of Protocol I".[59] Thus, the Protocol II also, according to France, becomes invalid in case the zone countries go against the statute of denuclearization.

China has signed and ratified the treaty. As a nuclear weapon state which is following 'non-first-use' policy, its guarantee has become very much valid to the Latin American States. It is only a signatory for Protocol II. After signing and ratifying Protocol II of the treaty in 1973 and in 1974 respectively, it issued a statement: "China will never use or threaten to use nuclear weapons against non-nuclear Latin American countries and the Latin American nuclear-weapon-free-zone; nor will China test, manufacture, produce, stockpile, install or deploy nuclear weapons in these countries or in this zone".[60] However, China expressed its reservation that the super powers, the US and the Soviet Union, should implement their undertakings: dismantling all foreign military bases in Latin America and refraining from establishing new bases, and prohibiting the passage of any means of transportation and delivery carrying nuclear weapons through Latin American Territory, territorial sea or air-space. Although these are not implemented by both the US and the Soviet Union, China has not changed its position.

The Soviet Union also signed and ratified the Treaty in 1978 and in 1979 respectively. It stated after signing the treaty that "the effect of Article 1 of the treaty extends, and specified in Article 5 of the Treaty, to any nuclear explosive device and that, accordingly, the carrying out by any party to the treaty of explosions of nuclear devices for peaceful purposes would be a violation of its obligations under Article 1 and would be incompatible with its non-nuclear status".[61] However, the Soviet Union stated further that if the parties are interested for PNE they can follow the instructions from IAEA. Regarding transport and transit problems, it mentioned that permitting the transit of nuclear weapons in any form would be contrary to the objectives of the treaty, especially to their obligations as laid down in Article 1. Also, the Soviet Union noted with the concern that if the non-nuclear status of the treaty was not maintained by any party of the treaty, the Soviet Union would reconsider its obligations under Protocol II of the treaty. In regard to the obligations undertaken by other nuclear weapon states, it stated that if the nuclear weapon states were not maintaining their obligations, it would reconsider its position.[62] However, the Soviet Union has been maintaining its nuclear infrastructure in Cuba. Two airfields, San Antonio de Los Banos and Jose Marti Airport, support regular Bear-D reconnaissance and nuclear-capable Bear-F ASW visits to Cuba. And Cienfuegos and Havana are used by Soviet naval forces. More detail is given in the appendix. The following section deals with Latin American States and their nuclear activities.

Latin American States and Nuclear Activities

There are twenty-six Latin American countries who have signed the treaty of Tlatelolco. And twenty-three of them have ratified the treaty. Only Argentina has not ratified. Brazil and Chile have signed and ratified, but both of them have not waived the entry-into-force provision, Article 28. Therefore, the treaty is in complete force, except Argentina, Brazil, and Chile, for twenty-three countries. Cuba is the only country which has neither signed nor ratified the treaty. Of all Latin American Countries, Mexico,

Argentina, Brazil, Chile, Peru, Cuba, Colombia, and Venezuela are involved in nuclear activities. Among these countries, only Mexico, Colombia and Venezuela are fully adhered to the treaty. However, the most advanced technology is with Mexico, Argentina and Brazil. They are nearing a technical capability to develop a 'explosive device'. Moreover, there are nuclear infrastructures with many Latin American Countries. For the purpose of this study, it is important to examine the nuclear activities of Mexico, Argentina and Brazil, and the nuclear infrastructures based in the zone.

Before examining their nuclear activities, it is important to note their attitude towards the treaty of Tlatelolco. On signing the treaty, Mexico stated that if technical progress makes it possible to differentiate between nuclear weapons and nuclear devices for peaceful purposes, it will be necessary to amend the relevant provisions of the treaty, according to the procedure established therein.[63] Thus, it reserved the right for peaceful nuclear activities even on the cost of amending the 'relevant provisions'. According to Mexico, therefore, the treaty is not complete in itself. Also, the statement emphasizes the greater freedom for contracting parties to do what they think peaceful nuclear activities. In case, the party finds the way apart from the prescription of the treaty provisions for peaceful activities, according to Mexico, the party can appeal, therefore, for a change of provisions. It argued, mainly on the basis that the treaty had to be changed according to the technical development in the zone.[64] It should be noted that in the early 1960s when Mexico was very much active for establishing NWFZ, although the idea was expressed first by Costa Rica in 1958 and it was formally introduced by Brazil in 1962, the nuclear technology was not well advanced in Latin America. However, in 1970s, Mexico, the only country fully adhered to the NWFZ agreement, joined the nuclear race in Latin America.[65]

Mexico started its nuclear programme in the late 1970s. Until the early 1970s, it had been utilizing both gas and oil for internal industrial use. However, in the late 1970s, when the government emphasized for producing more oil for export, it was, indeed, in need for finding out an alternative source of energy with which it could diversify its energy options. As of this reason, in 1979, the Portillo administration sorted out a plan for nuclear energy.[66] As a result, the United States, the country consuming approximately 70 per cent of Mexico's total oil, was approached by Mexican Government for nuclear assistance. Thus, in 1982, a nuclear power plant, 654-Mwe US-supplied unit, was set up. However, this plant was not fully completed due to the US restriction. Therefore, Medico applied to IAEA for enriched uranium for its power reactor. IAKA approached many countries including the US for getting enriched uranium. The US reconsidered to help Mexico in this respect, as IAEA requested it. It was agreed that the US would get natural uranium from France and get it enriched for supplying to Mexico. Also, Canada, France, Spain, and Sweden have been helping Mexico for its nuclear programme since the beginning of the 1980s.[67] For future Mexican pore units, Mexico is planning to utilize its uranium deposit. Mexico possesses significant uranium reserves. Unlike Argentina and Brazil, Mexico has been consistently using nuclear energy for peaceful purposes. However, it depends on the political decision of the Mexican Government which might change the situation in the future, as the recent nuclear activities of Mexico is directed towards the manufacture of heavy components.[68]

Argentina has signed the treaty but not ratified it. After signing the treaty it stated that the treaty allowed the parties to carry out "explosion of nuclear device" by their own means or in association with third parties. It pointed out that this explosion could be an explosion which involves devices similar to those used in nuclear weapons.[69] Thus, it recognized peaceful nuclear activities as a right of the contracting parties. And the effort for this, according to Argentina, can be through any means. Argentina's Nuclear Programme was started as the National Atomic Commission was created in 1950. The main purpose of establishing National Atomic Commission was to utilize the enormous uranium deposits. In 1956, Argentina purchased a reactor from the US. However, this reactor went in operation in 1958. It should be noted that as early as 1957, Argentina decided to develop research reactors indigenously.[70] Since then, Argentina has been following three important polices: (a) Emphasis on the goal of peaceful application of atomic energy; (b) Development of an independent nuclear capability, and (c) Careful assessment of international commitments in order to keep the country's options open. According to these policies, for Argentina, IAEA safeguards have been in effect since 1963. Argentine Ambassador to the UN, who participated in the discussion of the NPT, has summarized the Argentine point of view in the following terms: "The first value which cannot be overlooked is the protection of the security of each member of the international community. In the present state of the international panorama, with nuclear and non-nuclear countries, non-proliferation freezes the existing situation. Consequently, it is necessary than the states which do not have nuclear weapons are given effective guarantees by those who, because of their greater military power, have a primordial responsibility in the nuclear sphere".[71] He continued further: "The second fundamental value that must be protected when non-proliferation is reached, is technological progress, particularly in the developing countries, because this progress is the key to all economic and social development... (Argentina) cannot accept remaining in a subordinate position (in nuclear technology) especially when the bases of a nuclear technology, which our economic development requires, already exist in the country".[72]

Based on these policies, Argentina obtained power reactors, Atucha-I, Embalse and Atucha-II, uranium purification facility—Cordoba, uranium conversion facility, heavy water enrichment facility, fuel fabrication facility, reprocessing facility, and research reactors.[73] An account of Argentina's nuclear capability is given in the following table. It should be noted that, in 1978, Argentina's military leaders took decision to build the Elzeiza reprocessing plant, which would provide Buenos Aires with direct access to weapons-usable plutonium. Also, construction of the Pilcaniyen plant began under military leaders. However, these plans were slowed down as the democratic government was formed in 1983 by Raul Alfonzo, the nation's first democratically elected leader. Since 1983, Argentina has been supporting the non-proliferation and the nuclear programmes have been put under civilian control. Also, Argentina declared in 1983 that it would require all nuclear exports to be subject to IAEA safeguards in the recipient country.[74] It has to be noted that a decision to export heavy water to some of the third world countries has been taken by Commission National de Energies (CNEA) recently. According to CNEA, Argentina intends to build-up an industrial heavy water facility, which will make Argentina self-sufficient and sell the heavy water to third world countries. Moreover, Argentina has a plan to obtain enriched uranium from Brazil. According to this plan, the first delivery of enriched uranium will start in 1989. The first delivery planned is 5 tonnes of uranium enriched to 0.85 per cent.[75] Also, Brazil and Argentina have a plan to inaugurate the first stage of the Aroma nuclear demonstration plant in Ipero, a district in the interior of Sao Paulo State. This will be the first time that a parallel nuclear programme plant has been introduced publicly.[76]

Moreover, Argentina and Brazil have agreed to jointly research and develop technologies for separation, transport, and disposal of low, medium and high-level nuclear reactor wastes. The agreement was reached during the fifth plenary meeting on bilateral nuclear co-operation held on August 18-21 at San Carlos de Bariloche; Argentina.[77] Argentina has already begun site-specific design studies for a nuclear waste repository in the desolate Sierra del Medio region in Patagonia. Cierra Del Medio complies with Comissao Nacional de Energia Nuclear (CNEN) criteria for a repository, including rock stability and location away from earthquake zones, underground water and present and potential mining operations.[78] Brazil also has done extensive drilling, seismic testing and geologic mapping for a possible nuclear waste repository at Cachimbo in the Amazon jungle.[79] However, Argentina, unlike Brazil, is committed to reprocessing of spent reactor fuel at a commercial size plant to be built after 1995 at the Ezezia nuclear complex. Both sides agreed to set up a common market free of customs duties and paper work for nuclear instrumentation, that will likely be expanded to include other nuclear industries of the countries complementary and pool limited resources to develop new products and lower manufacturing costs for existing ones. And they also agreed to create an early warning system by both sides that could promptly notify and aid each other in case of radiological emergencies.[80] Apart from these nuclear activities, Argentina has selected combat aircraft able to deliver nuclear bomb such as A-49/Q Sky Hawk, Mirage 5P, Canberra etc. An account of Argentina's nuclear activities including selected combat aircraft is given in the foregoing table. The next section deals with Brazil's nuclear activities.

Brazil has signed the treaty of Tlatelolco, but it has not ratified it. However, while signing the treaty it stated that, according to the treaty (Article 18), signatories of the treaty have the right to carry out nuclear explosion including the one similar to those used in nuclear weapons. Thus, Brazil also, like Argentina, reserved the right of nuclear activities which would help develop its economic condition. Brazil's nuclear programme was initiated by National Research Council (Conselho Nacional de Pesquisas) in 1951. In 1956, National Atomic Commission (Comissao Nacional de Nergia Nuclear — CNEW) was established. Since then, all nuclear activities have been carried out under CNEN. In 1958, the first research reactor was constructed at Sao Paulo. In 1960, the second research reactor was built at the Belo Horizonte and the third one was built at Rio de Janeiro in 1965. The fourth reactor located in Belo Horizonte was completed in 1973.[81] However, after 1970, Brazilian nuclear policy was changed, as it started following an ambitious policy to become a Great Power eventually. Brazil's nuclear policy can be noted as an eminent diplomat, J.A. de Araujo Castro noted in 1971: "On various occasions... Brazil has sought to characterize what is now clearly looming as a firm undisguised trend towards the freezing of world power. And when we speak of power, we speak of not only of military power, but also of political power, of economic power, of scientific and technical power. The non-proliferation treaty... is the main instrument of this policy of freezing of World Power".[82] He continued: "The Treaty... established distinctive categories of nations: one comprising strong and therefore adult and responsible countries, and another comprising strong and therefore non-adult and non-responsible countries. Contrary to all historical evidence, the treaty starts from the premise that prudence and moderation are built-in features of power. It institutionalize inequality between nations and apparently accepts the premises that the strong countries will become ever stronger and the weak ones will grow ever weaker."[83]

As of these reasons, in 1975, Brazil signed with West Germany a nuclear transfer agreement. According to this agreement, West Germany agreed to provide Brazil up to eight 1300-megawatt nuclear power reactors, a pilot reprocessing plant, and a large-scale enrichment plant using the jet-nozzle technique. This agreement was highly controversial because it can provide Brazil with significant quantities of weapons—usable plutonium/highly enriched uranium.[84] The United States opposed this plan along with many countries which were co-operating for Brazil's peaceful nuclear technology.

However, it should be noted that Brazilian nuclear programme was supported by the US since the early 1980s. As a result, Brazil's first nuclear power reactor plant, Angra — a 626-megawatt, was supplied by the US in 1985. Since 1985, Brazil has been concentrating on indigenous nuclear technology with which it can co-operate with Latin American Countries. Also, it has proved its capability to acquire nuclear explosives in 1987. Brazil's President, Jose Sarney, has announced that nation's scientists have succeeded in enriching uranium for development of technology for use in power generation. It was understood that Brazil could develop the capability to enrich uranium to weapon grade quality.[85] However, Brazil has obtained power reactors, Angra-I and Angra–II, uranium purification facility, uranium conversion facility, enrichment facility, fuel fabrication facility, reprocessing facility and principal research reactors. Also, Brazil has selected combat aircraft to be able to deliver nuclear bombs. The next section explains briefly about the nuclear attitude of small states in Latin America. For, Chile, Cuba, Nicaragua, Venezuela, Columbia are considered.

Attitude of Small States

The treaty of Tlatelolco is in force for twenty-three countries, of all, twenty-two countries are small. Mexico, the only country to which the treaty is in force, had advanced nuclear technology. Nicaragua, Venezuela, Peru, Colombia and two other states—Chile and Cuba to which the treaty is not in force (Chile has signed and ratified but not waived the treaty whereas Cuba has neither signed nor ratified the treaty) — are interested for nuclear technology. They are all politically important countries. Among these, Chile is advanced state in nuclear technology, and Cuba is a Communist state which has nuclear infrastructure of the Soviet Union. Nicaragua is a politically disturbed Communist state in Latin America which has interest for nuclear technology. Peru, is having its own political significance, while Colombia has connection with the nuclear weapon power, the US. Chile's ratification of the treaty is conditional. That is, the treaty will not come into force for its territory until all appropriate Latin

American States have ratified and the relevant Protocols ratified by both states having territorial interests in Latin America: US, UK, France, and the Netherlands, and nuclear weapon states: US, Soviet Union, UK, France and China. The first condition is not met, as the very important state like Argentina has not ratified the treaty so far. Also, this condition includes Cuba and Chile. Cuba has not taken any decision about signing and ratifying the treaty. Chile has signed and ratified the treaty but not waived the entry-into-force provision, Article 28. Also, Chile's second condition is not met as Protocol I is not ratified by France. However, Chile has research reactor, La Reina, which is located in Santiago. The capacity of La Reina is 5 megawatt. La Reina is subject to IAEA safeguards.[86] Although, Chile's aspiration for nuclear technology is in low profile; it is remained to be seen in the future. Cuba is not directly related to the treaty.

It should be noted that because of the Cuban missile crisis in 1961-62, the idea of NWFZ in Latin America was proposed by Latin American Countries. However, the Soviet missile was withdrawn from Cuba. Cuba did not recognize the treaty as a practical one. However, it stated that it will become a party to the treaty only when the Guantanamo base ceases to be under foreign control. In 1903 a site covering 28000 acres at Guantanamo Bay was leased to the US as a naval station by the Cuban Government, the lease was renewed in 1934. Since 1960 the Castro Government has refused to accept the token 50000 annual rent and has pressured for the surrender of the base. But this problem is not solved so far. And the US has been still using Guantanamo Bay as its military base. As of this reason, Cuba is not interested to become party to the treaty. Moreover, Cuba has two VVER-440s power reactors which are under construction. The Soviet Union and Czechoslovakia are helping Cuba. IAEA Director General Hans Blix visited the construction site and inaugurated with Cuban President, Fidel Castro, the Center for Applied Nuclear Energy Research (CANER). IAEA assisted CANER for fund. VVER-440s may be subject to IAEA safeguards. For, negotiation is going on between IAEA and Cuba.[87]

Furthermore, Cuba has nuclear infrastructures of the Soviet Union. They are: two airfields, San Antonio de Los Banos and Jose Marti Airport which are bases for Bar-D reconnaissance and nuclear-capable Bear-F ASW visits to Cuba, and Cienfuegos and

Havana which are used by Soviet naval forces as major satellite ground stations and Soviet intelligence gathering facilities.[88] More detail is included in appendix F. Nicaragua, Venezuela, Peru and Colombia are small and significant countries in Latin America. They are all parties to the treaty. On signing the treaty in 1967, Nicaragua stated that it reserved the right to use nuclear energy for peaceful purposes such as the removal of earth for the construction of canals, irrigation works, and power plants. Also, it stated that it reserved the right to allow the transit of atomic material through its territory.[89] However, Nicaragua's nuclear ambition is not materialized as the present Sandinista Government has been politically disturbed by the United States. As far as its right to allow the transit of atomic material through its territory is concerned, it remained to be seen in the future. However, Nicaragua has nuclear infrastructures of the Soviet Union. Venezuela is a senior-member country which participated in the work of the Preparatory Committee of the Review Conference. And Venezuela is a country with highest per capita income. On signing the Treaty in 1967, Venezuela stated that Article 25; paragraph 2 of the Treaty should apply to Guyana. It should be mentioned that Article 25, paragraph 2 of the Treaty provides that no political entity should be admitted, part or all whose territory is the subject of a dispute or claim between an extra-continental country and one or more Latin American States, so long as the dispute has not been settled by peaceful means.[90] This dispute exists between Venezuela on the one hand and Guyana on the other. The UK has been using Guyana as its military bases. However, Venezuela has a research rector manufactured by International General Electric (IGE). This was awarded to Venezuela in 1957. The power capacity of this reactor is 3 MW. The cost of estimated project for this reactor is five million dollars. Also, Venezuela has one more research reactor, RVI which is located in Altos de Pips. The capacity of the reactors is 2 MW.[91]

Peru is a senior-member country in the Latin American NWFS. It participated in the work of the Preparatory Committee of the Review Conference. Peru has signed the treaty in 1967 and ratified it in 1969. Also, it has waived the entry-into-force provision, Article 28, in the same year. Since then, the treaty has been in force for Peru. Although Peru has shown little interest on nuclear technology, it has never given up. In fact, it has research reactor, RP-O. This reactor is located in Lima. The type of the reactor is recognized as Tank.[92] Colombia is also a senior-member country in Latin American NWFZ. It has signed the treaty in 1967 and ratified it in 1972. Also, it has waived the treaty in the same year. Since then the treaty has been in force for Colombia. On signing the treaty, Colombia made a declaration similar to the statement made by Nicaragua and Tobago. According to this, Colombia indicated its interest for peaceful nuclear energy for the removal of earth, the construction of canals, irrigation works, power plants, and so on. Also, Colombia indicated that it has the right to allow the transit of atomic material through its territory. However, Colombia has a power reactor which was manufactured by the American Machine and Foundry (AMF). The capacity of the reactor is 10 MW. The estimated project cost amounts to be 35000 dollars. This reactor was awarded to Colombia in 1962. Also, it has a research reactor, IAN-RI. It is located in Bogota. The type of the reactor is known as MTR. And the capacity of this reactor is 0.02 MW.[93] Uruguay also has one research reactor, RU.1 located in Montevideo. The type of the reactor is Lockheed and the capacity is 0.10 MW. Although there are many other small countries — Belize, Cuba, Dominica, Guyana, St. Vincent and the Gvenadines, St. Lucia and St. Christopher and Navis which are abstaining from nuclear power, they have their own political importance in the Latin American NWFZ. The following section deals with politics of the NWFS in Latin America.

Politics

Parties to conduct explosion including the explosion which involves devices similar to those used in nuclear weapons and does not describe procedures to be followed by the parties interested for such an explosion.[94] However, it says that any peaceful nuclear explosion must be in accordance with Article 1 of the Treaty, which prohibits the testing and use of nuclear weapons and Article 5 which defines a nuclear weapon as "any device which is capable of releasing nuclear energy in an un-controlled manner and which has a group of characteristics that are appropriate for use for warlike purposes".[95] But, Articles 1 and 5 do not explain clearly about nuclear device which can be used for warlike purposes and which can be used for peaceful purposes.[96] Therefore, there are different interpretations by different countries. For example, according to Argentina the treaty permits the PNE, whereas to Brazil, the treaty does not allow PNE because the development of devices only for peaceful uses is technically very difficult. And many other parties in the Latin American Zone, although recognize the right for PNE given by Article 18, they are doubtful about the technicalities with which a PNE can be carried out. For these problems, the treaty does not provide any solution. Despite, it allows indirectly the parties to interpret Article 16 according to their own understanding of the treaty which may go against the very interest of NWFZ in Latin America.

Moreover, the treaty is not clear about the zone of application or the geographical extent of the NWFZ. It says that the zone of application is confined to the territory of states for which the treaty is in force, which includes the territorial sea, air, space and other space over which the state exercises sovereignty in accordance with its own legislation (Articles 3 and 4).[97] Therefore, the zone of application depends on the contracting parties. On signing the Protocols the United Kingdom, the United States, France and the Soviet Union pointed out that they did not recognize any legislation which did not, in their view, comply with the relevant rules of international law.[98] The treaty does not state any rules in the provision of the treaty so as to solve this problem in case some parties do not agree to the view of the treaty. As of this reason, Brazil pointed out that the zone of application of the treaty depends on the "attitudes and behaviour of the nuclear-weapon powers". If the nuclear weapon states go by international law, there are possibilities for them, according to Brazil, to introduce nuclear weapons into the zone defined by the treaty of Tlatelolco.[99] However, this problem is not solved so far.

Moreover, the Tlatelolco treaty does not provide any provision to solve the transport and transit problem. This problem is important to be solved because it can go against the provisions of the treaty which prohibit nuclear weapon activities in the geographical extent of the NWFZ.[100] Also, it might go against the Protocol II which says that the nuclear weapon states should (a) respect the statute of denuclearization of Latin America in respect of warlike purposes; (b) not to contribute in any way to the performance of acts involving a violation of the obligations of Article 1 of the Treaty; and (c) not to use or threaten to use nuclear weapons against the contracting parties to the treaty. Venezuela and Chile raised this issue in the UN. They stated that the transport and transit of nuclear weapons in the area covered by the treaty is not mentioned in the text of the treaty. Therefore, according to them, "the qualifications in the statements of adherence to Protocols I and II of the Treaty of Tlatelolco thwarted the purpose of a denuclearized zone".[101] As of these reasons, except the Soviet Union and China, other nuclear weapon states consider that the treaty permits transport and transit in the zone. According to the Soviet Union and China, the transport and transit of nuclear weapons through the NWFZ is forbidden by the treaty. Also the treaty does not solve the problem of special report, and inspections that should be carried out by OPANAL.[102] According to Articles 15 and 16, which form part of the system of control established by the Treaty, the special on-site inspection should be carried out on the basis of "full and free access to all places and all information" granted by contracting parties. This is problematic in case a party thinks not to provide certain information to the OPANAL inspectors. To this effect Brazil stated at Montevideo, Uruguay, where the General Conference of OPANAL was held from 27 to 30 April, 1987: An example of this is the matter of industrial secrets. The inspections laid out in Article 16 could imply the risk that the indispensable confidentiality of certain industrial processes would not be sufficiently guaranteed, which would bring about the possibility of unjustifiable harm to the states involved. In the same fashion, the aforementioned inspections would not be restricted, as would be normal, to industrial and technological activities of a special nuclear nature, being able to extend, presumably, to innumerable sectors. This fact is particularly significant if we keep in mind that about eighty per cent of the components and material used in nuclear activities originate in non-nuclear industrial sectors.[103]

Argentine representative stated in the same conferences "My country has invested great efforts to achieve the development of Vanguard technology and, as I have said before, is inclined to share the benefits of this effort, but like any country which has a certain level of scientific and technological development, it could not allow such a broad dissemination of information with important economic value, leaving its industrial secrets unprotected".[104] Thus, an effective control system is not granted by the treaty. Also Articles 15 and 16 do not provide any mechanism to inspect the nuclear activities of nuclear weapon states. For example, it is impossible to verify the existence of nuclear weapons in Puerto Rico or Malvinas (Falkland Islands). Also the treaty faces problem relating to the conditions for the entry into force. This is a fundamental problem that the treaty faces at present. According to Article 28, the treaty will be complete when three conditions are met. The first condition is that all Latin American Republics must sign and ratify the treaty. The second condition is that all relevant states must sign and ratify the Additional Protocols. And the third condition is that safeguard agreements must be concluded with the IAEA. Thus, Article 28 requires the parties, who have signed and ratified, waive these three conditions. Unless and until the party waives Article 28, the treaty will not be in force for the party.[105] However, at present, there are twenty-three Latin American Countries who have exercised the option to bring the treaty into force. Both Additional Protocols have been signed and ratified by all relevant states, except France. France has signed but not yet ratified Protocol I. Cuba has yet to adhere to the treaty. Therefore, the treaty of Tlatelolco will be complete, if those conditions are met. The following chapter focuses on South Pacific nuclear-free zone.

NOTES AND REFERENCES

1. Tlatelolco is the name of a District in Mexico City where the treaty for the establishment of NWFZ in Latin America was signed. Parts of Central and South America where the languages of Spanish and Portuguese are spoken are called Latin America. Latin is the language of ancient Romans from which French, Spanish, and Portuguese were developed.
2. *United Nations General Assembly (UNGA), Official Records* (XVIII), Annexes, Agenda item 74, Document A/5145/Rev.I.
3. *Ibid.*
4. *Eight Nations Disarmament Conference* (ENDC), Document PV. 7, p. 9.
5. Alfonso Garcia Robles, *La denuclearization de la America Latina* (Mexico, 1966), p. 54.

6. UN Document A/C. 1/RV. 1339, November 18, 1963, p. 14.
7. See the Text of the Treaty in Appendix D.
8. See the Text of the Treaty on Appendix D.
9. *Ibid.*
10. *Ibid.*
11. Article 30 of the Treaty.
12. *Ibid.*
13. *Ibid.*
14. See Article 28 of the Treaty.
15. Article 25 of the Treaty.
16. Article 13 of the Treaty.
17. Article 4 of the Treaty.
18. *Ibid.* For more detail, see p. Miodray Mihajlovic, "Disarmament Non-Nuclear Weapon States and Security Guarantees", *Review of International Affairs* (Belgrade), Vol. 30, No. 692, Feb. 5, 1979, pp. 26-30.
19. *Ibid.*
20. Article 5 of the Treaty.
21. See, UN Special Report of the Conference of the Committee on Disarmament (USRCCD), *Comprehensive Study of the Question of Nuclear-Weapon-Free Zone in All its Aspects* (New York: UN, 1976), p. 36.
22. *Article18*, paragraph 2 of the Treaty
23. *Article18*, paragraph 3 of the Treaty
24. *Article 12*, paragraph 2 of the Treaty.
25. See *Article 16*, paragraphs 4 and 5 of the Treaty.
26. William N. Kincaid, "Challenges to verification: Old and New", Arms Control (Washington), Vol. 3, No. 3, December 1982, pp. 14-30.
27. Paul C. Szasz, The Law and Practices of the International Atomic energy agency (Vienna: IAEA, 1970), See also, Hans Blix, "Safeguards and Non-Proliferation, the AEA Efforts to counteract the spread of Nuclear Weapons", *IAEA Bulletin* (Ontario, Concord), Vol. 27, No. 2, summer 1985, pp. 3-8 *Bulletin*.
28. See *Article 12*, paragraph 2 of the Treaty.
29. OPANAL, Tenth General Conference, S/Information 374, 29 April 1987; also Benjamin Sanders, Safegu ards against Nuclear Proliferation in SIPRI Year Book 1975 World Armament and Disarmament (London: Tailor and Francis, 1975), p. 26; see also Allan McKnight, Atomic Safeguards: A Study in International Verification (New York: UN International Training and Research, 1971), pp. 1-8.
30. OPANAL, Tenth General Conference, S/Information 374, 29 April 1987.
31. For more detail relating to the problem of verification, See Allan S. Krass, Verification: How much is enough? (London: SIPRI, 1985), pp.-3-7.

32. See *Article 17* of the Treaty.
33. See *Articles* 5, 18 and 1.
34. See *Articles* 5, 18 and 1.
35. Albert Wholstetter, *et al.*, the Military Potential of Civilian Nuclear Energy (Chicago: The University of Chicago, 1977), p. 36.
36. See Kenneth N. Waltz, "The Spread of Nuclear Weapons: More May be Better", in James A. Schear, (ed.), *Nuclear Weapons Proliferation and Nuclear Risk* (London: International Institute of Strategic Studies, 1984), pp. 72-103.
37. See Stockholm Paper 6, The Right to Conduct Nuclear Explosions (Stockholm, SIPRI, 1975), pp. 12-14.
38. Additional Protocol I of the Treaty.
39. For detail see Articles 14, 15, 16 and 27 of the Treaty.
40. For detail see the Protocol II of the Treaty.
41. See Additional Protocol I of the Treaty.
42. *Ibid.*
43. Jozef Goldblat and Ragnhild Ferm, "Arms Control Agreements" in *SIPRI Year Book* 1984, *World Armaments and Disarmament* (London: Taylor and Francis, 1984), pp. 670-71.
44. *Ibid.*, pp. 671-72.
45. Memorandum by OPANAL Secretary General Gros Espials to the US Department of State, 7 February, 1980, reprinted in *International Herald Tribune*, 10 February, 1980.
46. *Ibid.*
47. William M. Arkin, *"The Treaty of Tlatelolco, Nuclear Weapons and Puerto Rico", Findings for the Bar Association of Puerto Rico Special Commission on the Nuclear Weapons Threat* (Washington, D.C.: Institute for Policy Studies, 184), pp. 1-17.
48. Jozef Goldblat and Ragnhild Ferm, "Arms Control Agreements", in *SIPRI Year Book,* World Armaments and Disarmament (Stockholm: SIPRI, 1984), p. 671.
49. *Ibid.*
50. *Ibid.*, p. 7.
51. *Ibid.*
52. Jozef Goldblat, n. 43, pp. 671-72.
53. See *Article 18* of the Treaty.
54. Jozef Goldblat and Victor Milan, *"The Falkland Malvinas Conflict-a Spur to arms Build-up"*, in *SIPRI Year Book,* 1983, *World Armaments and Disarmament* (London: Taylor and Francis, 1983), pp. 26-40.
57. *Ibid.*
58. See Max Hastings and Simon Jenkins, *Battle for the Falklands* (London: Pan Books, 1983), pp. 1-12.
59. Jozef Goldblat, n. 43, p. 670.
60. *Ibid.*
61. *Ibid.*, pp. 671-72.

62. Jozef Goldblat, n. 43, p. 670.
63. *Ibid.*
64. Jozef Goldblat, n. 43, p. 670.
65. John R. Redick, "The Tlatelolco Regime and non-proliferation in Latin America", *International Organization* (Boston), Vol. 35, No. 1, Winter 1981, pp. 103-37.
66. *New York Times*, 9 December, 1979, 24, April, 5 May, 1980.
67. *Nuclear News* (San Diego), February 1980; reprinted in *Strategic Digest* (New Delhi), vol. XVII, No. 12, December 1987, pp. 2350-51.
68. *Nucleonic Week* (New York), 24 January, 1980.
69. Jozef Goldblat, n. 43, pp. 669-70.
70. See Carlos Castro Madero, "Argentina's Nuclear Energy Programme", *Nuclear Europe* (Bucks), July-August 1983, pp. 31-33.
71. For a detailed study in this respect, see, Leonard S. Spector, *The New Nuclear Nations* (New York: Vintage Books, 1985), pp. 180-95.
72. J. M. Ruda, "La posicion Argentina en cuanto al Tratado sober la no Proliferation de las Armas Nucleares", Estrategia, 2, 9, 75-80, p. 77, cited from Onkar Marwah and Ann Schulz, (eds.), *Nuclear Proliferation and the Near-Nuclear Countries* (Cambridge, Mass: Ballinger Publishing Company, 1975), pp. 283-84.
73. *Ibid.*
74. See Richard Kessler, "Argentina May be Scaling down Heavy Water Production Plans", *Nucleonic Week*, May 16, 1985, p. 13.
75. Nuclear Engineering International (London), December 1987, *Reprinted in Strategic Digest*, Vol. XVII, No. 2, February 1988, p. 269.
76. *Foreign Broadcast Information Service* (FBIS) (Washington), Daily Report, Latin America, Friday 4 March, 1988, pp. 27-28.
77. *Nucleonic Week*, August 27, 1987; Reprinted in Strategic Digest, Vol. XVII, no. 12, December, 1987, pp. 2350-51.
78. *Ibid.*
79. *Ibid.*
80. *Ibid.*
81. For a detailed study, see, Leonard S. Spector, No. 71, pp. 196-209.
82. "The United Nations and the Freezing of Power", *United States Congressional Record*, August 4, 1971, pp. H 8016 cited from Onkar Marwah and Ann Schulz, (eds.), *Nuclear Proliferation and the Near-Nuclear Countries*, No, 72, p. 268.
83. *Ibid.*
84. Leonard S. Spector, n. 71, p. 197.
85. *The Hindu* (New Delhi), September 8, 1987.
86. See Daniel Pone Man, *Nuclear Power in the Developing World* (London: George Allen and Unwin, 1982), p. 42.
87. *Nucleonic Week*, November 19, 1987; reprinted in Strategic Digest, Vol. XVII, No. 1 January, 1988, p. 89.

88. See William M. Arkin and Fieldhouse, *Nuclear Battlefields: Global Links in the Arms Race* (Cambridge, M.A: Ballidger, 1985), p. 66.
89. Jozef Goldblat, n. 43, p. 669.
90. *Ibid.*
91. See Daniel Paneman, n. 86, pp. 41-42.
92. *Ibid.*, p. 42.
93. *Ibid.*, pp. 41-42.
94. See *Article 18* of the Treaty.
95. *Article 1* of the Treaty.
96. *Ibid.*
97. See *Articles 3* and 4 of the Treaty.
98. Jozef Goldblat, n. 43, p. 670-72.
99. *UN Department for Disarmament Affairs UNDDA*, The UN General Assembly and Disarmament 1984 (New York; UN, 1985), p. 138.
100. See *Protocol II* of the Treaty.
101. *UNDDA*, n. 99, p. 138.
102. For a detail study on transport and transit problem, see, Jozef Goldblat, *Arms Control Agreements; A Handbook* (London; Taylor and Francis, 1983).
103. Cited from Julio Cesar Carasales, "The Future of Tlatelolco 20 Years After it's Signature", *Disarmament* (New York), Vol. XI, no. 1, Winter 1987/88, p. 78.
104. *Ibid.*, pp. 78-79.
105. See *Article 28* of the Treaty.

4

Rarotonga Treaty: South Pacific Nuclear-Free-Zone

Background

South Pacific is an integral part of the Pacific Ocean. The Pacific Ocean is the largest in the world that consists of the area of over thirty million square miles of Sea stretching from the West Coast of America to Cape Town and South Africa. It shares 46 per cent of all the waters and 32.66 per cent of the earth's surface. Also, it is the deepest sea in the world. Geographically, it connects two continents of the globe: America and Asia. The Pacific basin Seaside countries are numbering more than forty. In the Pacific Ocean, there are raw materials: carbon, hydrocarbons, seaweed, and polymetallic nodules such as manganese, iron, nickel, copper and cobalt.[1] Because of these reasons, it has been passing through many phases of power struggle that attracted a number of nuclear installations of the US after the Second World War. Russia operates twenty per cent of its Delta and Typhoon class submarines including the long range submarine based nuclear missiles in the Pacific. The US has its nuclear connections in Japan (Okinawa), South Korea, Philippines, Guam and Australia.

Apart from these forces, the US also operates its SLBMs in the Pacific through Norwegian Sea, the Bering Sea, and underneath the Arctic. It has deployed eight Trident submarines in the Pacific Ocean, started deployment of 4000 Sea-Launched Cruise Missiles (SLCM) including 758 nuclear-armed ones, continued towards its target of a 600 ship Navy including 15 aircraft carriers, and revamped four battleships. These forces are extended to the US Pacific Fleet, which is covering the Indian Ocean as well.[2] Further, the US tests nuclear weapons in Pacific area. Due to such testing people in Marshall Island suffer from radiation hazards. It also established its impact area for incoming missiles at Kwajalin Atoll. The UK tests its nuclear weapons in Australia and at Christmas Island (New Zealand).[3] China tests its ICBMs in Kansu province that fly over the south of Kiribati. It should be noted that Russia too tests its SLBMs in Pacific. It launches these missiles from north of Moscow to their impact area on the Kamchatka Peninsula over flying the sea of Okhotsk and from Tyuratam to east of the Aral Sea.[4] Therefore, the South Pacific Forum (SPF), which comprises thirteen countries, Australia, New Zealand, Solomon Islands, Tonga, Vanuatu, Cook Islands, Fiji, Kiribati, Nauru, Niue, Papua New Guinea, Tuvalu, and Western Samoa have decided to keep at least the South Pacific free of nuclear activities.

History

The idea for establishing nuclear-free-zone was expressed by the Australian Labors Party (ALP) in 1960s. It was supported by the New Zealand, which pursued a strongly anti-nuclear stance in its foreign policy: banning port visits by nuclear armed ships, opposing of the French nuclear tests in the South Pacific, supporting of the proposal for Indian Ocean zone of peace, and laying the groundwork for a regional nuclear-zone. In 1975 New Zealand demanded the UN along with Fiji to consider a nuclear-free-zone proposal for South Pacific. In effect, the UN General Assembly adopted a resolution 3477(XXX) on 3 July, 1975.[5] The resolution called upon all concerned parties to consult about the ways and means to establish NFZ in South Pacific. New Zealand and Fiji were joined by Papua New Guinea as co-sponsor to present a draft resolution to the UN. The UN adopted a resolution in the first committee on 28 November by a vote of 94-0, with 18 abstentions; and in the General Assembly on 11 December by a vote of 110-20 (Resolution No. 3477). China supported the resolution. But all other nuclear powers, the UK, France, the USA and the Soviet Union expressed that this proposal would interfere with the rights of navigation.[6]

After Labor Party's defeat in the 1975, the National Party Government of Robert Muldoon (1975-84) did not take up the initiative very seriously. Malcolm Templeton, the New Zealand

Permanent Representative to the UN at the time, had revealed that the new national government abandoned the idea of nuclear-free-zone initiative.[7] In 1967, Muldoon described that without the assurance of nuclear weapon countries; a mere declaration of a nuclear-free-zone would remain an empty gesture. In March 1976, Australia and New Zealand, therefore, declared in the Sixth Pacific Forum meeting in Rotorua, that a regional NWFZ would respect the freedom of the high seas and the existing security arrangements, especially ANZUS. Thus, the conservative governments of Australia and New Zealand have not only delayed the NWFZ treaty but also have pursued a SPNFZ for the purposes of establishing an alibi rather than achieving a genuine progress.[8] After the defeat of the conservative parties in both Australia and New Zealand, the Labor Party's Governments have taken up their initiative. In Australia, the ALP Government announced its intention to promote a SPNFZ shortly after assuming office in March 1983. Thus, the Fourteenth South Pacific Forum meeting held in August 1983 took up this Australian demand and condemned the continued French nuclear testing in the South Pacific.[9]

At the 1984 Forum meeting in Tuvalu, Heads of Government agreed on the desirability of establishing a nuclear-free-zone in the region at the earliest possible opportunity in accordance with a set of principles endorsed by the meeting. These principles are:[10]

(i) The South Pacific countries should be free to live in peace and independence and to run their own affairs in accordance with the wishes and traditions of their people;

(ii) South Pacific Countries should enjoy peaceful social and economic development free from the treat of environmental pollution;

(iii) South Pacific Countries would acknowledge existing international treaties, organizations and regional arrangements, such as the Charter of the United Nations, the nuclear non-proliferation treaty and the law of the sea, which contributes to their objectives;

(iv) There should be no use, testing or stationing of nuclear explosive devices in the South Pacific;

(v) No South Pacific country could develop, manufacture, receive from others, acquire or test any nuclear explosive device;

(vi) Nuclear activities of South Pacific countries should be in accordanc with applicable international principles and treaties, notably the non-proliferation treaty, and take into account regional arrangements;

(vii) South Pacific sovereign rights to decide for themselves their security arrangements and such questions as the access to their ports and airfields by vessels and aircraft of their countries.

Based on these principles, on 6 August, 1985, at the sixteenth South Pacific Forum meeting held in Rarotonga, Cook Islands, and the South Pacific Forum Countries adopted a nuclear-free-zone treaty for South Pacific.[11] This treaty was signed and ratified by ten forum countries. They are: Australia, Cook Islands, Fiji, Kiribati, New Zealand, Nauru, Niue, Papua New Guinea, Tuvalu and Western Samoa. Solomon Islands, Tonga, and Vanuatu are not the signatories of the treaty. The full text of the Rarotonga treaty is given in Appendices.

Scope of the Treaty

The Rarotonga Treaty includes a preamble, sixteen articles, four annexes, and three protocols. The preamble notes about the fundamental aims of the treaty. It says that the parties to this treaty are "united in their commitment to world at peace; gravely concerned that the continuing nuclear arms race presents the risk of nuclear war which would have devastating consequences for all people"; and "convinced that all countries have an obligation to make every effort to achieve the goal of eliminating nuclear weapons, the terror which they hold for human kind and the threat which they pose to life on earth".[12] And it continues that the parties are "Believing that regional arms control measures can contribute to global efforts to revise the nuclear arms race and promote the national security of each country in the region and the common security of all"; and "determined to ensure, so far as lies within their power, that the country and beauty of the land and sea in their region shall remain the heritage of their peoples and their descendants in perpetuity to be enjoyed by all in peace".[13] Thus, the preamble, after reaffirming the importance of the NPT, Sea Bed and Outer Space Treaty, reads that the parties to the treaty are "determined to keep the region free of environmental pollution by radioactive wastes and other radioactive matter".[14] The articles of the treaty may be described briefly as follows: Article 1 defines the usage of terms and Articles 3 and 4 explain about the parties' undertakings regarding the renunciation of nuclear explosive devices and peaceful nuclear activities respectively. Article 8 establishes the control systems, while Articles 9 and 10 pointed out the procedures for the control system. And procedure for amendment, signature and ratification, withdrawal, reservations, entry into force and depository functions is explained from Articles 11 to 16 respectively. Annex 1 explains about the area bounded by a line, while Annexes 2, 3 and 4 deals with IAEA safeguards, consultative committee and complaints procedure. Obligation of the States having territories within the limits of the South Pacific zone is provided in Protocol I. Protocol II is created for nuclear weapon states to undertake not to use or threaten or use nuclear explosive device against the zone countries, while Protocol III created for nuclear explosive device anywhere within the South Pacific nuclear-free-zone.[15] For the purpose of this study, it is important to examine some important provisions of the Rarotonga Treaty. Therefore, obligation of the contracting parties, zone of application, definition of nuclear explosive, system of verification and control and additional protocols are examined below.

Obligation of the contracting parties is dealt with in Articles 3 to 7. According to Article 3, the parties undertake not to "manufacture or otherwise acquire, possess or have control over any nuclear explosive device", and "not to take any action to assist or encourage the manufacture or acquisition of any nuclear explosive device by any State" and Article 4 says that the parties undertake not to provide "source or special fissionable material, or equipment or material especially designed or prepared for the processing, use or production of special fissionable material for peaceful purposes", to nuclear weapon or non-nuclear weapon states unless adequately safeguarded. According to Article 5 of the treaty, the parties should "prevent in its territory the stationing of any nuclear explosive device". Article 6 requests the parties "to prevent in its territory the testing of any nuclear explosive device", and "not to take any action to assist by any state". Finally, according to Article 7 the parties undertake not to dump "radioactive wastes and other radioactive matter" at sea in the zone, not to assist such dumping by any one.[16]

Nevertheless, obligation of the contracting parties provided by those five articles does not prohibit all nuclear activities. For example, activities for nuclear energy such as bio-medical and research uses of nuclear technology are not banned. Also, some direct weapons involvement and weapon related activities are unaffected.[17] The main objective of those obligations, therefore, is only to control certain activities, test and dumping of radioactive wastes and other radioactive matter at the zone. The presence of nuclear weapons, or their manufacture and testing anywhere within the territories of South Pacific States, up to the twelve miles sea limit, are not seriously considered, as Article 5 states that "each party in the exercise of its sovereign rights remains free to decide for itself whether to allow visits by foreign ships and aircraft to its ports and airfields, transit of its airspace by foreign aircraft, and navigation by foreign ships in its territorial sea or archipelagic waters, in a manner not covered by the rights of innocent passage, archipelagic sea lane passage or transit passage of straits".[18] Moreover, those articles do not control missile testing. There is no mention about delivery system in which the missile is an integral part. Thus, the obligation of the parties is to ban only direct nuclear weapon presence on land while not prohibiting weapons related activities or the transit of nuclear-armed ships or aircraft.[19]

Zone of application is defined in Annex 1. According to this, the boundaries of the SPNFZ generally follow the territorial limits of the South Pacific Forum members. To the east, the SPNFZ is joined with the Latin American Zone at 115 degree west; its southern boundary coincides with the outer limit of the Antarctic Treaty at 60 degree south; its western boundary is formed by Australia's and Papua New Guinea's western borders; and its northern boundary is formed generally by the equator, with a few ups and downs to fit certain specified contours. Essentially, therefore, the SPNFZ ranges from 115 degree east to 115 degree west, and from the equator to 60 degree south. Thus, the Rarotonga adjoins the Latin American and Antarctic zones, contributing on its part to a very big NWFZ in the southern hemisphere in general. It should be noted that Africa and Indonesia are the only areas in the entire southern hemisphere left out of NWFZ. The treaty covers the 'territory' of member countries of South Pacific Forum, those who have signed the treaty. The 'territory' refers to internal waters, territorial sea and archipelagic waters, the Sea-Bed and sub-soil beneath, the land territory and the airspace above them. There is one very significant qualification to this general prohibition. The treaty specifically allows each state to make an exception for nuclear weapons that may be aboard ships that are visiting its ports or navigating its territorial sea or archipelagic waters, and for weapons that may be aboard aircraft that are visiting its airfields or which are transiting its airspace.[20] It should be noted that the treaty does not compel signatories to allow such involvement but leaves the decision to the state concerned. The treaty also does not contravene the activities, which are protected by the international law with regard to freedom of seas. (See the Map)

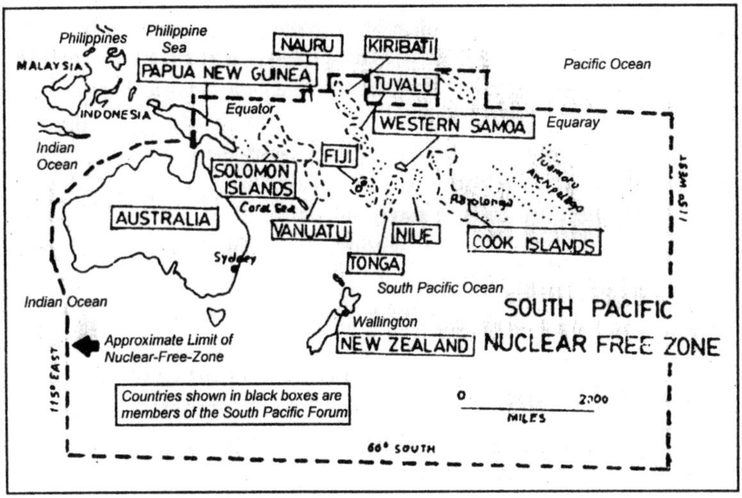

Definition of nuclear explosive is given in the Article 1. It reads: "Nuclear explosive device means any nuclear weapon or other explosive device capable of releasing nuclear energy, irrespective of the purpose for which it could be used". And it continues: "The term includes such a weapon or device in unassembled and partly assembled forms, but does not include the means of transport or delivery of such a weapon or device if separable from and not an indivisible part of it".[21] It should be noted that the Tlatelolco treaty prohibits only nuclear weapons not related activities including peaceful use of nuclear energy, whereas Rarotonga treaty prohibits all matters related to any nuclear explosion including PNE. However, it permits the delivery systems, which can be used for both nuclear and conventional warfare. The South Pacific Countries to cope up with the international understanding of PNE in particular adopted this position. For instance, in the early 1960s both the US and the Soviet Union engaged in PNE to excavate harbors or canals, recover underground mineral resources—notably oil and natural gas, and to establish underground heat reservoirs for use in supplying steam for civil works. However, since the 1970s, when the NPT came into force and when India tested its device (in 1974), both the US and the Soviet Union argued that there was no difference between nuclear weapons and nuclear explosives.[22] However, the NPT allows PNE (Article V) for non-weapon states mentioning about the potential benefits from any peaceful applications of nuclear explosion.[23] It should be noted that the Rarotonga treaty is the only treaty drafted in accordance with the NPT principles. Tlatelolco treaty came into force before NPT. However, South Pacific Forum countries do not utilize the NPT provision. Instead, they adopted a position to convince both the US and the Soviet Union. Therefore, the right for PNE is not granted to the contracting parties.

System of verification and control is established by the treaty in accordance with an important principle contained in the 1975 report of the UN ad hoc experts' group on nuclear-weapon-free zones. It should be noted that the Rarotonga treaty is the only treaty, which carefully reviewed the 1975 report of the UN as all other treaties came into force before the UN report. According to the UN report, the task of verifying a NWFZ agreement would fall into two main categories. "One is to ensure that zonal states do not develop or produce nuclear weapons. The other is to ensure that the zone is effectively free of nuclear weapons coming from outside sources and such weapons are withdrawn if they are present in the zone".[24] In effect to these categories, the Rarotonga treaty gives these responsibilities to both the Director of the South Pacific Bureau for Economic Co-operation (DSPBEC) and the IAEA. DSPBEC is the organization based in Suva, Fiji. It serves as secretariat to the South Pacific Forum. Also, it has administrative responsibilities under the control system of verification includes: reports by a party of any significant event within its jurisdiction affecting the implementation of the treaty, and exchanges of information on matters arising under or in relation to it: consultative committee, to be convened by the Director from time to time, to consider any matter arising under the Treaty or to review its operation; the compulsory application of IAEA safeguards to peaceful nuclear activities; and a complaint procedure.[25]

Also, the treaty makes provision for special inspections in the event of and alleged breach of the treaty by a party to it. International inspectors appointed by the consultative Committee should carry out these inspections. These inspectors are subject only to the direction of the Consultative Committee. For carrying out an inspection the countries of the zone should co-operate.[26] It should be mentioned that, in regard to this provision, the Australian Parliament passed a Bill, which gives to the treaty inspectors an appropriate power under Australian law to enable them to carry out their inspections. If a party considers that there are some activities against the provision of the treaty, it can complain to the Director. In case, the matter is not solved, the party can request the Director to convene the Consultative Committee. In the Consultative Committee, the party should give an account of evidence. If the evidence is convincing, the Consultative Committee will warrant a special inspection. For, the Committee has the right of appointing three inspectors. If the party is not convinced with the special inspectors, it can send its representatives along with them. The party complained of should co-operate with the team to carry out the inspection. After inspecting, the special inspectors should report in writing to the Consultative Committee.[27]

According to Annex IV of the treaty "if the Consultative Committee has decided that the Party complained of is in breach of its obligation under this treaty, or that the above provisions have not been complied with, or at any time at the request of either the complaint or complained of Party, the Parties shall meet promptly at a meeting of the South Pacific Forum".[28] Finally, South

Pacific Forum will decide upon any action. In case, if general body of the South Pacific Forum, it can decide, if it likes to do so, to withdraw from the treaty. However, there are technical problems to verify the nuclear activities in the South Pacific region. For example, Australia is the only country, which has been utilizing nuclear materials in the zone. Having an enormous deposit of uranium, it has been trading its uranium with many countries. And the rest of the countries in the South Pacific are incompetent in nuclear technology.[29] Therefore, Australia, having a strong US based nuclear infrastructure can dominate the verification process.

The Rarotonga Treaty creates three additional protocols. Protocol 1 is for signature by the states which are having territorial possession in the South Pacific region: France, the United Kingdom, and the United States. France has three overseas territories. They are: French Polynesia, New Caledonia, and Wallis and Futuna. The UK has Pitcairn Islands and the US has American Samoa and Jarvis Island. Protocol 2 is for signature by nuclear weapon states: US, Soviet Union, UK, France, and China. Protocol 3 is for signature by the states, which are testing nuclear explosive device in the South Pacific region: France, UK, and US. The Soviet Union and China have signed the protocols and France, the UK and the US have refused to sign. Additional Protocol 1 has six Articles. Article 1 says: "Each party undertakes to apply, in respect of the territories for which it is internationally responsible situated within the South Pacific Nuclear Free Zone, the prohibitions contained in Articles 3, 5 and 6, in so far as they related to the manufacture, stationing and testing of any nuclear explosive device within those territories, and the safeguards specified in Article 8 (2) (c) and Annex 2 of the Treaty".[30] Article 2 provides the right to the states to alter its obligations, while 3 and 4 state about the name of the states to be signed and ratified respectively. Article 5 explains about the duration of the treaty. According to this, Protocol 1 is of a permanent nature and shall remain in force indefinitely. Moreover, it says that the party shall have the right to withdraw from Protocol 1. Finally, Article 6 says that protocol 1 shall enter into force for each state on the date of its depositary of its instrument of ratification.[31]

Additional Protocol 2 comprised seven Articles. According to Article 1, the nuclear weapon states should undertake "Not to use or threaten to use any nuclear explosive device against: (a) Parties to the Treaty; or any territory within the South Pacific Nuclear-Free-Zone for which a state that has become a party to Protocol 1 is internationally responsible". And Article 2 of the Protocol 2 says that the nuclear weapon states, "Undertake not to contribute to any act of a party to the Treaty which constitutes a violation of the Treaty, or to any act of another Party to a Protocol which constitutes a violation of a Protocol". Article 3 gives the right to the states to alter any of their obligations specified in the protocols of the treaty. Articles 4 and 5 are concerned about the parties to the Protocols and the ratification procedure. And entries into force of the treaty are provided in Articles 6 and 7 respectively.[32] This Protocol is signed by the Soviet Union and China. However, they do not ratify it. The US, the UK and France have refused to sign it. Protocol 3 comprises five Articles. Article 1 says: "Each party undertakes not to test any nuclear explosive device anywhere within the South Pacific Nuclear-Free-Zone". Article 2 provides the right to the parties, as it provides in Protocols 1 and 2. Articles 3 and 4 state about the signature and ratification of the treaty by the US, the Soviet Union, the UK, France and China, while Article 5 explains about the duration of the treaty.[33] This protocol is signed by the Soviet Union and China. Other states have not signed any protocols of the treaty at present. The list of South Pacific States that have signed or ratification of protocols of the treaty by the nuclear weapon states, status of IAEA safeguards agreements for parties to the treaty, are given in the following Table.

Attitude of Nuclear Weapon Countries—United States

In 1975 when SPNFZ proposal was made by Fiji and New Zealand, the US had opposed to the idea. Since then, the US had maintained that the SPNFZ did not meet the criteria developed by US for judging free zone proposals. Those criterion are[34]: intra-regional initiation; effective prohibition of the development of nuclear explosive devices by zonal states; participation by all important regional states; provision for verification of terms of the NWFZ treaty; non-disturbance of existing security arrangements; respect for international airspace and international straits and the right

States that have signed or Ratified the Treaty of Rarotonga (April 1987)

Country	*Date of Signature*	*Date of Ratification*
Australia	Aug. 6, 1985	Nov. 12, 1986
Cook Islands	Aug. 6, 1985	Oct. 28, 1986
Fiji	Aug. 6, 1985	Oct. 4, 1985
Kiribati	Aug. 6, 1985	Oct. 28, 1986
New Zealand	Aug. 6, 1985	Nov. 13, 1986
Nauru	July 10, 1985	Apr. 13, 1987
Niue	Aug. 6, 1985	Dec. 5, 1986
Papua New Guinea	Sept. 9, 1985	–
Tuvalu	Aug. 6, 1985	Jan. 16, 1986
Western Samoa	Aug. 6, 1985	Oct. 20, 1986
Additional Protocol 1		
China, People's Republic of France	Dec. 1986	
United Kingdom		
United States		
USSR	Dec. 1986	
Additional Protocol 2		
China, People's Republic of	Dec. 1986	
France		
United Kingdom		
United States		
USSR	Dec. 1986	
Additional Protocol 3		
China, People's Republic of France	Dec. 1986	
United Kingdom		
United States		
USSR	Dec. 1986	

Treaty of Rarotonga safeguards agreement

Country	*Signed but not in Force*	*In force*
Australia		x
Cook Islands		x
Fiji		
Kiribati	x	
New Zealand		x
Nauru		x
Niue		
Papua New Guinea		x
Tuvalu		
Western Samoa		

Source: Embassies of Australia and New Zealand, Washington, D.C., for latest information, *see* SPRI Year Book series till 2005.

of innocent passage through territorial seas; and non-international concerning the rights of zonal parties under international law to grant or deny transit privileges, including port calls and over-flight, to non-zonal states.

However, the South Pacific Forum countries, especially Australia played a great role to meet these criteria and made all other countries accept. Still then, agree to two-hundred miles exclusive economic zones. Strategically the Rarotonga Treaty does not penalize the US, which does not have nuclear weapon bases in the South Pacific and has no apparent plans for introducing them into American Samoa. Thus, there should be no strategic loss from Rarotonga ratification. Also, the projected free zone except for certain off-sets does not extend into the North Pacific where the US has major strategic assets, notably the missile-testing site at Kwajalein in Palau, Guam. Also, the US has major strategic locations in Palau, Clark Air Force Base and Subic Bay facilities in Philippines.[35] Also, the US has Trust territories under the permission of the United Nations. They are: Marshall Islands and Federated States of Micronesia. In these states, especially in northern Marianas and in Palua, the "nuclear allergy" movement of South Pacific Countries is spread. Some of the groups in the movement demand the US to abolish its nuclear infrastructures in the Pacific. Because of these reasons, the US is opposed to any nuclear free move in the Pacific in general.[36] For example, former Secretary of Defense, James Schlesinger said: "In the full spectrum of the term, the US must remain a Pacific power. Politically, economically and militarily it is in our national interest to be capable of maintaining the current balance among the United States, the Soviet Union, Japan and the Peoples' Republic of China in the Pacific, as well as to be able to uphold our commitments to our smaller allies in the area." He continued[37]: "To do this requires a credible presence, particularly in the military sense, to demonstrate our resolve, to add substance to our political endeavors, to protect our economic interest, and to deter major conflict." However, the US suggested the following criterion specifically relating to the South Pacific Nuclear Free Zone. They are[38]: (1) The initiative should come from the region concerned; (2) All states in the region should participate; (3) There should be adequate verification; (4) Existing security arrangements (ANZUS) should not be disturbed; (5) The proposal should prohibit the development or possession of any nuclear explosive device by parties to the treaty; and (6) The treaty obligations must be consistent with existing international law, and specifically not contravene, the principle of freedom of navigation of the high seas and the right of innocent passage through territorial seas.

Also, the US noted that these criteria were maintained in the foreign policy approach towards South Pacific basically because of the increasing Soviet influence in the South Pacific.[39] The Rarotonga treaty meets the criteria one, five and six of the US. And criteria two that all states in the region should participate is not met because of the French territory, Vanuatu. As far as the criterion third is concerned, the arms control move of South Pacific Countries well set in the framework of both NPT and the model of Tlatelolco thereby assuring the verification guarantee. Finally, the criterion four seems to be much concerned in the US expressed its dissatisfaction on certain issues particularly in the wake of New Zealand's denial for American sub-marine visiting its port. According to the US the New Zealand's anti-nuclear politics would ultimately result for dissolving the military alliance, ANZUS.[40] Thus, it was reported in April 1986 that the US had adopted a tough uncompromising stand towards SPNFZ. According to US, the Rarotonga treaty would directly benefit Soviet global objectives to the detriment of US interests. Moreover, the US pointed out that the SPNFZ could create a serious precedent for the establishment of interlocking NWFZ, which would impede the free movement of US forces around the world.[41]

The US has contingency plans to create bases for nuclear armed ships and planes on Babethuap in Palau, on Tinian and also prospects for the US seeking facilities for nuclear armed B-52s in a crisis at the Darwin airfield in Australia. Moreover, it has access with bases in Philippines through which about half of Asia's oil and 80 per cent of its strategic materials pass. According to the US these bases are against the Soviet Navy, which is operating in the Pacific. The Soviet Navy, with a base at Cam Ranb Bay in Vietnam, has been expanding in the area. Subic is the primary port, training area and logistics support base for the US Seventh Fleet; its ship repair facilities are said to be the best in Asia.[42] Clark, home of the thirteenth US Air Force, is the staging point for strategic airlift to the Indian Ocean, including the air and naval support base on Diego Garcia. The US also has use of four other communications, radar and recreation facilities in the Philippines.

There are about 16,000 US servicemen stationed in the country, including 9,122 air force personnel and 5,908 in the navy, plus tens of thousands of sailors visiting at any given time. A 25-year lease was covered under a Military Base Agreement (MBA) originally signed in 1947.[43] The lease ends in 1994 after which either party can abrogate the agreement with year's notice. Clark covers, 3,760 hectares and Subic 6,303 hectares of prime agricultural and commercial land in Central Luzon. The constitutional provision on nuclear free Philippines is very clear which can be interpreted for accepting American bases as well as opposing them. Despite of the opposition, the US has been building up, with government support, a 27 million dollar urn-way at Clark and 6 million dollars worth of quarters and other improvements at Subic, which are aimed to strengthen their smaller facilities stretching from Guam to perhaps Singapore.[44]

Moreover, the US is facing problems already from the Trust Territory of the Pacific Islands, as it has a plan as a potential replacement for the facilities at Subic Bay. However, the trust territories are trying to free themselves from military influence of the US. As of these reasons, the US wants, at least, to keep control over foreign, defense and fiscal affairs. For this purpose, the US has proposed certain plans known as compact of free association.[45] This was placed before the people of the four micro-entities of Micronesia. One entity, the Northern Marianas, opted for Commonwealth status with the US on the lines of Puerto Rico. The other three will not have sufficient international personality in legal terms to join the UN if the US is permitted to terminate the trusteeship. Especially Palau has refused to accept associated status with the US on terms including acceptance of the nuclear defense.[46] The 8000 voters of the total population of 15,000 have repeatedly refused to amend their Constitution's 'nuclear-free' clause to enable the introduction of nuclear substances, weapons or ships in their land, sea or air space. Also, they have opposed the American nuclear tests in Bikini, Enewetak and Rangelap since the beginning. Also, at the Kwajalein Missile Base in another Micronesian entity, the Marshall Islands, the traditional land-owners protested against US testing of missiles from

Vandenberg Air Base in California. The US wants to have strategic base in Marshall Islands as it has in Puerto Rico.[47]

Furthermore, Australia and New Zealand have opposed both the French and American activities in the Pacific along with the support of Melanesian as well as Micronesian people. Australian Government reported that because of its hosting of US satellite surveillance and communications facilities, Australia was rendered vulnerable to Soviet attack.[48] New Zealand has questioned the very presence of the US in the Pacific. Its opposition was registered as it refused to accept the American ship to its port. Further, Papua New Guinea, which is opposed in the Decolonization Committee of the UN, has argued for finding out extraordinary procedure so as to free the Pacific Islands from outside powers: Britain, France and United States. And Fiji, although it has reversed the position of banning nuclear capable vessels in 1982, is not satisfied with outside powers. It should be noted that Fiji was pressurized by the US to reverse its 1982 decision. Vanuatu, known as the Toung Turk of the Pacific, has been consistently supporting Melanesian independence movements.[49] And the decision taken by South Pacific Forum to leave the right to each sovereign nation for deciding whether or not to permit transit of such weapons and nuclear-powered vessels within their land, sea and air space was realized by the US that it would create problems for its testing missile delivery systems at Kwajalein. More importantly, the US was not satisfied with the individual right given by South Pacific Forum.[50]

Therefore, the US maintains that the Rarotonga treaty for nuclear free South Pacific will affect the American strategy in the Pacific in general. Also, signing the Protocols of Rarotonga treaty would, according to the US, become a prelude to other regional demands, like the question of decolonization, to pressurize the US not to make use of the Islands even for missile testing purposes.[51] Because of these reasons, the US is not willing to sign the protocols. However, the United States has signed four nuclear free zone agreements, covering South America (Tlatelolco Treaty), Antarctica, Outer Space and the Sea-bed. But the accords are designed to prevent proliferation of nuclear weapons in areas where none are stationed or where nuclear threshold nations have declined to sign the Nuclear Non-proliferation Treaty.

France

In South Pacific, there are three French overseas territories. They are: French Polynesia, New Caledonia, and Wallis and Futuna. The French Polynesia is a group of Islands. It consists of 130 Islands. The total surface area of French Polynesia is 4200 sq. kms. New Caledonia consists of the Loyalty Islands, the Walpole and pains islands, and the uninhabited chesterfield islands. The total surface area of New-Caledonia is 19103 sq. kms. The overseas territory of Wallis and Futuna consists of two main islands of Wallis (area) and Futuna (Mooru). The total surface area is 274 sq. kms. These territories are very important both economically and strategically. For example, the mineral wealth of New Caledonia includes nickel, chrome, iron, manganese and cobalt.[52] However, France has started its nuclear test in the Pacific as the Algerian crisis forced the French nuclear testing programme to move from Sahara in 1966. Since 1966, France has exploded its nuclear bombs in the Pacific atmosphere. Between 1966 and 1970s, France has shifted its nuclear tests to Mururoa Atoll. More than forty bombs are exploded including the prototype of a neutron bomb.[53] It should be mentioned, environmental damage and accidents occurring at the test center. The French Government denied most of these reports. On July 6, 1979, two test site workers were killed and two were injured. But the French Government stated that it was a non-nuclear accident involving the explosion of a solvent used in decontamination work. Also, French Government denied the following incidents: On July 25, a bomb became struck halfway down a 1-km. test shaft. It was exploded and, therefore, created tidal wave. On March 11-12, 1981, a storm exposed buried radioactive waste from pre-1975 atmospheric tests. On September 29, 1981, an underwater crack had developed in the atoll and was leaking radioactive materials.[54] In October 1981, trade union federation representing test site workers stated that the atoll sank by about 2 cms. after each explosion, and had sunk by about 1.5 meters since 1975. On December 21, 1981, the territorial government called for a suspension of the tests pending an independent scientific inspection of the atoll because of the leakage. And finally, in October 1983, a group of scientists from Australia, New Zealand and Papua New Guinea had carried out a limited inspection of Mururoa. France also neglected this report.[55]

In French Polynesia, France maintains an estimated 3000 troops and a full complement of marines, paratroopers, naval and air forces. These forces can be deployed to any flash point in French territories. It is important to note that the US and allied forces, during World War II, used New Caledonia as a base. More importantly, France noted with the concern, therefore, that the support of SPNFZ might lead for the decolonization of its overseas territories.[56] It should be mentioned that within the framework of its existing colonial doctrine, France has permitted limited constitutional reform in these territories, thus, allowing greater powers of self-government and local administration but not independence.[57] According to France, the anti-nuclear protest could turn into a political movement for decolonization of its territories. This happened in the case of an "anti-nuclear-protest-movement" that spread throughout Oceania, which has been clearly aligned with a political movement for freedom struggle.

On the other hand, on the eve of the Rarotonga meeting, a French official, Jean Michael Baylet, visited Papua New Guinea, Fiji, Tonga, Western Samoa and Vanuatu to explain the Government's position on nuclear testing and self-rule in French Pacific possessions. He informed the self-rule in French Pacific possessions. He informed the South Pacific Forum members that France would carry out nuclear-testing beneath Mururoa Atoll/and it would not sign the protocols of the treaty.[58] French position in SPNFZ has resulted in because of the following factors: first, French Government consistently demonstrated the will to sustain and improve France's nuclear deterrent forces; second, although British and the US opposed France's successfully to adhere to the/Limited Test Ban Treaty, they have given public evidence that they wish France to cease its underground nuclear testing programmes; third, the unfavourable prospects for a comprehensive test ban (CTB), and even for a super powers test moratorium, tend to minimize any injury to France from criticisms of testing; fourth, regional scientists permitted by France to study Mururoa on a limited basis found that nuclear tests posed no health or environmental dangers.[59]

Although French Government used these factors as an advantage for carrying out its nuclear tests in the South Pacific, most of the South Pacific Countries denied outrightly the French decision. New Zealand campaigned against it. As a result, most of the South Pacific Countries joined with New Zealand to oppose the French testing in Mururoa Atoll. Specifically the Greenpeace movement was very much against the French decision. Greenpeace, founded in 1969, has been engaged in protest activity against French nuclear test since 1972. A converted 40-metre fishing vessel, known as The Rainbow Warrior sailed into Auckland harbor on 7 July, 1972. The Rainbow Warrior, a converted 40 meters fishing vessel, sailed into Auckland harbor on 7 July, 1985 to prepare as the flagship of an anti-nuclear protest against the French at Mururoa. France sunk the Rainbow Warrior in the Auckland harbor, killing one crew member.[60] This event has focused international attention on French nuclear testing in the region. In the late 1985 France opened negotiations with Greenpeace, in order to agree on a means to pay compensation for physical damages and loss of life. In early 1986, France paid up and apologized.[61]

The French nuclear test in the South Pacific began with a 25-30 Kt atmospheric explosion on 2 July, 1966. By 1974, France had carried out 41 atmospheric tests in all. Australia and New Zealand terminated atmospheric testing with a successful action against France at the World Court. And the series of underground testing began with a 5 Kt explosion at Fangataufa Island on 5 June, 1975. The Rainbow Warrior episode has strengthened the commitment of New Zealand and other South Pacific states (1) to an anti-testing policy in opposition to France; (2) improved perceptions of the Lange government, domestically and abroad; (3) given further impetus to Wellington's banning of nuclear-related vessels from New Zealand ports, and gained some additional world sympathy for the stance; and (4) increased French dedication to nuclear explosive testing, thereby lengthening the odds against French ratification of the Rarotonga Protocols.[62]

When the 1975 test was opposed by people, a French military General said: "...Because in order to have a credible nuclear armament, it is necessary to increasingly improve it, and to do this it is necessary to conduct tests, there is no limit to the Pacific Experimentation Center's existence and presence in French Polynesia".[63] Also, it had exploded a 150 Kt device at Mururoa Atoll on 9 May, 1985, the sixty-ninth in the underground series.

It is to be noted here that the US and the Soviet Union signed a Threshold Test Ban Treaty in 1974 which prohibits underground tests of more than 150 Kt yield. The first test in 1986 was conducted on 26 April, and had an estimated yield of 4 Kt.[64] France did not agree to budge on the issue of nuclear testing at Mururoa. It should be mentioned here that French President Mitterrand witnessed Mururoa test on 13 September, 1985. On his return to Paris, Mitterrand told that France would continue to test in order to maintain the credibility of its '*force de frappe*' "for as long as it is judged necessary".[65] This proved the French opposition to the SPNFZ.

The United Kingdom

On 20 March, 1987, the United Kingdom announced its position on SPNFZ, as the Ministry of State at the UK Foreign and Commonwealth Office provided a written answer to the House of Common in which it was stated that it "would not serve the national interest" to sign the protocols. And it continued saying that the United Kingdom had no intention of "testing, manufacturing, or basing" nuclear weapons on Pitcairn Island, the only territory under British jurisdiction in the area covered by the protocols.[66] The United Kingdom has had a long historical and cultural association with all South Pacific Countries. Most of the Pacific countries were British colonies and all have had close association with the United States in recent years. It should be noted that in the 1950s, the United Kingdom had carried out its nuclear tests at three sites in Australia: the Monte Bello islands, Emu Field and Maralinga. In July, 1984, the Australian Government established a Royal Commission to inquire into the consequences of British nuclear test in these sites.[67]

However, the British decision was announced after the United States took decision not to sign the Rarotonga treaty. Therefore, it is to be understood that the United Kingdom has a strategic interest in South Pacific *vis-à-vis* the United States. Since most of the British colonies in the Pacific are now with the United States, it is viewed that the UK would go along with the American decision in this regard. Therefore, in future, it is expected that the United States and the United Kingdom would co-operate in the strategically important twenty-first century Pacific. It has to be noted, however, that additional protocols of the Tlatelolco treaty for NWFZ in Latin America was signed and ratified by the United Kingdom. Noting the British position on Latin American NWFZ, the New Zealand Prime Minister, Lange, stated: "Adherence to the Protocols is but a small step from the adoption of that position (not to act inconsistently with the Protocols), yet to the South Pacific Countries adherence would be a gesture of great symbolic and substantive importance".[68] Thus, the UK has opposed the SPNFZ treaty.

China and Russia

On 10 February, 1987, China signed the SPNFZ treaty but reserved its right to reconsider them. Chinese Ambassador to Fiji, Chaozhu, who signed the treaty protocols, said the area could be nuclear-free only if other big powers accepted their special responsibility. Chaozhu said China would reconsider its stand if other nuclear powers took any action that changed the status of the security of China.[69] It should be mentioned that China is the only country which supported the idea of NFZ in South Pacific proposed by Fiji, New Zealand and Papua New Guinea in 1975. Although the Soviet Union abstained from voting in 1975, now it is in support of SPNFZ.

In February 1986, the South Pacific Forum sent a group of delegates to the Soviet Union to discuss about the South Pacific nuclear-free-zone with the Soviet Foreign Ministry officials. The Soviet Foreign Ministry informed the delegates that "creating nuclear-free-zone really ensures the making of the territories of the signatory states into a zone completely free from nuclear weapons". Also, in 1986, the Foreign Minister Shevardnadze announced the Soviet decision to sign the protocols of the treaty to the Fijian Prime Minister, Ratu Sir Kamiese Mara, who is also Chairman of the South Pacific Forum that "we fully share the South Pacific Countries' concern over nuclear explosions which continue to resound in their region". He further informed: "Signing by the Soviet Union of protocols the treaty of Rarotonga represents a good example of co-operation between the USSR and South Pacific countries in the interests of peace and security in the region". He wrote, "...Signing by the Soviet Union of protocols to the treaty of Rarotonga represents a good example of cooperation between the USSR and South Pacific Countries in the interests of peace and security in the region. We are ready to co-operate further, to combine efforts in solving common problems which are of concern to our countries ".[70] It should be noted that the Soviet Union's acceptance was phrased to exclude port calls by nuclear armed vessels. According to the Soviet Union, this position is taken basically because of the US military influence in the Pacific especially in Guam.[71]

Conversely, the Soviet decision on signing the treaty of Rarotonga is a political move, as it is interested to influence the Pacific Islands in the future. The Soviet Union is relying on commercial and scientific programmes to gain influence access in the South Pacific. It has already signed a one-year fishing access agreement with the Pacific Island state of Kiribati. Although the agreement is not renewed, it may help further the Soviet Union to improve its relations with other Island states. In early 1987, Vanuatu negotiated an agreement that permits Soviet access to that island state's ports and possibly airfields. However, for the Soviet Union, a strong security alliance is yet to be born in the South Pacific region.[72] As of these reasons, the Soviet Union has been in support of the South Pacific nuclear-free-zone. The following section focuses on Australia.

Australia's Nuclear Activities

Australia is rich in uranium. It has been exporting uranium to several countries in the world. Australian uranium was explored by the UK in 1940, as the UK was interested for nuclear weapon programmes at that time. The Australian mines were opened in the 1950s. Although these mines are closed now, there are two other mines opened and functioning currently. The huge uranium deposit was discovered at Roxby Downs in South Australia in 1975. As a result, Australia has one-third of the world's economically recoverable uranium.[73] Australia, however, is a non-nuclear weapon country, which is involved in selling enormous uranium in the world. For example, the US, South Africa, Israel, the UK, France and China are connected with the uranium business of Australia. Apart from its uranium activities, Australia has many US military bases, which are inter-related with the nuclear weapon related activity in the Pacific. It is also a major partner in the security alliance, ANZUS.[74]

The first US Navy became operational in 1967. Since then, the US has increased its bases in Australia. Today, there are more than forty military bases, which are interconnected with the nuclear plan of the US. For the purpose of the study, it is important to note some of the bases, which are re-establishing the NFZ in South Pacific. They are: radio communications base of the US Navy at North West Cape, military space research center at Pine Gap, space communications center in Nurrungar, and installation of an anti-submarine sonar on Christmas Island. US Navy at North West Cape, the radio communications base, maintains communication with US bases on the Pacific Island of Oahu, Guam, the Philippines and Diego Garcia. This also helps to communicate with the US nuclear submarines deployed in the Indian Ocean. Recently, these facilities at North West Cape have been equipped with new system, which can communicate with the US military satellites.[75] Thus, the US Navy in South Pacific connects the 'star wars' layers, which are to be established for carrying out a mission of attacking or killing incoming Soviet ICBMs.[76] Also, the military space research center at Pine Gap, which was established in 1969, helps both the navy and space related commanding centers in the Pacific as well as Indian Ocean.

The space communication center in Nurrungar is used to communicate with ground station of military space communication centers in the Southern Hemisphere. This is the principal center through which the US ICBMs can be operated. The installation of anti-submarine sonar on Christmas Island is used for helping the US armed forces, which are specifically employed for carrying out a military mission in the Pacific. The US armed forces are also assisted by the Indian Ocean based installation on Cocos Islands. Besides, there is an agreement between Australia and the US, which permits the US nuclear aircraft in a crisis period. This agreement also permits the US to place three B-52 bombers and KC-135 flying tankers in an alert position in order to fulfil the Pacific War mission. It should be noted that the US has 160 military bases in the Pacific. These bases are indirectly involved with Australian bases.[77]

As counter forces in the Pacific, the Soviet Union has a number of alternative strategic nuclear delivery vehicles

(SNDVs). They include the single-warhead ss-11 Sego ICBMs, the MIRV ed ss-18 ICBMs, various SLBM carried by FBM submarines operating near Vladivostok or Petropavlovsk, or strategic bombers such as the Tu-95 Bear and Tu-22M Backfire.[78] The Soviet forces are mainly targeted towards North West Cape, Pine Gap, and Nurrungar. An account of American nuclear facilities in Australia is given in the Appendix 7.

Attitude of New Zealand

Since the early 1960s, New Zealand has played a major role for establishing SPNFZ. Antarctic treaty in 1959, Outer Space treaty in 1967, Tlatelolco treaty for Latin America NWFZ in 1967, and Non-proliferation treaty (NPT) in 1967 have attracted New Zealand to work towards the objectives of establishing nuclear free Pacific in general. Therefore, New Zealand was opposed to nuclear tests carried out by the US and the UK.[79] Protest movements were spread all over the country. As a result, the US and UK ceased all nuclear testing in the Pacific by 1960. In the same year, France started atmospheric nuclear testing programme in the French Polynesia. New Zealand registered a case against France in the International Court of Justice in 1973. This was supported by Australia. As the court's order was in favour of New Zealand, France withdrew its atmospheric nuclear testing in 1974—the year when France signed the Limited Test Ban Treaty, which was formulated to control atmospheric test at that time. However, France began underground testing at Mururoa Atoll in early 1975. New Zealand started, therefore, to campaign against French underground nuclear tests, and requested the South Pacific Bureau for Economic Co-operation (SPBEC), which was established in 1972, to extend its support. As SPBEC, the major economic forum started supporting the idea of New Zealand, the South Pacific Forum Fisheries Agency, set up in 1978; the South Pacific Commission which has over twenty-five government members, including the metropolitan states of the UK, France and the US extended their support to SPBEC.[80]

However, in the late 1975, New Zealand proposed a draft

resolution to the UN in which the idea of SPNFZ was expressed. Australia, Fiji and Papua New Guinea supported this resolution. Later, Fiji and Papua New Guinea joined with New Zealand to sponsor this resolution to the UN General Assembly.[81] This move was very much opposed by the US. The US stated that the nuclear free idea would harm the security alliance, ANZUS. When the US posed its argument against SPNFZ by citing ANZUS, New Zealand started registering its opposition to ANZUS in the beginning of the 1980s. In 1984, David Jange, Prime Minister of New Zealand stated that ANZUS was not a nuclear-related security alliance, and that New Zealand, did not wish to use nuclear weapons for its security purposes. Thus, New Zealand protested against the US nuclear-armed ship movements in the South Pacific. US nuclear-armed warships had visited New Zealand ports since the 1960s.

In the same year, Rainbow warrior, the Green Peace ship, which was sent to Auckland harbor in protest against French underground nuclear test in Mururoa Atoll, was sunk by France killing the ship's photographer.[82] In the summer of 1984, when the US took a decision to send the USS Buchanan to visit New Zealand after a March ANZUS exercise, New Zealand demanded the US to declare whether the ship carried nuclear weapons. The US did not agree to give testimony. The Deputy Assistant Secretary, James A. Kelley, said[83]: "It would be unreasonable to expect the United States to ease an adversary's tracking and targeting problem by identifying which of our ships have the greatest capability. Identification or restriction of the area of movement and operations would increase the vulnerability of such ship and limit their usefulness. It would weaken deterrence and might increase our adversaries' temptation to resort to force, including the application of conventional military power." However, New Zealand refused port access to the USS Buchanan on February 4, 1985.[84]

In protest against New Zealand's decision, US representative Molinari argued[85]: "They say they made the gesture as a way of reducing the risk of nuclear war. Yet, do you reduce the risk of nuclear way by destroying a regional alliance that has kept the nuclear peace for four decades? Do you promote peace by denying military co-operation to the one country in the world committed to, and most capable of, preserving that peace?" Furthermore, a Retired US Navy Admiral Gene La Roque, head of the Washington-based Center for Defense Information, told New Zealand in a television interview that "American strategy—and this is documented—is to keep the fighting as far as possible from the United States in hope that a 'limited' war can be fought and finished in a foreign theater without recourse to massive nuclear strikes between the United States and the Soviet Union".[86]

Nevertheless, Prime Minister Lange did not change his decision and he informed the UN Conference on Disarmament held in Geneva in May 1985: "My government will, indeed must, respond to the concern of New Zealanders about the continuing escalation of the nuclear arms race. We shall reflect, in our policies, their hopes and their determination that the nuclear weapons states will heed the calls which the international community has for so long made on them, and which in recent years have fallen on stony ground. The people and Government of New Zealand have rejected participation in the nuclear arms race".[87] Thus, both French and American attitude towards the New Zealand's initiation of SPNFZ have come to an end, and New Zealand's idea came into practice as South Pacific Forum countries signed the Rarotonga treaty in August 1985 and ratified it in 1986. Endorsements of the Soviet Union and China have helped New Zealand to consolidate its position further in the South Pacific. Furthermore, in support of SPNFZ, Prime Minister David Lange introduced a bill in Parliament on 12 February, 1987, to ban all nuclear weapons from New Zealand, describing that it would be a real measure of arms control.[88] (See the Table)

Attitude of Small States

There are eleven small states which are included in the South Pacific Forum: Cook Islands, Fiji, Kiribati, Nauru, Niue, Papua New Guinea, Solomon Islands, Tonga, Tuvalu, Vanuatu, and Western Samoa. Of ensure there is all, eight states are agreed to the establishment of South Pacific nuclear-free-zone in the Pacific. The states not agreed to the treaty are: Solomon Islands, Tonga and Vanuatu. Before discussing about their attitude, it is important to note the overall development in the Pacific. In the Pacific, there are more than 900 islands and reefs. They have been used by the US, the UK and France, as nuclear test sites. For example, Marshall

Island had been used by the US since 1946. Because of the UN initiation to prevent the American testing programme in the late 1945, the US had shifted to northern Atolls of Bikini and Eniwetok, which were severely contaminated by radiation.[89] Also, islands like Rongelap and Utirik Atolls were accidentally affected by the fallout of American test in the northern Atoll. Kwajalin Atoll, the central island among these groups in the Pacific was used in the early 1980s. More than 8000 residents of this island were forced to shift by the US to nearly Ebeye islet. Other US tests took place in the then British territory of the Gilbert Islands (now Kiribati and part of Kiribati—Kiribati is included in SPNFZ), and at Johnston Island, a US possession near Hawaii.[90] (See the Table)

Table

	No. of Delivery Vehicles	*Range (N.M.)*	*Throw Weight Thousand Ibs*	*No. of Warheads*
ICBMs:				
SS-11 Sego	570	5700	2	1
SS-18 Mod.1	50	7450	16	1
SS-18 Mod. 2	68	6850	16	8
SS-18 Mod. 3	50	10000	16	1
SS-18 Mod. 4	140	6850	16	10
SLBMs:				
SS-N-16 Mod. 1		1300	1.6	1
SS-N-6 Mod. 2	464	1600	1.6	1
SS-N-6 Mod. 3			1.6	2
SS-N-8	298	4300	1.8	1
SS-N-18 Mod. 1			2.5	3
SS-N-18 Mod. 2	176	4050	2.5 1	
SS-N-18 Mod. 3			2.5	7
Bombers:				
Tu-22 M Backfire	75	3075	4	2
Tu-95 Bear	113	4000	8	4

Source: Desmond Ball and RH Mathams n. 78, p. 46, for latest information, see SPRI Year Book series till 2005.

Conversely eight island states are agreed to the treaty of Rarotonga. They signed the treaty in 1985. They did the ratification of the treaty in different times. Fiji and Nauru have ratified in 1985 and 1987 respectively, whereas all other countries except Papua New Guinea have done it in 1986. All of them have contributed for the establishment of South Pacific nuclear free zone. For example, Cook Islands had hosted the Forum countries in Rarotonga where the sixteenth session of the South Pacific Forum adopted the treaty of Rarotonga (the session took place in Awarna, the administrative draft resolution to the UN along with New Zealand and Papua New Guinea in the same year. Kiribati, the small state which is scared of Chinese ICBM test in the Pacific, is also a supporter of nuclear free zone since the beginning, as it has signed the treaty in the same day, 6 August, 1985, when Fiji and New Zealand have signed. Nauru has contributed for establishing South Pacific nuclear free zone, as it produced first notable paper on the dumping of nuclear waste in the Pacific. In that paper, Nauru made a particular reference to the Pacific. Based on the study, Nauru suggested that the London dumping convention on nuclear waste be amended and the forum agreed that Japan be told.[91]

More importantly, Nauru's initiation to stop the dumping of nuclear wastes helped other South Pacific states to carry forward a programme, which would stop French nuclear tests in the Pacific.[92] Niue, the Polynesian country, is a consistent supporter, as it has advocated, since the beginning, for a modest proposal, which was originally proposed by both Australia and New Zealand. Also, it proposed for even more flexible SPNFZ, which would serve the interest of all contracting parties. Papua New Guinea, being a signatory among Melanesian countries to the treaty, did not ratify the treaty. But it has advocated for more radical treaty than the present one. Also, Papua New Guinea's contribution for the treaty dates back to 1975 when it joined both New Zealand and Fiji to propose a draft resolution to the UN. It should be noted that Papua New Guinea has become independence. Tuvalu is the first country, which has ratified the treaty. It has ratified the treaty on 16 January, 1986. Tuvalu's contribution to the Rarotonga treaty came, as it hosted the Forum countries in 1984 when the leaders of the Forum countries met at Funafuti.

In this meeting, Tuvalu assisted all other states to draw a set of principles as a basis for SPNFZ. Western Samoa, a Polynesian state, has argued for a more radical treaty than the present one.[93] Solomon Islands and Vanuatu are Melanesian countries. Tonga is a Polynesian country. Since the beginning both Solomon Islands and Vanuatu have argued for radical treaty, whereas Tonga advocated for a more modest one. Vanuatu is the only state, which is very much against the SPNFZ. Also, it has signed an agreement with the Soviet Union, which permits Soviet access to island state's ports.[94] It is of the view that SPNFZ cannot be fully achieved unless and until the nuclear activities of big powers in the Pacific are stopped in general and nuclear activities of South Pacific Countries, especially Australia, are stopped in particular. Also, Vanuatu has denied permitting the access for American warships.

Politics

The twenty-first century is termed as a 'Pacific Century'. Economic and military activities are directed towards the Pacific region, which is therefore a hotbed for the political activities of the world in the ensuring years of twenty first century. The future of the Pacific politics for the US, the UK and France—the big powers of the world is brighter as they have their colonial states. The Soviet Union and China are interested in the region as they have already initiated the process by supporting the SPNFZ; and in the case of the Soviet Union by signing agreements with Kiribati and Vanuatu, and nuclear agreement with Australia in the case of China.[95] The US has acquired Hawaii, Guam and American Samoa in the Pacific. Thus, in the Pacific, the US has a strong base. US Navy has, therefore, become the controller of these islands. In this context, the US Navy as an American Lake refers to the Pacific Ocean.[96]

Moreover, the US has consolidated its position in Marshall Island, which is used for testing its missiles from California. Palau, a small island state, which has achieved a nuclear free constitution for itself, has not been released by the US, as the US likes to dominate the foreign policy of Palau and it refuses to accept the full independence to this state. Both Marshall and Palau were trusteeship territories of the US permitted by the UN in 1947. Although the trusteeship is ended, the freedom of these states is not granted.[97] Apart from freedom of these relations, the US is in good terms with Australia. Its nuclear infrastructures are well as forces assigned for Indian Ocean. The UK has relations with

Australia since 1901, the year when Australia was granted independence. Australia helped, therefore, the nuclear weapon programme of the UK by opening its uranium mine to UK. Also it permitted the UK to test nuclear weapons in Christmas Island, which was then part of their Gilbert and Ell ice Islands colony.[98] France has French Polynesia in the Pacific where it has been involved in nuclear tests.

Because of these reasons, the South Pacific Countries have decided to restrict the influence of these big powers and consolidate the unity of South Pacific Countries economically and politically, if not militarily, in the future. Thus, the SPNFZ move in the Pacific has become a first step to see so that the Pacific islands are released from the influence of the big powers and the nuclear free Pacific is achieved in general in the twenty-first century. For this objective, there are two regional alliances working in the South Pacific.[99] They are the South Pacific Forum (SPF) and the Nuclear Free and Independent Pacific Movement (NFIPM). The first of these is an alliance of thirteen nations, which has achieved the treaty of Rarotonga. Their attitudes are already discussed in the earlier sections of this chapter. However, the Labor political parties both in Australia and New Zealand deserve to be noted. Both the Labor parties have long held anti-nuclear position.

In Australia, the Labor Party (ALP) showed its anti-nuclear tendency as it protested against the Australian Government permission in the 1940s for the UK to mine the uranium in South Australia. It also opposed the decision taken by the Anglophile Conservative Prime Minister Robert Menzies, who permitted the UK to test its nuclear weapons in Christmas Island in 1952. Since then, ALP has evolved a strategy to achieve nuclear free status of the Pacific. The New Zealand Labor Party (NZLP) has developed its political strategy at the grassroots level since 1950s. Since then, NZLP has been taking strong measures against both French nuclear tests in Mururoa Atoll and American nuclear activities in the Pacific.[100] Rainbow warrior and USS Buchanan issues are the examples for its tactful protest restriction against France and the US. Thus, the NZLP is the force behind the signing of SPNFZ treaty.

The Nuclear Free Independent Pacific Movement (NFIPM) is spread all over the Pacific. In Australia, NFIPM began in the

1940s, as the aboriginal people have opposed uranium mining on their land. They along with the Church people, union members and peace groups, protested massively at Roxbury Downs, in the South Australian desert, potentially a large uranium mine in the world.[101] They have argued for focusing the attention of the people that the uranium mining would cause the environmental hazards especially the possible contamination of water in the Great Artesian Basin. In 1976, a national one-day Railway strike was staged by some local trade unions against uranium export as well as mining at Mary Kathleen. In 1981 the Waterside Workers Federation staged a blockade of uranium shipment at the Drawin Wharf for seven weeks. These forceful movements were used by the ALP, as ALP could succeed in the 1983 election.[102] Since 1983, the Hawke Government has supported the nuclear free idea of the NFIPM. NFIPM in Australia has declared 96 nuclear free zones in Australia representing over 56 per cent of the population by 1986. The first declaration in this respect came in 1975, as Fitzroy, the local jurisdiction, declared it nuclear free.[103]

In New Zealand, there is a strong peace movement. By January 1986, the peace movements covering 65 per cent of the people in New Zealand declared 100 municipal nuclear free zones. NZLP is a part and parcel of the peace movement. Therefore, David Lange, the Prime Minister of New Zealand encouraged the effort of peace movements in various ways. He declared in the UN that the New Zealand Government policy would reflect the peace-loving people of New Zealand. He observed further, when he was asked to describe New Zealand's stance on nuclear issue: "We live in a part of the world which does not have a strategic imperative for nuclear arms, and for us to be welcoming them is in fact an escalation".[104] Thus, the NZLP has played a role for strengthening the peace movement in New Zealand. Apart from these movements in the Pacific, there are peace movements in Japan too. By January 1986, there were 638 nuclear free zones all over Japan including in Tokyo and Kyoto district. Kobe, Kiyose city and Tokyo have declared their harbors off limits to visiting military vessels especially nuclear weapon ships. More importantly, the movement is also widespread in the small island states in the Pacific. As a result, Fiji, Micronesia, Hawaii and Vanuatu have been very much active. Palau has nuclear free Constitution. All these movements are directed towards the achievement of nuclear free Pacific in the future.[105] As a first step, the SPNFZ was achieved in 1985. However, for the purpose of the study, it is important to understand the complications and the politics of the Rarotonga treaty.

Rarotonga treaty is not prohibiting all nuclear activities of the zone countries. The main of the treaty is to ban the dumping of radioactive wastes. Other activities for nuclear energy, bio-medical and research uses of nuclear technology, for example, are not banned. Even as an arms control agreement the treaty has significant limitations. Some direct weapons involvement and weapons related activities are unaffected by this treaty.[106] Thus, in a full meaning, it cannot be said Rarotonga treaty is established for a nuclear weapon free zone, let alone the broader concept of a nuclear free zone. However, the Australian Government, as a sponsor of the treaty, has given the impression that the treaty is the beginning of the achievement for peace in the South Pacific. Australian Labor Government has given this impression because of convincing electorates who were in support of Disarmament activities for peace. At the same time, by the same treaty the Australian Government had a plan of convincing the majority of the electorates who are in support of ANZUS.[107]

New Zealand and other small island states are also of the opinion that the Rarotonga treaty is an instrument with which they can secure their political interest in (the South Pacific). However, the treaty can be disputed. First, the treaty has failed in the beginning itself, as France was not prepared to stop testing its nuclear devices in the South Pacific Country. The American nuclear weapons can reach any part of the Pacific from Guam. Therefore, there are debates on border issue particularly relating to the northern border of the SPNFZ where Guam is situated. Some of the member states argue extension of the north of equator to include US Trust Territory of the Pacific Islands and extend to east to include the French territories in the South Pacific.[108]

Third, the provision of the treaty which prohibits the South Pacific Countries from developing, manufacturing, receiving from others and acquiring and testing any nuclear device can be noted. This provision defines nuclear explosive device as the any kind, peaceful as well as explosive. But, it excludes the existence of all weapon related nuclear infrastructure. For example, Australia has entertained American bases for a long time now. Because of this reason, the treaty does not in any way conflict with Australia's defense arrangements, notably ANZUS.[109] By just excluding 'nuclear device' alone, it is impossible to justify the concept of NWFZ. That is why, the whole world at this point of time, till the time the nuclear war breaks out, can be recognized as a NWFZ. Keeping the option open for the bases of nuclear weapon countries means the impracticable nature of NWFZ. In South Pacific, this may lead to a misunderstanding between small and big states. Already Kiribati, which has signed and ratified is not satisfied with the recent happenings in the SPNFZ. Papua New Guinea and Vanuatu are also actively observing the activities of both Australia and New Zealand. Australia, as the biggest among all both geographically and technologically, should stop certain unwanted activities in the region; otherwise, the small states including New Zealand may feel that Australia is blackmailing them in this region.[110] Already, New Zealand has shown its dis-satisfaction over the activities of Australian Government in the basic issues like Rainbow Warrior, USS Buchanan and ANZUS which are the problems still the New Zealand is faced with the US.

Fourth, the province of the treaty allows the South Pacific Countries to retain their rights to decide for themselves, such questions as the access to their ports and airfields by vessels and aircraft of other countries. This provision is interrelated, however, which is already discussed. By this, Australia justifies the existence of the nuclear related bases. Noting that this is its rights. Thus, the treaty of Rarotonga leaves a number of nuclear weapon related infrastructures in Australia. US command, control and communication (C3) facilities are deployed at Nurrungar, Paingap and North West cape in Australia.[111] Moreover this provision does not provide the control the role of nuclear support facilities, nuclear power generation and the export of strategic mineral uranium in this region.[112]

Fifth, the treaty is not prohibiting the transit of ships capable of carrying the nuclear weapons through high seas of the region. The reason given for this is that the parties to the treaty don't have and are unlikely in the foreseeable future to have the capability for effectively monitoring and verifying the transit of ships capable of carrying nuclear weapons. This problem can be understood as New Zealand faced with the USS Buchanan ship. New Zealand, if it had monitoring capacity, it would have monitored itself to identify what type of ship it was, instead of asking the owner of the ship, the US. However, for this purpose the treaty would have developed certain provisions to jointly put an effort to monitor in and around the region. But, it does not. Thus, it shows the seriousness of the treaty. Sixth, it gives the right to the parties to call a nuclear-armed ship to their ports. For this weakness, the treaty indicates that there are beyond the legal jurisdiction of the South Pacific States because these activities are already protected by international law. Because of these reasons, the advocates of the treaty argue that the treaty is right in leaving the problem to the parties to solve, as the treaty respects the international law of the sea and the international law of the airspace.[113]

Thus, the treaty depends upon the international law for transit problem and the UN for the definition of explosive devices. Peaceful nuclear activities and verification in the zone, are therefore, not well defined by the treaty. Because of these reasons, the treaty is more of a political exercise than a practical one in the Pacific Ocean. The following is concerned with the comparison of both the Tlatelolco and Rarotonga treaties.

Tlatelolco and Rarotonga—A Comparison

Both the treaties are aimed at establishing NWFZ in inhabited areas. Therefore, comparing each other, for the purpose of this study, is very important. They have both similarities and difference. Similarities can be noted as follows. Both the treaties are:[114] (a) Prohibiting the acquisition, manufacture, testing and stationing of nuclear weapons, (b) Applying to inhabited areas of the world, (c) Permitting peaceful uses of nuclear energy, (d) Relying on IAEA inspection to verify that nuclear materials and facilities are not diverted under certain circumstances, (f) Respecting rights in international law to freedom of the seas, innocent passage of ships and freedom of over flight for aircraft, (g) Allowing individual parties to decide upon port visits by foreign ships that are nuclear powered or that carry nuclear weapons (implicitly for

Tlatelolco and explicitly for Rarotonga), (h) Including protocols to commit nuclear weapon states to respect weapons against their parties, and (i) Providing an organization to carry out the treaty; OPANAL for Tlatelolco and the Directorate of the South Pacific Forum for Rarotonga.

The differences are as follows: (a) Zone of application:[115] Tlatelolco covers a large land area with some oceans, where as Rarotonga is primarily oceanic with one continent, Australia and many islands, (b) Nuclear testing: Rarotonga explicitly bars testing of any kind of nuclear explosives. Tlatelolco permits tests of peaceful nuclear explosives, (c) Peaceful nuclear explosives: Tlatelolco recognizes and permits tests of peaceful nuclear explosives subject to certain strict conditions whereas Rarotonga does not make any distinction between military and peaceful explosives and bars both, (d) Status: Tlatelolco treaty is not in effect for Argentina, Brazil, Chile and Cuba. Whereas Rarotonga is fully in effect for all of its members, (e) Nuclear exports: Rarotonga commits its parties not to export nuclear materials to any country unless covered by strict non-proliferation measures including IAEA safeguards. Tlatelolco does not, (f) Dumping of radioactive wastes: Rarotonga obliges parties not to dump radioactive wastes at sea anywhere within the zone and to prevent the dumping in their own territorial seas as well as to support a regional convention against such dumping within the region, (g) Withdrawal: Tlatelolco permits a party to withdraw after three months notice, whereas Rarotonga requires twelve months, (h) Protocols: Rarotonga includes a protocol to commit the nuclear weapons states not to test nuclear explosives within the region. Although the objectives of both the treaties are formulated in good faith for the cause of helping out the UN for attaining nuclear Disarmament in general, they are not fully practicable since the nuclear weapons countries have not adhered to them in the real sense. As a matter of fact, they remain as nuclear-free-zones in paper. Practically there are reportedly nuclear weapons related activities in both the zones. The following chapter is concerned with the politics of nuclear-free-zones.

NOTES AND REFERENCES

1. For a detailed study on the Pacific, *see* Cultural Department of Embassy of Chile to Singapore, *Chile and the Pacific* (Singapore: Inter Office Services, 1986), pp.177-200.
2. Tom Stefanick, *Strategic Anti-Submarine Warfare and Naval Strategy* (Toronto: Lexington Books,1987), pp. 56-57.
3. Walter Pincus, "Pacific Experience Shows Difficulty of Cleaning up Radiation", *Washington Post*, April 18, 1978, pp.2-8; the UK sent two navy weather boats in 1958 to observe the nuclear tests in the Pacific. Those two boats were Pukaki and Rotoiti.
4. See *Asia Yearbook* 1985, south Pacific (Hong Kong: *Far Eastern Economic Review*, 1985), pp. 98-101; also *see Canberra Times*, August 7, 1985.
5. See *United Nations Disarmament Yearbook* 1982, vol.7 (New York, UN, 1982), p. 264.
6. *Ibid.*
7. Malcolm Templeton, "Novelty, Gestures and Direction in Foreign Policy; Thoughts from the Twentieth Foreign Policy School", in H. Gold ed., *New Directions in New Zealand Foreign Policy* (Auckland: Benton Ross, 1985), p. 142.
8. F.A. Mediansky, "Nuclear Free Security in the South West Pacific", *Australian Outlook* (Canberra), No. 39, August 1985, pp. 77-83.
9. *Australian Foreign Affairs Record* (Canberra), No. 54, August 1983, pp. 408-09.
10. "Communiqué of the South Pacific Forum Relating to South Pacific Nuclear-Free Zone Treaty, 5-6 August 1985", *Disarmament, A Periodic Review by the UN*, Vol. VIII, No. 3, Winter 1985, pp. 169-70.
11. *Ibid.*
12. See the Preamble of the *South Pacific Nuclear Free Zone Treaty* in Appendix E
13. *Ibid.*
14. *Ibid.*
15. See *the Text of the Treaty.*
16. See the *Articles 3 to 7* of the Treaty.
17. See Greg Fry, "Towards a South Pacific Nuclear Free Zone", *Bulletin of the Atomic Scientists* (Illinois), June-July 1985, pp. 16-20.
18. *Article 5 of the Treaty.*
19. See Greg Fry, n. 17, pp. 16-20.
20. See *Annex 1 of the Treaty.*
21. *Article 1 of the Treaty.*
22. See John P. Holdren, "Nuclear Power and Nuclear Weapons: The Connection is Dangerous", *BOAS*, Jan. 1983, pp. 40-45.
23. For detail about NPT, *See* Chapter five of the Book.

24. UN Special Report of the Conference of the Committee on Disarmament (UNSRCCD), *Comprehensive Study of the Question of NWFZ in its Aspects* (New York: UN, 1976), pp. 43-44.
25. See *Article 8 of the Treaty.*
26. *Ibid.*
27. See the *Annex 4 of the Treaty.*
28. *Ibid.*
29. Michael Denborouglo, (ed.), *Australia and Nuclear War* (Sydney: Croom Helm,1983), pp. 44-48.
30. See *Protocol I* of the Treaty.
31. *Ibid.*
32. See *Protocol II* of the Treaty.
33. See *Protocol III* of the Treaty.
34. *US Department of Defense,* Appropriations for 1976, Sub-committee on Appropriations (Hearings), House of Representatives, 94th Congress (Washington: US Government Office Printing, 1975), p. 397.
35. A Survey of Some Issues is to be found in Jonathan M. Weisgall, "Micronesia and the Nuclear Pacific", *School Advanced Studies (SAIS) Review,* (Washington), No. 5, Summer-Fall, 1985, pp. 41-56.
36. For a Survey of Nuclear-Related Infrastructures and Nuclear Arms Development, *See* William Arkin and Richard W. Field house, *Nuclear Battle Field* (Cambridge: Ballinger, 1985).
37. *Development of Defense,* n. 34, p. 397.
38. *International Herald Tribune* (Paris) Feb. 12, 1987.
39. For a good study in this regard, *See* John C. Torrance, "Coping with the Soviet Pacific Threat", *Pacific Defense Reporter* (Victoria), June 1983. p. 27.
40. *See* Milton Cockburn and Amanda Buckley, "Pacific treaty has US worried", *Sydney Morning Herald,* 8 August, 1985, p. 1.
41. Geoff Kitney, "US gets tough with Australia over Nuclear-Free-Zone", *National Times* (Sydney), 25 April, 1986, p. 5.
42. *International Herald Tribune,* February 12, 1987.
43. "Will the US Have to Go"?, *Asia Week* (London), Vol. 4, No. 11, March 14, 1988, pp. 25-27.
44. *Ibid.*
45. *See* Allen Cameron, "The Strategic Significance of the Pacific Islands: A New Debate Begins", *The Third World Quarterly* (London), Vol. 19, No. 3, Fall 1975, p. 1024.
46. *See* Melvyn Krauss, "The New Zealand Syndrome Spreads", *The New York Times,* February 17, 1985.
47. *See* Milton Cockburn, n. 40, p. 1.
48. Geoff Kitney, "US gets touch with Australia over Nuclear Free Zone", *National Times,* 25 April 1986, p. 5.

49. Walter Lini, Australia and the South Pacific: A Vanuatu Perspective, *Australian Outlook* (Canberra), No. 38, August 1982, pp. 29-31.
50. *See* Secretary of State George P. Shultz, "On Alliance Responsibility" (address given at the East-West Center, Honolulu, Hawaii, July 17, 1985), *Current Policy,* No. 724 (Washington, D.C.: Department of State, 1985).
51. *International Herald Tribune,* February 12, 1987.
52. For a detailed study in this regard, see, *Cultural Department of Embassy of Chile* to Singapore, n. 1, pp. 177-200.
53. *See* Sue Rabbitt Roff, "New Caledonia: Decolonisation and Denuclearisation in the Pacific", *Third World Quarterly,* Vol. 8, No. 1, January 1986, pp. 621-38.
54. *Keesing's Contemporary Archives Record of World Events (KCARWE),* (Harlow, Essex), Vol. XXXI, No. 5, May 1987, pp. 33854-55.
55. *Ibid.*
56. Rabbit Roff, n. 53, p. 626.
57. For example, the Nuclear Free Pacific Conference, held in April 1975, in Suva, Fiji, decided the problem was not simply a matter of French testing in the Pacific but "the Continuing existence of colonialism and imperialism in the Pacific", *Pacific Island Monthly* (Sydney), Vol. 46, No. 9, September 1975, p. 28.
58. *International Herald Tribune,* January 17-18, 1987.
59. *The Washington Post,* August 29, 1984.
60. Ramesh Thakur, "A dispute of many colours: France, New Zealand and the 'Rainbow Warrior' Affair", *The World Today* (London), December 1986, pp. 209-215.
61. *International Herald Tribune,* March 14, 1986.
62. *See* Greg Fry, n. 17, pp. 18-20.
63. Cited from E. Soula, "France and the Pacific", *Pacific Monthly,* Vol. 49, No. 9, September 1975, p. 9.
64. "South Pacific Nuclear Free Zone", *France, Facts and Figures* (Wellington: Embassy of France, June 1985), pp. 13-16.
65. *The New York Times,* September 16, 1985.
66. *International Herald Tribune,* 21 March, 1987.
67. Brian Hocking and John Warhurst, "Australia and Britain: Drifting Apart"?, *The World Today,* December 1986, pp. 244-45.
68. Cited from David McDowell, "The Teaty of Rarotonga", *Disarmament* (New York), Vol. XI, No. 1, winter 1987/1988, pp. 93-104.
69. *Amrita Bazar Patrika,* 11 February, 1987.
70. *International Herald Tribune,* February 12, 1987.
71. The Island of Guam annexed from Spain in 1898 and considered US territory, the Island has been turned into a major strategic outpost of the US in the Pacific. Nuclear missile submarines and B-52 strategic bombers with nuclear weapons aboard are based there. The list of basic military facilities set up on the island includes

air bases in the Gulf of Apra, a naval aviation base in Agan, and an air base in Anderson. During the US aggression in Indo-China US bombers tock off from the Anderson base to carry out barbarous bombing of towns and villages in Vietnam, Laos and Kampuchea. The US military bridgehead on Guam poses a constant threat to vast areas of the Pacific and to national liberation movements in Asia. Guam lies at about 15 degree north and is central to the American nuclear war plan in the Pacific. Some experts argue that Guam is geographically South Pacific country, see, *G. Pry*. No. 17, pp. 63-66.

72. See US Department of Defense, Soviet Military Power 1987, Reprinted in *Strategic Digest* (New Delhi), Vol. XVII, No. 6, June, 1987, p. 1113.
73. For a detailed study in this regard, *see*, Paul Dibb, "World Political and Strategic Trends: Their Relevance to Australia", in Paul Dibb, (ed.), *Australia's External Relations in the 1980s: The Interaction of Economic, Political and Strategic Factors* (New York: St. Martin's Press, 1983), pp. 28-43.
74. The security treaty *between* Australia, New Zealand, and the United States (ANZUS) is regarded as a forerunner of the larger Pacific pact. Twice in the preamble and in Article 8, the treaty explains that the co-ordination of defense efforts are agreed 'pending the development of a more comprehensive system of regional security in the Pacific'. *See* Trevor R. Reese, Australia, New Zealand, and the United States. *A survey of International Relations 1941–1968* (London: Oxford University Press, 1969), p. 126.
75. William Arkin, "Tomahawkj Ominous New Deployment", *Bulletin of Atomic Scientists* (BOAS)(Illinois), Vol. 40, No. 4, 1986, pp. 16-22.
76. For an excellent study dealing with the outer space connection, *see*, Andrei V. Kozyrev, "Outer Space and Universal Security", *Disarmament* (New York), Vol. 10, No. 2, Summer 1982, pp. 38-49.
77. William M. Arkin, n. 75, pp. 18-20.
78. Desmond Ball and R.H. Mathams, "The Nuclear Threat to Australia", in Michael Denborough (ed.) *Australia and Nuclear War* (Sydney: Croom Helm Australia, 1983), p. 46.
79. See Greg Fry, "Australia, New Zealand and Arms control in the Pacific Region", in Desmond Ball, ed., *The ANZUS connection* (Sydney: George Alllen and Unwin, 1985), pp. 106-08.
80. *Ibid*.
81. *UN Disarmament Year Book* 1982, n. 5, p. 264.
82. Greenpeace, founded in 1969, has been actively involved in protest activity against French nuclear tests since 1972. The Rainbow Warrior incident made Greenpeace movement well known to the whole world. For solving this problem between France and New Zealand, the UN took an active role. As a result, New Zealand has accepted

to release the French officers who were involved in sinking the ship, and France has accepted New Zealand's claims for separation of the ship and its demands for apology. Captain Prieur and Major Mafart were sent from New Zealand jail to the French Polynesian island of Hao for a period of three years; France gave seven million dollars for separation and French Prime Minister tendered a formal and unconditional apology to Prime Minister of New Zealand. See, *Ramesh Thakur,* No. 35, pp. 211-12.

83. *Hearing Before the subcommittee on Asian and Pacific Affairs* of the Committee on Foreign Affairs, House of Representatives, 99th Congress, March 18, 1985 (Washington: US Government Printing Office), p. 155.
84. *International Herald Tribune,* 5 February 1985.
85. *Hearing,* n. 83, p. 155.
86. New Zealand Nuclear-Free-Zone Committee (NZNFZC), "Nuclear Free", *Journal of NZNFZC* (Wellington), March/April, 1985, p. 16.
87. *Washington Post,* 4 May, 1985.
88. *Washington Times,* 13 February, 1987.
89. *See* Walter Pincus, "Pacific Experience shows Difficulty of Cleaning up Radiation", *Washington Post,* 18 April, 1978, p. A-2.
90. See *Kissing's Contemporary Archives Record of World Events* (KCARWE), Vol. XXXII, No.2, 1986, pp. 34170-72.
91. *Asia Yearbook* 1985, n.4, pp. 98-101.
92. *Ibid.* France is the only country which is actively involved in nuclear testing in the Pacific. The latest nuclear test was carried out on 17 June, 1988. By October 1984, the year when the South Pacific countries were concerned about establishing SPNFZ, Francè had already carried out 113 nuclear tests in the Pacific, 45 of them atmospheric and 68 of underground.
93. *Communiqué of the South Pacific Forum relating to South Pacific Nuclear-Free zone Treaty,* n.10, pp. 169-70.
94. *US Department of Defense,* n. 72, p. 1113.
95. Nuclear agreement between China and Australia was signed in 1987. This Agreement covers the exchange of nuclear and non-nuclear materials, equipments and technology as well as conditions governing reprocessing of Australian Uranium and recycling of recovered plutonium. The agreement also can cover the transfer of Swiss spent fuel or high level waste to China. See, *Nucleonic Week* (New York), 24 December, 1987.
96. See Peter Hayes, *et al., American Lake, Nuclear Peril in the Pacific* (New York: Penguin Books, 1986), pp. 49-74.
97. See Harold Jackson, "Victims of the Nuclear Colonists", *Manchester Guardian Weekly,* 15 July, 1984.
98. *Ibid.*

99. Greg Fry, n. 79, pp. 106-08.
100. Ramesh Thakur, n. 60, pp. 210-12.
101. *See* Paul Dibb, n. 73, pp. 29-31.
102. *See* Gregory Fry, "Regionalism and International Politics of the South Pacific", *Pacific Affairs*, Vol. 54, Fall 1981, pp. 455-89.
103. *Washington Post*, 14 January, 1986; also Michael Paugh, "New Zealand—A Nuclear Free Model", *The World Today*, March 1986, pp. 40-41.
104. "New Zealand Assails US Ship Ban Reaction", *The Sun* (Baltimore), February 27, 1985, p. 4.
105. *Washington Post*, 14 January, 1988.
106. *See* William M. Arkin and Richard W. Fieldhouse, "Focus on the Nuclear Infrastructure", *Bulletin of the Atomic Scientists*, June 1985, pp. 11-15.
107. Gregory Fry, n. 102, p. 488.
108. *See* Greg Fry, n. 17, p. 18.
109. For a good study in this regard, see, Desmond Ball, *A Suitable Piece of Real Estate: American Installations in Australia* (Sydney: Wale and Ironmonger, 1980), pp. 88-98.
110. *See* Desmond Ball, n. 78, p. 46.
111. William M. Arkin, n. 36, p. 80.
112. John P. Holdren, n. 22, pp. 40-45.
113. *See* David McDowell, n. 68, pp. 93-104.
114. *See* the texts of the treaties in Appendices
115. *Ibid*.

5

Politics of the Nuclear-Weapon-Free Zone

Background

International action to prevent the spread of nuclear weapons was started by signing up the nuclear non-proliferation treaty (NPT) that had initiated steps towards the creation of nuclear non-proliferation regime. In addition to the NPT, there are a number of other arms control treaties, which are also in support of creating such non-proliferation regime.[1] For example, the treaty Banning Nuclear Weapon Tests in the Atmosphere, in Outer Space and Under Water commonly known as the Partial Test Ban Treaty (PTBT) and the Treaties of Tlatelolco and Rarotonga can be noted. Nevertheless, the NPT is the center of all these treaties. It can be understood by the basic provisions of the treaty, which set out the fundamental obligations for the creation of non-proliferation regime. Article 1 reads as follows: "Each nuclear-weapon state party to this treaty undertakes not to transfer to any recipient whatsoever nuclear weapons or other nuclear explosive devices directly or indirectly, and not in any way to assist, encourage or induce any non-nuclear weapon state to manufacture or otherwise acquire nuclear weapons or other nuclear explosive devices". And the Article II reads: "Each non-nuclear-weapon state party to this treaty undertakes not to receive the transfer from any transferor whatsoever of nuclear weapons or other nuclear explosive devices or of control over such weapons or explosive devices directly or indirectly, not to manufacture or otherwise acquire nuclear weapons or other nuclear explosive devices; and not to seek or receive any assistance in the manufacture of nuclear explosive devices".[2] For maintaining these fundamental obligations, both the nuclear and non-nuclear weapon states have accepted four important points. They are:[3]

> "Non-nuclear weapon states ratifying the treaty pledge not to manufacture or receive weapons and peaceful nuclear explosives. (Both nuclear weapons and peaceful nuclear explosives are prohibited); to verify that they are living up to this pledge, non-nuclear weapon states also agree to accept International peaceful nuclear activities (an arrangement known as "full-scope" safeguards); all countries accepting the treaty agree not to export nuclear equipment or material to non-nuclear weapon states except under IAEA safeguards and nuclear weapon states agree not to assist non-nuclear weapon states in obtaining nuclear arms; all countries accepting the treaty agree to facilitate the fullest possible sharing of peaceful nuclear technology. (In practice this is a pledge by the advanced nations to help less developed countries build peaceful nuclear programme). All countries accepting the treaty agree to pursue negotiations in good faith to end the nuclear arms race and achieve nuclear disarmament under international control. (In practice this applies to the United States and Russia)".

However, the treaty does not prohibit parties from accumulating nuclear weapons material (highly enriched or plutonium) as part of their peaceful nuclear energy or research programmes as long as the material is subject to IAEA inspection.[4] This means parties to the treaty can become capable of producing nuclear arms without violating the terms of the treaty.[5] If an interested party desires to make nuclear sales to countries that are not parties, such as India or Argentina (even if these countries have unsafeguarded nuclear facilities), it can be interpreted that the treaty permits this activity too. The items exported by any party should be placed under IAEA safeguards. For example, US sales of nuclear fuel to South Africa, which has at least one unsafeguarded nuclear installation, are permissible under the treaty as long as the fuel were placed under safeguards in South Africa.[6] In the late 1970s and early 1980s, China also sold nuclear materials to Argentina, India, Pakistan and South Africa without requiring the application of IAEA safeguards.[7] The non-nuclear weapon states—Argentina, Brazil, India, Israel, Pakistan and South Africa—are not party to the treaty. They have unsafeguarded nuclear activities. Libya and Iraq, two additional potential nuclear weapon states are parties to the NPT. In the review conferences of NPT held in 1975, 1980 and 1985, the complaints of non-nuclear weapon states were focused on two important elements of the treaty: Article IV, which calls for the (fullest possible transfer of nuclear technology for peaceful purposes and Article VI, which, along with the treaty's preamble, obligates nuclear weapon state parties to "pursue negotiations in race and calls upon them to continue negotiations to achieve a comprehensive nuclear test ban.)[8] However, these problems are not completely solved.

Meaning of Nuclear-Weapon-Free

At present, there are three treaties which are concerned with the definition of nuclear weapon. They are: NPT, Tlatelolco and Rarotonga. Article IX of the NPT says: "For the purpose of this treaty, a nuclear weapon state is one which has manufactured and exploded a nuclear weapon or other nuclear explosive devices prior to January1, 1967".[9] Therefore, according to the NPT, there is no other nuclear weapon state except the five. That means the explosive devices relating the states without these devices can be considered as a nuclear weapon free states. This definition, thus, invalids the argument that 'horizontal proliferation' or the spread of nuclear weapons to the third world/non-nuclear countries, especially to Argentina, Brazil, India and Pakistan are establishing the non-proliferation regime. According to Tlatelolco treaty "a nuclear weapon is any device which is capable of releasing nuclear energy in an uncontrolled manner and which has a group of characteristics." However, it recognises the importance of the 'link' between both the peaceful as well as nuclear explosive of a device, as the type of devices is not explained in the treaty. The treaty of Rarotonga explains, "...Any nuclear weapon or other explosive devices capable of releasing nuclear energy, irrespective of the purpose for which it could be used".[11] It is not clear, however, in the Rarotonga treaty whether treaty really means of covering all types of devices. Thus, these treaties are failed to define exactly what do they mean by nuclear free is recognized by all the treaties on the basis of the principles of the UN, as seen in the first chapter. Since they depend upon the UN principle for nuclear free status, they are also abiding by the UN definition of nuclear weapon. According to the UN, nuclear weapon usually means nuclear bombs and warheads'.[12] Therefore, the 'nuclear free' efforts of both the Tlatelolco and Rarotonga can be stated as the efforts for making their region free of nuclear bombs and warheads. Thus, the UN recognizes these two nuclear free 'or' nuclear weapon free zones as the efforts of strengthening the non-proliferation regime.

For the purpose of the study, it is important to know the other components of nuclear weapon systems. Because these components are part and parcel of weapon system without which the nuclear explosive power is useless. For example, in Australia, there are several installations such as navigation aids for submarines, communications-intercept and direction-finding antennae that can be used for target acquisition and sonar arrays. Especially, they can be used in connection with maritime patrol aircraft carrying nuclear depth charges and by attack submarines. Thus, in general, they serve for carrying out a nuclear war in the Pacific. Although the South Pacific is declared as nuclear free zone, according to nuclear war strategy, these installations would be targeted by the Soviet Union.[13] Also, in Latin America NWFZ, there are nuclear weapon related installations. Therefore, the definition of NWFZ covering only bombs and warheads is not acceptable to many Third World countries.[14] But the supporters of this definition are in view that the bombs and warheads are only made for war purposes and therefore, it should be considered first rather than all other components. Till the time the zone which is not having, according to them, the bombs and warheads, and which is having all other components can be considered as a NWFZ. They hold the view further that it is very difficult to define the "nuclear free" concept, therefore one should accept the most dangerous element like bomb and warheads first to be controlled in the zone and the rest should be put under the IAEA control. According to them, if a member country of NWFZ wants to abolish the installation of all components, which may be used in nuclear warfare and which may therefore become nuclear target in war, it should raise this question bilaterally with the nuclear state concerned. Many South Pacific Countries have raised the issue of American installations in Australia. Some argue that since the installations are difficult to be defined and their uses are much interrelated, the components, which are deployed only for the purpose of war, for example delivery vehicles, should be scrapped.[15] Thus, the definition of nuclear-weapon-free zone is not clear, as the nuclear weapon itself is not defined properly.

Peaceful Nuclear Energy and the Connection

The peaceful nuclear explosive programme was started at the Lawrence Radiation Laboratory, University of California during the late 1950s, which was known as "Plowshare" programme.[16] The same peaceful nuclear explosive programme was also carried out by the Soviet Union in the same period. It was called in the Soviet Union as "the programme of the use of commercial underground nuclear explosion".[17] It was believed in both US and Soviet Union that the peaceful nuclear programmes were definitely related with nuclear weapons programmes. Therefore, the NPT, which was sponsored by nuclear weapon States—US, Soviet Union and UK—is very restrictive. However, the Tlatelolco Treaty gives the non-nuclear states the right to use nuclear energy for peaceful purposes, in particular for their economic development and social progress. Article 18 says: "The contracting parties may carry out explosions of nuclear devices similar to those used in nuclear weapons".[18] This recognizes the fact that there is a close relation between the nuclear explosion for peaceful purposes and the nuclear explosions for weapon programme. However, the peaceful nuclear explosions could be divided into two categories:[19]

1. Mining operations for the recovery of natural resources. Among the various uses were envisaged: the fracturing of oil and gas recovery; the blasting out of cavities to store

of oil and gas recovery; the blasting out of cavities to store gas or oil or nuclear wastes from spent fuel; the leaching of copper and other minerals from ore-bearing rock; the crushing and fracturing of ore; the removal of overburden and uncovering of mineral rock for strip mining; and putting out run-away oil and gas well fires by sealing them off with an underground explosion.

2. Excavation operations and earth moving by catering explosions. Among the operations envisaged here were the excavation of canals, harbors, mountain passes and highways; the diversion of rivers; and the building of dams and water reservoirs.

The non-nuclear weapon states, which are bound with IAEA safeguard system face problem to get these peàceful nuclear technologies for their social progress. Especially, it is believed by the countries which are not agreeing with the NWFZ concept that once a individual state or a region declares itself as a nuclear-free zone, it implies that they lose their right of using nuclear technology for any purpose. For instance, countries committed to the concept of NWFZ lag to get the nuclear technology whereas the countries in the same zone such as Brazil, Argentina and Mexico, which are not satisfied with the concept, get more support for their peaceful nuclear activities.[21] However, the connection between peaceful nuclear power and nuclear weapons can be understood as Warren Donnelly explains "that both utilize the energy produced by the fission of uranium or plutonium atoms. The difference is that in a power reactor the concentration of fissionable material in the nuclear fuel is low and the reactor is designed to produce a slow, sustained reaction to make steam, turn a turbine, and generate electricity, while a nuclear weapon utilizes material with a much higher concentration of fissionable material, and is designed to produce an uncontrolled, explosive reaction."

He continues: "Uranium enriched to 3 per cent U-235 is sufficient to fuel a nuclear power reactor; weapons require either uranium enriched to 90 per cent U-235 or relatively pure plutonium separated from the spent fuel of a reactor". Thus he points out that "it is generally accepted today that the conceptual design of a nuclear bomb is within the capabilities of most nations."[22] If a country has either uranium-235 or plutonium-239, it can go for nuclear weapon programme (see the following diagram).

Routes to Nuclear Weapons

1. Direct Routes

All these operations may be done under military control on a small scale and secretly at a cost of about 1 million per atomic bomb.

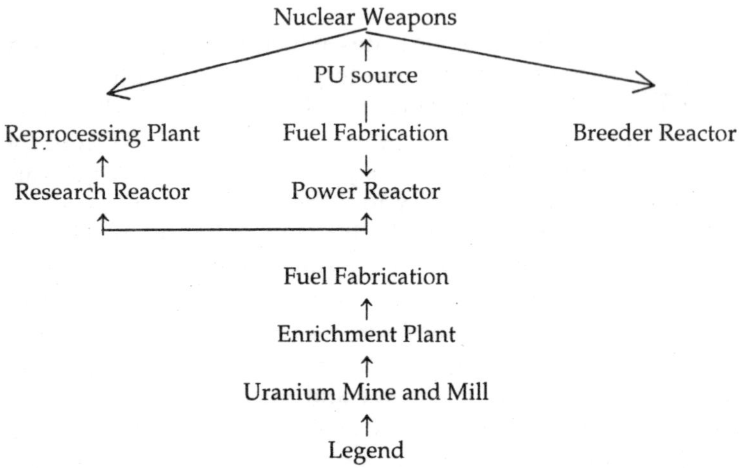

2. Indirect Routes

The nuclear explosives may be produced as byproducts of a peaceful power. The marginal cost of a nuclear explosive device may be no more than a few hundred thousand American dollars.

Source: Stockholm International Peace Research Institute Yearbook 1981, *World Armaments and Disarmament* (Stockholm: Francis, 1981), p. 7. Enriched uranium (over 40% U-235) and weapon grade plutonium (over 90% Pu-239) are needed for making atomic and hydrogen bombs respectively.

Verification System

IAEA and regional organizations are responsible for the verification of NWZ. Regional verification set-up is made by both the Tlatelolco and Rarotonga treaties. They are Agencies for the Prohibition of Nuclear Weapons in Latin America (OPANAL) and the South Pacific Bureau for establishing a programme of on-site inspections, audits and inventory controls known as "safeguards". It verifies the transfers of nuclear materials from one country to another based on certain agreements designed to ensure that they will be used only for peaceful purposes. The objective of IAEA is set out in Article II of the IAEA's statutes. It says: "The Agency shall seek to accelerate and enlarge the contribution of atomic energy to peace, health and prosperity throughout the world. It shall ensure, so far as it is able, that assistance provided by it at its request or under its supervision or control is not used in such a way as to further any military purpose".[23]

Article III, A, 5 gives the right to the agency "to establish and administer safeguards designed to ensure that special fissionable and other materials, services, equipment, facilities and information made available by the agency or at its request or under its supervision or control are not used in such a way as to further any military purpose; and to apply safeguards, at the request of the parties, to any bilateral or multilateral arrangement, or at the request of a state, to any of that state's activities in the field of atomic energy."[24] Thus, the IAEA does two jobs: co-operating for peaceful nuclear energy and verifying the materials in order to stop the weapon programme of the country which uses the materials for peaceful purposes. Therefore, it can be stated that the IAEA also recognizes the close connection that the materials used for peaceful purposes can also be used for weapon production. Technically, it is feasible to divert nuclear materials even from closely guarded facilities, and the IAEA might well not even be able to detect their disappearance.[25]

The problems that the Agency faces can be noted as follows: (1) It uses seals and cameras in the installation of particular country which uses the materials under safeguard agreement; (2) IAEA inspectors are not present in the installation; (3) Enrichment and reprocessing facilities are not under the IAEA system; (4) Certain types of facilities such as fuel fabrication, reprocessing and enrichment installations which uses materials in the form of powers, liquids or gases are difficult to safeguard; (5) It conducts only fewer inspections at safeguard installation; (6) IAEA inspector cannot make unannounced visits the installation of the country which uses the materials under safeguard agreement; and (7) The country which uses the materials under safeguard agreement can also reject particular IAEA inspectors.[26]

Regional Agencies: the Agency for the Prohibition of Nuclear Weapons in Latin America (OPANAL) and the South Pacific Bureau for Economic Co-operation. They work towards the objective of preventing the member countries of the zone from violating the treaties.[27] For, both agencies agree to 'full-scope' safeguards (i.e. IAEA accounting and inspection measures on all of a nation's nuclear activities). They also face problems like the IAEA. OPANAL, for example, has not solved any problem, although there are reports by zone countries against the nuclear activities of other countries. Especially the British involvement in the Falkland war can be noted.[28] This issue is discussed already in the third chapter. In the case of South Pacific Bureau for Economic Co-operation is yet to establish its credibility. Apart from the IAEA and the regional agencies, there is a group known as Nuclear Suppliers Group (NSG), which is also part of the verification system established by the present proliferation regime. The US, Soviet Union, Australia, Canada and West Germany, France, Japan, the UK, held a meeting in London in 1975. The London meeting focused on two important issues. The first was, if and under what conditions technology and equipment for enrichment and reprocessing (the most sensitive parts of the nuclear fuel cycle from a weapon proliferation perspective), shall be transferred to non-nuclear states.

The second issue was whether transfers should be made to states, which do not agree for IAEA safeguards. France and West Germany opposed this move, as they had already contracts with some countries (Pakistan and South Korea in the case of France, and Brazil in the case of West Germany). However, the London meeting adopted a "Trigger List" which enlisted the material, which can be transferred. These materials, according to the NSG agreement, should be transferred based on understandings of the recipient countries that they would not use the material for weapon production. These guidelines are adopted by supplier countries.[29] However, the effort to control the sensitive materials is not very effective. (See the Table)

World Nuclear Facilities

Country	*NPT Signer*	*Enrichment Plant*	*Reprocessing Plant*	*Breeder Reactor*	*Unsafeguarded nuclear facility*
Argentina	X	–	S	–	–
Australia	S	–	–	–	–
Brazil	X	–	S	–	–
Canada	S	–	–	–	
Chile	X	–	–	–	–
Columbia	Not Ratified	–	–	–	–
China	X	S	–	–	–
Cuba	X	–	–	–	–
Egypt	S	–	–	–	S (Soviet Union Reactor)
India	X	–	–	–	S (Canada's Reactor, US heavy water)
Indonesia	S	–	–	–	–
Iran	S	–	–	–	–
Iraq	S	–	–	–	–
Israel	X	–	–	–	S (France's Reactor, Norway Heavy Water)
Japan	S	S	S	S	–
Libya	S	–	–	–	–
Mexico	S	–	–	–	–
Pakistan	X	–	S	–	S (Belgium)
Philippines	S	–	–	–	–
South Africa	X	S	–	–	S (West Germany)
South Korea	S	–	-	–	–
Soviet Union	S	S	S	S	–
Taiwan	S	–	–	–	–
Thailand	S	–	–	–	–
Turkey	S	–	–	–	–
United States	S	S	–	–	–
Uruguay	S	–	–	–	–
Venezuela	S	–	–	–	–
Zaire	S	–	–	–	–

Source: Jack Dennis, No. 1, pp. 350-351, for latest information *see* SIPRI Year Book till 2005.

Concerns of the States within the Established Zones

According to the Treaties of Tlatelolco and Rarotonga, there should be total absence of nuclear weapons in the zone and the states within the zone should share more responsibility than the states outside the zone. Therefore, they undertake the obligations that they will not develop, test, produce, possess, or acquire nuclear weapons in the territory under their jurisdiction and that they will not permit anybody to store, install, or deploy such weapons in their territories. In addition, they should agree not to give, seek, or receive any assistance in the development or renounce all military uses of nuclear energy.[30] Although Argentina and Brazil have accepted the Tlatelolco Treaty and the IAEA safeguards, they have been increasingly involving in accumulating plutonium. They are having uranium too (see chapter 3). It should be understood that the Alamogordo and Nagasaki bombs were plutonium bombs while the one at Hiroshima was a uranium 235(U-235) bomb. It is generally considered that 5 to 7 kilograms of Pu are needed for a small bomb of the Nagasaki size and 10 to 15 kilograms of U-235 for a small bomb of the Hiroshima size. The yield of each of these two bombs was in the 15 to 20 kilotones range, i.e. the equivalent of 15,000 to 20,000 tons of high explosive.[31] If the countries located in the zone have acquired fissionable material and nuclear explosive, the NWFZ is impracticable. In the case of South Pacific nuclear free zone, Australia can be noted. Australia has nuclear weapon related infrastructures deployed by the US.

Thus, the existence of the NWFZ depends upon each and every member of the zone. If any one of the states is not co-operating the objective of the Treaty for a total absence of nuclear weapons, the NWFZ cannot be achieved. Moreover, it should be understood that the states either outside or inside zone have nuclear weapons, there will be an impact on any NWFZ in the world because of the incalculable destructive power of nuclear weapons.[32] For instance, the Preamble of the Tlatelolco Treaty says: "In the name of their peoples and faithfully interpreting their desires and aspirations, the Governments of the States which sign the Treaty for the Prohibition of Nuclear Weapon in Latin America... convinced that nuclear weapons, whose terrible effects are suffered, indiscriminately and inexorably, by military forces and civilian population alike, constitute, through the persistence of the radioactivity they release, an attack on the integrity of the human species and ultimately may even render the whole earth uninhabitable".[33] Although all Latin American Countries and South Pacific Countries are convinced about the danger of nuclear weapons in general, they have failed to have any provision in the Tlatelolco treaty or Rarotonga for reducing outside nuclear weapons. Both the main articles and the protocols of the Treaties say nothing about the existence of nuclear weapons. (See the Map).

Existing Nuclear Arms and Infrastructure

Nuclear arms and infrastructures are with nuclear weapon countries: US, Soviet Union, UK, France and China. At the time of signing the NPT in 1970 (three years after the Tlatelolco Treaty which was signed in 1967) the US had 1054 intercontinental ballistic missiles (ICBMS), 656 submarine-launched ballistic missiles (SLBMS), and 650 bombers—2360 strategic delivery vehicles in all. The Soviet Union had 850 intercontinental ballistic missiles (ICBMS) and 195 bombers—1045 strategic vehicles in all.[34] Both the NPT and NWFZ treaty could not do anything against these forces, although the NPT aimed for the complete absence of nuclear weapons and the NWFZ treaty called absence of nuclear weapons and the NWFZ treaty called upon nuclear weapon states to pursue negotiations in good faith on effective measures relating to cessation of the nuclear arms race.[35] As a result, by the end of 1984, the US had 9,000 strategic nuclear warheads, 1,045 ICBMS, 568 SLBMS and 328 strategic bombers. New US strategic plan includes two land-based ballistic missile (MX and Midget man), a new sea-launched ballistic missile (the Trident II or D-5), 3 version of low-flying cruise missiles (sea, land and air-launched), 2 new bombers (B 1 and stealth), a whole new generation of new nuclear warheads, and "star wars" anti-missile system in space. Soviet nuclear forces includes 7,000 strategic nuclear warheads, 1,400 ICBMS, 980 SLBMS, and 350 strategic bombers. And also, Soviet plans include 7,000 strategic bombers. And also, Soviet plans include at least two ICBMs, (SS-X-24 and 25), and a new

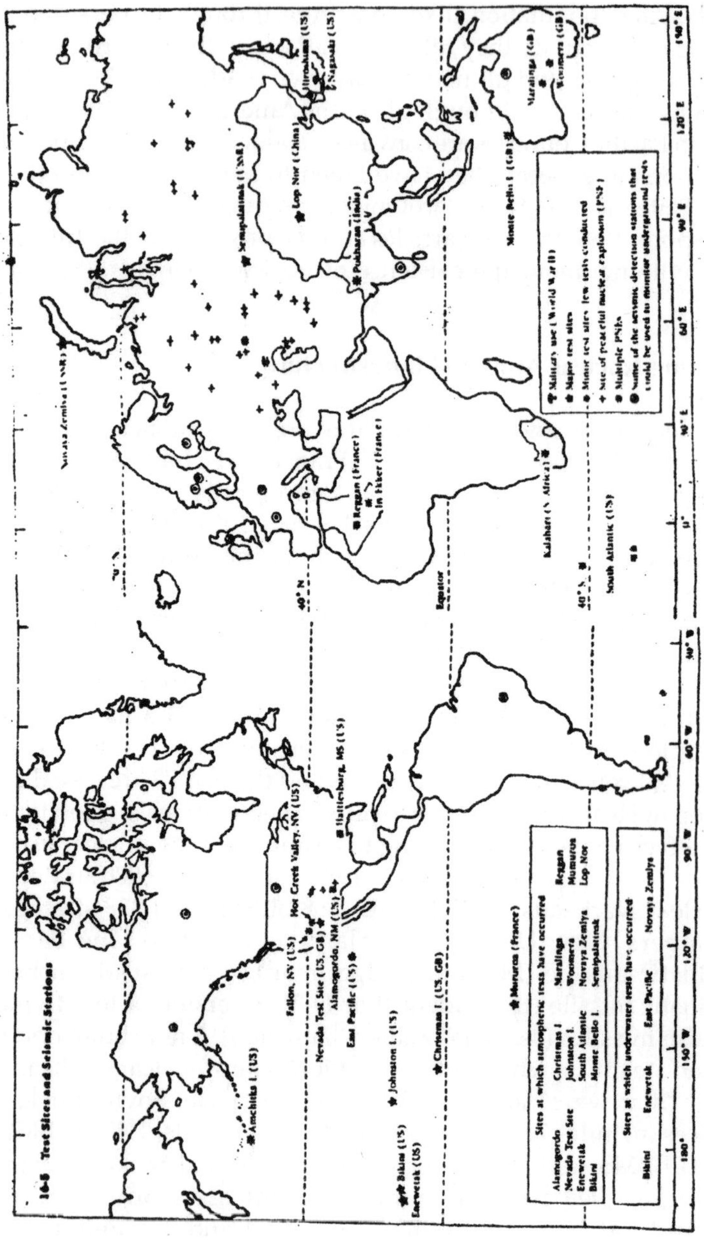
16-8 Test Sites and Seismic Stations
Amchitka I. (US)
Bikini (US)
Enewetak (US)
Johnston I. (US)
Christmas I. (US, GB)
Mururoa (France)
Fallon, NV (US)
Hot Creek Valley, NV (US)
Nevada Test Site (US, GB)
Alamogordo, NM (US)
East Pacific (US)
Hattiesburg, MS (US)
40° N
Equator
40° S
Novaya Zemlya (USSR)
Semipalatinsk (USSR)
Lop Nor (China)
Pokharan (India)
Hiroshima (US)
Nagasaki (US)
Reggan (France)
In Ekker (France)
Kalahari (S. Africa)
South Atlantic (US)
Monte Bello I. (GB)
Maralinga (GB)
Woomera (GB)
Military use (World War II)
Major test sites
Minor test sites (few tests conducted)
Site of peaceful nuclear explosion (PNE)
Multiple PNEs
Some of the seismic detection stations that could be used to monitor underground tests
Sites at which atmospheric tests have occurred
Alamogordo
Nevada Test Site
Enewetak
Bikini
Christmas I.
Johnston I.
South Atlantic
Monte Bello I.
Maralinga
Woomera
Novaya Zemlya
Semipalatinsk
Reggan
Mururoa
Lop Nor
Sites at which underwater tests have occurred
Bikini
Enewetak
East Pacific
Novaya Zemlya
180°
150° W
120° W
90° W
60° W
30° W
0°
30° E
60° E
90° E
120° E
150° E

SLBM (SS-NX-23), a new strategic bomber (Blackjack), cruise missiles, and hunter-killer satellites.[36] Both the US and the Soviet nuclear warheads are ever increasing since 1984. The United Kingdom, France and China also have their own forces. The United Kingdom has an arsenal of between 200 and 5,000 warheads, China above 3,000 and France between 100 and 200. Their warheads are also increasing in number.

Moreover, the Rapid Deployment Forces (RDF) of US—navy: aircraft carrier battle groups (3), and amphibious ready group (1) which typically consists of three to five amphibious ships including fighter wings (10) each consists of approximately seventy-two aircraft; ground forces: marine amphibious forces (2) each consists of a ground combat division, a tactical fighter wing and sustaining support and army combat divisions (5) each division consists of 16,000 to 17,000 soldiers—would endanger the NWFZ. RDF, in a situation that will be suggested by US, can be used against any part of the world including NWFZ.[37] RDF is composed of integrated and "dual-capable" units equipped with tactical nuclear as well as non-nuclear weapons. For example, B-52, the nuclear capable US aircraft deployed in Diego Garcia and the two aircraft carrier groups stationed in the Arabian Sea south of Pakistan's Makran coast would make NWFZ concept meaningless for South Asia.[38]

Furthermore, nuclear infrastructures—such as scientific research, information gathering and early warning surveillance—are installed in many NWFZ countries. The NWF treaties (Tlatelolco and Rarotonga) ignored all these forces. William M. Arkin explains:[39] the main flaw in existing nuclear-free policies or nuclear free zone proposals is that they set up a system whereby non-nuclear warheads, while the infrastructure is ignored. In the 1950s and 1960s when nuclear weapons were large and difficult to transport or assemble, the mere restriction of warheads might have made sense as an arms control initiative. But today warheads are small and light weight and require minimal upkeep. Virtually every ship and airplane available to the nuclear powers can carry them anywhere on earth, as long as the intelligence, targeting, basing, training place to support them.

The nuclear infrastructure can be categorised into eight sectors—the arsenals are the ships, aircraft, guns, missiles and warheads, and the bases used in training, maintenance and supply of nuclear forces; the facilities for the production of nuclear warheads and related fissionable materials; the research, development and testing complex; the surveillance systems which gather information on and monitor the adversary's nuclear weapon systems; the early warning system of radars, satellites and information processing stations; the communications system which links all these; the command structure which plans and controls nuclear war; civil defense. These facilities are with many countries. For example, West Germany, Canada, Italy, UK, Japan, Turkey, South Korea, Greece and Philippines are leading countries in this respect. West Germany alone has 241 nuclear facilities.[40] Also nuclear infrastructures are deployed in some NWFZ countries: Antigua (located in the Latin American NWFZ), Australia (located in the South Pacific NWFZ), Argentina (located in the Latin American NWFZ), Barbados (located in the Latin American NWFZ), Panama (located in the Latin American NWFZ), Puerto Rico (located in the Latin American NWFZ) and Virgin Islands (located in the Latin American NWFZ). These are all deployed by US. The Soviet Union has its infrastructure in Cuba[41] (see the Appendix F).

Developing Countries and NWFZ

The treaties of Tlatelolco, Rarotonga, Antarctic, Outer Space and Sea-bed are signed by third world countries. Also, most of the NWFZ proposals are proposed, for establishing NWFZ, in Third World countries. There are eight proposals. Of all, five proposals are for establishing NWFZ in Third World countries: Africa, Mediterranean, Indian Ocean, South Asia, Middle East (see chapter 1). More than forty-third world countries are located in the proposed NWFZ. The established NWFZ: Latin America and South Pacific have more than thirty. There is no nuclear-free zone or NWFZ established among nuclear weapon countries: US, Soviet Union, UK, France and China. Although, China is a third world country, it has nuclear weapons and it does not belong either to established or to proposed nuclear free zone region. However, the attitude of third world countries is an important factor for strengthening both the NWFZ and the nuclear non-proliferation region. Argentina, Brazil and Mexico are major Third World countries in the Latin America NWFZ. They are involved in nuclear activities for peaceful purposes (see chapter 3).

The treaty is not in force for Argentina and Brazil. Both the countries are not satisfied with the NWFZ concept.[42] Since the treaty leaves these big countries in the region, which are having certain sensitive nuclear materials, the Latin America NWFZ is not practically established. Also, they are not satisfied with the nuclear weapon countries and their attitudes towards Latin America NWFZ. Especially, Argentina had reported to the OPANAL about the British nuclear involvement in the Falkland war. But, this issue was not solved properly by the OPANAL. Therefore, Argentina is very much opposed to the NWFZ. They are not signatories of the NPT. According to them the NPT is not an instrument, which treats all the countries, both nuclear and non-nuclear equal.[43]

In South Pacific nuclear-free zone, there are island states, which are not agreeing with the American nuclear installation in Australia (see Chapter 4). Thus, countries such as Vanuatu, Tuvalu, Kiribati and Western Samoa are not fully agreeing to the South Pacific nuclear-free zone. Most of the Third World nations in South Pacific have signed only for the purpose of avoiding the influence of the big powers in their region. They are more bothered about decolonization than denuclearization. Although, the peace-movement in this region is united on the issue of nuclear tests and nuclear dumping they are working towards the objective of freeing all Pacific island nations from the US, France and the UK.[44] For example, in the proposed zones: Africa, South Asia, there are countries like South Africa, India and Pakistan. Their attitudes towards NWFZ are as follows. South Asia, but it has involved in sensitive nuclear activities. India does not agree to the concept of NWFZ. It has opposed Pakistani proposal in the UN. India's viewpoint is that NWFZ is not practical one because of the increasing nuclear arms proposed by nuclear weapon countries, which can reach any part of the world today. It has proposed recently in the UN for nuclear free universe by 2010.[45] According to this, a universal nuclear free move should be initiated by all members of the UN. Therefore, it does not believe in the regional approach for nuclear arms control, especially regional NWFZ.

Sea and Outer Space Connection

Both the United States and Soviet Union have been operating their nuclear forces at the Baltic, the Barents, Arctic, Black Seas and etc. These forces are part and parcel of deterrence—Mutual Assured Destruction (MAD), the ability of each to destroy the aggressor even after having absorbed a first strike which is focused towards Europe in particular and which is operational for general war in the world by connecting the Atlantic, Pacific and Indian Ocean through land and air routes.[46] The nuclearization of the sea was started in the 1960s, as the United States deployed US carrier-borne fighter bombers and Polaris submarines. In the same period, the Soviet Union deployed anti-ship, air, surface and sub-surface bombers. Followed by these forces, the deployment of submarine launched Ballistic Missiles (SLBM) of both the Soviet Union and the United States marked the deterrent controversy at stake, by increasingly improving the range and accuracy of their SLBMs which can reach NWFZs. The US Polaris was close to Soviet waters by moving through NATO controlled waters, supported by facilities in Greenland, Iceland, Britain and Norway. Therefore, the Soviet Union countered by deploying its forces near the US homeland—which was contributed to the Cuban missile crisis in the 1960s.[47]

When the Soviet moves in the sea near the US homeland was created eve and cry in the West, especially in the US, the Soviet Union concentrated in the Arctic. Especially the Soviet effort impressed equally in the fields of chemical oceanography, water salinity, temperature and oxygen measurements, water biological and aerial aero magnetic data gathering, gravity charts and ice dynamics investigations. Improving its sea power both in research for civil and military purposes, the Soviet Union had deployed the first Delta-class submarines, with inter-continental range missiles that could be fired from Soviet territorial seas in 1972. The special character of the Delta class is that it can facilitate surfacing and firing prospects through certain ice thickness and reach Latin America NWFZ. As a counter measure, the United Stated deployed forty US warheads assigned to every Soviet city. Thus, the increase of American warheads in the Barents and adjacent Arctic water attracted more Soviet SLBM fleet in the late 1970s. The United States deployed in the same period the supportive underwater devices in Atlantic, North Sea and Norwegian waters.[48]

As a result, in the beginning of 1980s, the United States took lead in stealth bomber designs to thwart Soviet radar, stealth cruise missile design and SMART targeting technology in general, and counterforce intercontinental ballistic missile guidance prospects, known as MX. These forces are designed to serve the nuclear forces deployed in the land or sea.[49] Although these forces are branded as counter forces for Soviet, SS-20 missiles, the US Pershing II and cruise missiles are peculiar forces having the procurement of additional nuclear super carriers as nuclei for new exceptionally potent naval strike forces connecting the land, air and sea. Especially, cruise missile, the low flying and escapable from the Soviet Union radar, can reach the target at any cost by over flying on land or on the surface of the seawater. Also, a wide range of communication system with the specific mission for commanding, controlling and communicating all related installations in sea, outer space and land are dispersed by the US at sea. These forces confirmed the US superiority in the sea wars[50]. Thus, the US forces in the Barent and Arctic seas serve the reinforcements and supplies in different stages of the different war scenarios, aiming to win a limited nuclear war either in land or in sea. Today, there are more than 15000 nuclear warheads in the naval forces of the nuclear weapon countries[51]. They can reach both the Latin America NWFZ and the South Pacific nuclear-free zone. In the UN Special Session on Disarmament held in July 1988, the US has denied to include the sea-based nuclear arms in the arms control Agenda.

Nuclear controversy is expanded to Outer Space, as the US has declared star wars programme on 23 March, 1983. ABM and Outer Space Treaty are violated or interpreted in a different way today in order to implement the star wars programme by 1994 [52]. If American scientists, (more than fifty per cent of the scientists in US are in the opinion that the star wars cannot be separated from nuclear war) succeed in deploying star war weapon system based on nuclear or non-nuclear energy that will endanger the whole world. Non-nuclear method of implementing the star wars programme, as the US Government claims to be so, would create a nuclear dimension because the nuclear systems which are already based on both land and sea are involved in any type of war, either planned or accidental. This scenario principally would affect the NWFZ in the future[53]. However, it is important to note the recent development in regard to the non-nuclear deterrence of the US. The notion of non-nuclear deterrence war declared by the US on 23 March, 1983, as President Ronald Reagan stated:[54]

> "I have reached a decision, which offers a new hope for our children in the 21st century... isn't it worth every investment necessary to free the world from the threat of nuclear war? We know it is... America does possess now the technologies to attain very significant improvements in the effectiveness of our... non-nuclear forces... with these who gave us nuclear weapons, to turn their great talents now to the cause of man-kind and world peace, to give us the means of rendering these nuclear weapons impotent and obsolete... This could pave the way for arms control measures to eliminate the weapons themselves ... our only purpose—one all people share—is to search for ways to reduce the danger of nuclear war."

In this connection, the former Soviet Union has declared its interest in January 1986, as Mikhail Gorbachev noted as follows:[55] "The Soviet Union proposes that a step-by-step consistent process of ridding the earth of nuclear weapons be implemented and completed within the next 15 years, before the end of this century... Our proposal on this subject can be summarized as follows: Stage one. Within the next 5 to 8 years the USSR and the USA will reduce by one half the nuclear weapons that can reach each other's territory. As for the remaining delivery vehicles of this kind, each side will retain no more than 6,000 warheads... The first stage will include on the complete elimination of medium-range missiles of the USSR and the USA in the European zone—both ballistic and cruise missile—as a first step towards riding the European continent of nuclear weapons." With regard to the second stage, he stated that it will include all other nuclear powers to join the process of nuclear Disarmament and stage three will eliminate all remaining nuclear weapons. Thus, by the end of 1999, according to Soviet proposal, there will be no nuclear weapons on earth. Adding to that Mr. Gorbachev stated: "A universal accord will be drawn up that such weapons should never again come into being... Thus, we propose that we should enter the third millennium without nuclear weapons...".[56] Thus with the notion of non-nuclear deterrence and the nuclear-free world by the beginning of 21st century, the INF treaty was signed by both the US and the Soviet Union on 8 December, 1987.

According to the INF treaty, both the US and Russia had agreed to destroy all their land-based medium-range nuclear missiles, ranging from 500 to 5000 kms. The agreement was signed after two summits in Geneva (1985) and Reykjavik in 1986. However, the process is still continuing now in the Unified Europe facing a lot of hurdles because of differences in agreeing on withdrawal of tactical forces. Although the American Pershing missiles stationed in West Germany, Tomahawk and cruise missiles in Britain, West Germany, Italy and Belgium were withdrawn, still certain technical problems in relation to defusing the bombs are continuing. Russia has eliminated silo-based, SS-4 rockets, SS-12, SS-23 and the SS-20 missiles from the former East Germany. However, the non-nuclear connection of both the US and Russia in Europe would undermine the INF treaty and will go against the European interest in the coming years. The next chapter, being the conclusive one, evaluates new initiatives for comprehensive nuclear free world.

NOTES AND REFERENCES

1. Nuclear non-proliferation treaty was signed in 1968. According to the treaty, non-nuclear-weapon states agree neither to seek nor to acquire technology or materials for nuclear weapons production, while weapon states pledge not to transfer same to non-weapons states. Parties to the treaty include Egypt, Iran, Iraq, Libya, Syria, but not Argentina, Brazil, Chile, Cuba, France, China, India, Israel, Pakistan, Saudi Arabia. Non-proliferation regime or system is a set of rules, regulations, norms, understanding, procedures and institutions that attempt to regulate the international spread of nuclear technology and to constrain the ability of states to acquire a nuclear-weapons capability or detail, see, Jack Dennis, "Nuclear Weapons Proliferation" in Jack Dennis, (ed.), The *Nuclear Almanac—Confronting the Atom in War and Peace* (Mass: Addison-Publishing Company, 1984), pp. 320, 354, 357 *id* 360.
2. See *the text of the NPT* in Appendix G.
3. *Ibid.*
4. "Natural uranium contains less than one per cent of U-235, the isotope which is readily fissionable. Most of natural uranium is comprised of U-238, which is not readily fissionable. In order to be usable in nuclear weapons as well as in most power reactors/ uranium must be "enriched" to obtain a higher concentration of U-235. For use in a nuclear power reactor/uranium must be enriched

to about 3 per cent U-235; for weapons use, uranium must be 90 per cent U-235 or greater. Enrichment plants are large, very expensive and require huge amounts of electricity. Only a handful of countries now have enrichment plants. Plutonium is the other material that can be used to make a nuclear explosive. Can also be mixed with uranium to fuel some types of power reactors. Plutonium is a man-made material—it does not occur in nature. It is formed in a nuclear reactor when U-238 atoms capture a neutron. However, for the plutonium formed first be separated from residual uranium and fission products by chemical "reprocessing". This involves chopping up the irradiated uranium, dissolving it in strong acid, and separating out the plutonium. Like enrichment plants, reprocessing plants are expensive and difficult to build and only a few countries in world have them. See, Warren Donnelly, *Pakistan and Nuclear Weapons* (Washington per cent Environment and Natural Resources Policy Division, Congressional Service, 1987), pp. 889-90.

5. *See* Albert Wholsetter, "Spreading the Bomb Without Quite Breaking the Rules", *Foreign Policy* (Washington) Winter 1976-77, pp. 36-56.
6. *See* Dan Smith, Africa's Nuclear Capability (London: World Campaign Against Military and Nuclear Collaboration with South Africa, 1980), pp. 9-11; IABA safeguards and related issues are discussed in a section of this chapter entitled "Verification system".
7. For Chinese nuclear policy see, Harry Gelber, *Nuclear Weapons and Chinese, Policy,* Adelphi Papers, No. 99 [London: Institute for International Strategic Studies (IISS), 1973], pp. 1-36.
8. Christine Audgins, "NPT Review Conference Off to a Smooth Start as Old Issues Predominate", *Nucleonics Week,* September 5, 1985, p. 7; see also Ernest Hass, "Why Collaborate? Issue-Linkage and International Regimes", *World Politics* (Princeton), vol. XXXII, 1979/80, pp. 14-28; for full text and the status of the NPT see Appendix G.
9. *Article IX* of the NPT.
10. *Article V* of the Tlatelolco Treaty.
11. *Article I* of the Rarotonga Treaty.
12. *United Nations,* treaty series, Vol. 402, No. 5778, pp. 76-78.
13. Desmond Ball and R.H. Mathams, "The Nuclear Threat to Australia", in *Australia and Nuclear War* (Sydneyt Croon Helm, 1983), pp. 38-54.
14. Markey and Waller, *Nuclear Peril, The Politics of Proliferation* (Cambridge: Publishers, 1982), p. 45.
15. Albert Wholsetter, n. 5, pp. 36-56.
16. Gerald Johnson, "Plowshare at Cross Roads", *Bulletin of the Atomic Scientist,* Chicago), Vol. 26, n. 6, June 1970, p. 83.
17. See V.S. Smelyanov, in the Peaceful Use of Nuclear Explosions", in Stockholm International Peace Research Institute (SIPRI) (ed.), *Non-Proliferation Problem* (Stockholm: SIPRI, 1974), p. 217.
18. *Article 18* of the Treaty of Tlatelolco.

19. William Epstein, *The Last Chance, Nuclear Proliferation and Arms Control*. (New York: The Free Press, 1976), p. 175.
20. See Robert K. and Joseph Nye, *Power and Interdependence! World Politics in Transition* (Boston: Massachusetts Institute for Technology, 1977), p. 36.
21. For a good study on the economics of nuclear power, see, William C. Potter, *Nuclear Power and Non-Proliferation, An inter-disciplinary* Perspective (New York: Gunn and Hain Publishers, 1982), pp. 99-130.
22. Warren Donnelly, n. 4, p. 890.
23. *Arms Control and Disarmament Agency* (ACDA), Arms Control and Disarmament Agreements (Washington Government Printing Office, 1980), pp. 83-88. "Safeguards agreements required by the NPT have entered into force for 68 countries. For 44 non-nuclear weapon states party to the treaty, the relevant safeguards agreements have not yet entered into force; however, none of these states have significant nuclear activities", *ibid.*, p. 88.
24. *Ibid.*
25. *See* for an argument in this line, Albert Wholsetter, *Swords from Plowshares The Military Potential of Civilian Nuclear Energy* (Chicago: University of Chicago Press, 1977), pp. 234-36.
26. Leonard Spector, *The New Nuclear Nations* (New York: Vintage Books, 1985) p. 236.
27. See *the Text of the treaties* in Appendices.
28. Joseph Gallacher, "Article VII, The Treaty of Tlatelolco and Colonial Warfare in the 20th Century" in Ian Bellany, Coito. Blacker and Joseph Gallacher,' (eds.), *The Nuclear Non-proliferation Treaty* (London Frank Cass, 1985), pp. 80-81.
29. Lewis Dunn, *Controlling the Bomb: Nuclear Proliferation in the 1980s* (New Haven, Conn.: Yale University Press, 1982), p. 88.
30. *See* the preamble of the Treaty.
31. SIPRI Yearbook 1981, *World Armaments and Disarmament* (London: Taylor and Francis, 1981), p.121.
32. Albert *Wholsetter et al., Moving Toward Life in a Nuclear Armed Crowd?* (Los Angeles: Pan Henriotics, 1975), p. 2.
33. *See* the *Preamble of the Treaty.*
34. *UN Comprehensive study on the question of Nuclear weapons* (New York: UN, 1981), pp. 21-35.
35. UN Special report of the conference of the committee on Disarmament, Comprehensive *study of the question of Nuclear Weapon-Free-Zones in all its aspects* (New York: United Nations, 1976), p. 99.
36. SIPRI yearbook, 1984, *World Armaments and Disarmament* (London: Taylor and Francis, 1984), pp. 23-40.
37. Jasjit Singh, Threat of Nuclear Weapons, in K. Subramanyam, (ed.), *India and the Nuclear Challenge* (New Delhi: Lancer International, 1986), pp. 76-78.

38. *Ibid.*, p. 78.
39. William M. Arkin and Fieldhous, *The Nuclear Battlefield, Global Links in the Arms Race* (Cambridge: Bellinger Publishing Company, 1985), pp. 169-71.
40. *Ibid.*
41. *Ibid.*
42. Joseph Gallancher, n. 28, pp. 80-81.
43. *Ibid.*
44. Ramesh Thakur, "A dispute of many colors: France, New Zealand and the 'Rainbow Warrior' Affair", *The World Today* (London), December 1986, pp. 209-215.
45. *The Hindustan Times* (New Delhi), 28 July, 1987.
46. *See* Tom Stefancic, *Anti-submarine Warfare and Naval Strategy* (Toronto: Lexington Books, 1987), pp.156-60.
47. *Ibid.*
48. *Ibid.*
49. Tom Stefanick, n. 46, p. 156.
50. *Ibid.* "Command, control and communications is the term used to describe a system of input, processing, decision-making and execution for military forces and operations. Being a 'system', it is largely composed of electronic aids—sensors, computers and communications links—but the central feature remains human decision-making. C^3 supports the routine administrative decision-making to budget and allocate resources in peace time, to monitor the worldwide political and military situation, and for contingency planning, training and exercises .... There are three distinct components of the C system: (a) command authorities, nuclear control systems and common centers to analyses data, make decisions, carry out directions and control forces; (b) sensors, including intelligence systems, providing inputs of warning and attack characterization; and (c) communicate ions links to distribute warning data, and ensure the proper execution of commands". *See*, SIPRI Yearbook 1984, World Armaments and Disarmament (London, 1984), pp. 455-66.
51. Williams M. Arkin, "The Nuclear Arms Race at Sea", *Neptune papers I* (Washington: Greenpeace, 1987), pp. 14-18.
52. UN, *Disarmament: Problems Related to Outer Space* (New York: UN, 1987), pp. 4-14.
53. *Ibid.*
54. *International Herald Tribune* (Paris), 24 March, 1983.
55. Mikhail Gorbachev, *For a Nuclear Free World* (Moscow: Novosti, 1987), pp. 11-12.
56. *Ibid.*

6

Conclusion

> *"The Nuclear Non-Proliferation Treaty (NPT) based regime has not kept pace with the march of technology and globalization... Delegates at the month long Conference of NPT held on 27 May, 2005 could not furnish the world with any solution to the grave nuclear threats we all face... There are cracks in each of the Treaty's pillars—non-proliferation, disarmament and peaceful uses of nuclear technology—and each of these cracks requires urgent repair."*
>
> — Kofi Annan, UN Secretary-General

The increasing involvement of nuclear weapon countries in many regions of the world poses a great danger to the world in general and to the nuclear-free zones of different regions in particular. Therefore, a new universal nuclear non-proliferation regime based on order of peace and non-violence is required to be achieved. In this regard, Gandhian philosophy on peace and non-violence had been thought about by eminent persons of the world. In the early 1950s, Albert Einstein stated that Gandhian philosophy would be the lighthouse for the future generation, which would not only help formulate order for local peace but also for the international one.[1] The former President of South Africa, Nelson Mandela in 1999 pointed out that the twenty first century would be the Gandhian century. Major initiative in realization of the relevance of Gandhian principles came into being when the United Nations (UN) has termed the twenty first century as the century of peace and dedicated the first decade of it for the development of peace and non-violent approaches of Mahatma Gandhi. Against this brief background, this chapter explores the possibility for creating new world.

Present World Order—An Analysis

Present world order is originated based on violence. The concept, violence, is defined as aggression, fighting, hostility, war, violent behaviour, brutality, cruelty, sadism and bloodshed. Of all, war is considered as the highest level of violence since it causes both physical and mental damages. Many eminent scholars have analyzed the concept of war and its impact on both national and international politics. For instance, Kautilya in his wrings, expressed that human nature was essentially aggressive that would further establish or invite the same from others consequently leading to war. Aristotle brought such school of thought into history of international relations. He recognized war as a force for acquisition of land, animal and men of others and identically exposed it as a system of violence that would never help in establishing peace among nations.[2] In the same line of thought, Rousseau, in his book titled *The Social Contract*, criticized war as a source of permanent violence based on which negotiated settlement among nations were impossible. In continuation of understanding the concept of war, Karl Von Clausewitz in his book, *On War*, noted that war was only a part of political violence and, therefore, it could be handled through political intercourse between nations for the cause of establishing political peace. He emphasized on the importance of having world order based on humanistic consideration not on the experiences of inhuman wars. The history of present world order is noted as follows:[3]

Treaty of Westphalia (1648)

It set the foundation of the nation-state system, which was the result of wars between princes of Protestants and Catholics in Europe leading to the collapse of the Holy Roman Empire.

Treaty of Utrecht (1773)

Balance of power and alliances came into being after this treaty. It was the result of war among European nations such as England, France, Holland and Spain.

Congress of Vienna (1815)

It established protocols among nations after the succession war of Polish (1733), the war of Austrian succession (1740), the Seven years war (1756-63), the French Revolution (1789), and finally, the defeat of Napoleon in Waterloo war in 1815.

Treaty of Versailles (1918)

It was signed at the end of First World War and helped create the League of Nations. Former President of the US, Woodrow Wilson played a leading role in creating this organization.

The United Nations (1945)

Although it was established even before the end of the Second World War, it was because of the usage of atomic bombs by the US in Japanese cities of Hiroshima and Nagasaki, the importance of such organization was much realized by many countries of the world. Former President of the US, Franklin D. Roosevelt was instrumental in creating the UN in co-operation with the then Prime Minister of the UK, Winston Churchill.

The present world order emerged on the basis of war, as noted above, not only contributed suspicion and tensions among nations but also made the nations pursue war as an ultimate instrument for settling disputes by making the world body like UN much helpless in exploring the other means for conflict resolution more effectively. As a result, it has brought in so many bad elements neglecting the peace, prosperity and human development in the world particularly at the cost of poor nations. Prominent among such elements brought by the violent order includes 'balance of power', 'deterrence' and 'cold war'. In the name of balance of power, the US and former Soviet Union were dominating by equally dividing the world and generating supports among nations for their respective political and ideological interests. It also promoted power blocs and military alliances creating theatres of war. Europe was the first victim for such politics of super powers immediately after Second World War. Because of the reason, thousands of weapons including chemical, biological and nuclear, were produced and deployed in different parts of the world in the name of deterrence.

Even after the collapse of Soviet Union, unification of Europe and the crumple of cold war, there are still hundreds of such weapons in the stockpiles of the big powers, which are more than sufficient to destroy the entire globe. Because of such ongoing arms race, social, economic, political and environmental problems were neglected resulting in more than fifty wars occurring every year. According to Robin Clerk, during 1860–1900, A.D. 0.4 per cent of the world population was killed in wars and during 1900 to 1949 A.D.; it went up to 2.01 per cent. Keeping this trend in view, he estimates that during 2000–2050 A.D. 40.5 per cent of the world population will die in wars.[4] For example, due to wars in the developing countries, fifty thousand people are killed, more than a million are becoming homeless and a million children are undernourished every year. Apart from annihilating humanity, it spreads permanent economic problems especially among the helpless poor countries in Africa, Asia and Latin America. Economic disparity between haves and have-nots (developed and developing countries) are, therefore, in increasing scale, establishing a biased economic order neglecting the plight of the poor countries.

An eminent economist, Alfred Marshall states: "The present world economy is biased and inhuman". Its inhuman face can be seen, as one looks at the staggering military expenditure of the world nations. According to Roy Barman, military expenditure of the world has passed over one billion a day in 1977 reaching 400 billions a year which is approximately 50 million dollars an hour and roughly 100 dollars for each human being on earth.[5] Unmindful of poverty ridden countries, the big powers are making plans for distributing world resources in an unequal way making enduring economic imbalance. Due to such economic plan of dominant powers, the resources of the developing countries were indiscriminately being used for the advantages of developed countries. It is stirring to note that 20 per cent of the world population enjoys 86 per cent of the world resources and 225 individuals of the world possess 47 per cent of the wealth of the present world.[6] The developed countries have more number of such affluent people amassing wealth. Since the wealth of the world is concentrated in few hands, the economic problems of the world community are so complex in nature especially in finding mechanism for equitable economic distribution.

Such economic affluence of individuals dominates the political powers and makes the situation more dangerous. It is reported that affluent individuals fund ninety-nine per cent of the political parties of the present world and misuse the governance making the politics immoral. As of the reasons, there are more than 700 political wars recorded in the history of international relations until the beginning of the Second World War. All these wars took the toll of a billion lives.[7] In the Second World War, humanity was forced to witness an unprecedented destruction due to the usage of atomic bombs by the American Government in Japan. According to reports, the US used the war situation to demonstrate its capability and planned to dominate the world after the war. No system could prevent such plan of US. Rather many countries were in support of it. During the period of war, the US also, as noted by many, misused the human potential of renowned scientists of the world in Manhattan Project, New York. Group of scientists escaped from Europe fearing to Hitler under the leadership of Albert Einstein were provided with political asylum for the purpose of producing atomic bombs. After successful production of atom bombs code named, 'little boy' and 'fat man', the US took decision to use them on Japanese cities, Hiroshima and Nagasaki on 6 and 9 August, 1945 respectively.[8] Such unilateral attitude of the US during the Second World War has imposed on the world the deterrent approaches misguiding all the nations involved in the game of deterrence.

Vicious Cycle of Deterrence

Instead of investing money on science and technology that would help people escape from both manmade as well as natural calamity like the tsunami, the world is spending much on unwanted armories creating a vicious cycle of violence involving various nations produce gigantic weapons. For example, the military expenditure of the big powers per year can be cited here: US (295 billion dollars), Russia (60), China (40), France (35), Britain (35), Germany (30) and Japan (45).[9] By spending this much amount, they spread their military forces in various regions of the world. The US has its forces all over the world. Apart from having positioned 1,100,000 military personnel within US, it has in Western Europe (1,10,000), Japan (90,000), Russia/Europe (10,000), Middle East (30,000) and Latin America (13000). Thus, totally it has 2, 53,000 forces, acquiring sizeable amount of money from the national budget.[10] Many poor countries of the world are in the quagmire of spreading violence in the name of deterrence that guarantees neither peace nor security to the people. It is important to understand the game of deterrence started by the US in a little more elaborative way, as it is the central one to be analyzed for the cause of evaluating a new world order based on peace and non-violence.

Deterrence, as a concept, simply means persuading an opponent not to attack by having enough forces to disable the attack and/or launch a punishing counter attack. It needs, therefore, numerous nuclear forces to be produced and deployed against enemy. As of the reason, the US did so in the late 1940s deploying nuclear forces in Europe with the intention of preventing the Communist aggression. For the first time in the history of war, it adopted a forward base strategy and staged its short range nuclear missiles—Thor and Jupiter—in West Europe in 1948. For its war plan with the Soviet Union, it had also organized North Atlantic Treaty Organization (NATO) in 1949. As a result, the Former Soviet Union had encountered the American plan by placing SS-20 missile and by forming up Warsaw Treaty Organization (WTO) aligning with East European countries. Such game made both the super powers produce various weapons. For understanding its dynamic cycle of violence, the American deterrent policy, which lies on the following doctrinal approaches, can be noted:[11]

Massive Retaliation

It was followed during the 1940s, the period when the US was the sole nuclear power. It provided the rights of using all means to win over the enemy—the former Soviet Union, which had exploded its atomic device in 1949. Due to these doctrinal approaches, many atomic bombs were produced by both the super powers and because of that all other nations like the United Kingdom, France and China had produced similar weapons systems.

Mutual Retaliation

It was followed through out 1950s. In this period, the former Soviet Union had become equal, if not fully, by at least breaking the US nuclear monopoly. As a result, NATO, the military organization, formed up in 1949 had started deploying the American nuclear missiles in and around West Europe. For encountering NATO, the Warsaw Pact arrangement was made in East Europe with the help of the former Soviet Union.

Flexible Response

It was enunciated when the former Soviet Union had become so powerful in technological front, especially in the field of space by developing Sputnik in 1957 that was considered by Americans as the gateway for missile development. Due to this doctrine, in the 1970s many missiles including Inter Continental Ballistic Missiles (ICBMs), Submarine Launched Ballistic Missiles (SLBMs) and Air Launched Cruise Missiles (ALCMs) were produced and deployed in different parts of the world.

Mutual Assured Destruction (MAD)

It was followed from late 1970s as the Soviet Union led in the field of Anti Ballistic Missiles (ABMs) technology by producing destructive weapons equal to that of the American's. This doctrine led for various complications in the world instigating regional wars, especially in the Middle East. Most of the arms control agreements failed due to over ambition of super powers' strategy.

Mutual Assured Survival (MAS)

It was originated in 1980s with the objective of defending certain targets from the Soviet attack. In this context, the President Ronald Reagan declared the 'star wars programme' on 23 March, 1983. This is what now being described as the most important doctrine of the twenty first century, which allows an array of weapon system in the name of National Missile Defense (NMD) and the Theater Missiles Defense (TMD).

It should be noted here that all these doctrines of the US are not systematically analysed and put in right frame of their time by the implementers of the doctrine themselves.[12] Just for interpreting the nature and objectives of their plans, they are being considered and followed according to the convenience of interpretation not for logical consequences by sticking to time line. However, one can see in the doctrinal approaches of the US nothing but various developments and deployments of different kinds of nuclear weapons. In addition, the doctrines including the MAS, encourages blindly the ongoing nuclear arms race in the name of defense and it involves all other countries in the theatre of warfare. The following table shows the warring capability of world nations.[13]

As a result, a little attention was paid for human development during the cold war period, as the super powers were concentrating on war games in the name of balance of power, cold war, deterrence etc. At present, the political as well as the economic situations are fast changing. Because of that, the present order is in transition. Nevertheless, there is much to be done for making the present world order more violence free. Certain elements are still highly motivated and greed based that may result in misuse of human potential and in creation of vicious cycle of war in the name of competition or in a modern parlance called *deterrence* once again. Therefore, the world nations should work together for establishing peace-centric world order in the present century. Before evaluating such a new order, an inquiry on the relevance of Gandhian principles is pertinent here. The following section is devoted for the purpose.

Efforts for Replacing the Concept of Deterrence

Many diplomats of the present world appreciate Gandhian principles. For instance, Henry Kissinger notes that Gandhiji's life was inspired by truth, which had no boundary in space and time and which could only be the base for the edifice of peace and non-violence in the world. Kenneth E. Boulding notes, "... The idea of the non-violent resistance associated with the name of Gandhi... Is a powerful method of bargaining for a social contract...Non-violence is more sophisticated in its philosophy... It is perhaps the most important political idea of the world."[14]

Ballistic Missile Capabilities of the World Nations

Country	*Range (Miles)*	*Potential Targets*
United States[a]	13,000	(World)
Russia[a]	13,000	(World)
China[a]	13,000	(World)
Britain[a]	4,600	(World; Submarine-launched)
France[a]	3, 700	(World; Submarine-launched)
North Korea[b]	800 (3000?)	South Korea, Russia, China, Japan)
India[a, c]	150 (1500)	Pakistan, (China, Afghanistan, Iran, Turkey)
Pakistan	175 (400)	India
Iran[b]	300 (1250)	Iraq, Kuwait, Afghanistan, (Israel, Egypt, Turkey, Saudi Arabia, Russia, India)
Saudi Arabia	1700	Iran, Iraq, Syria, Israel, Turkey, Yemen, Egypt, Libya, Sudan
Israel[a, c]	900	Syria, Iraq, Saudi Arabia, Egypt
Iraq[d]	370	Iran, Kuwait, Saudi Arabia, Syria, Israel
Syria	370	Israel, Jordan, Iraq, Turkey
Egypt	175 (280)	Libya, Sudan, Israel
Yemen	175	Saudi Arabia
United Arab Emirates	175	Saudi Arabia, Iran
Afghanistan	175	Pakistan, Tajikistan, Uzbekistan
South Korea	150	North Korea
Vietnam	175	China, Cambodia
Belarus	300	Russia, Ukraine, Poland
Ukraine	300	Russia, Belarus, Poland, Hungary, Romania
Bulgaria	300	Serbia, Albania, Turkey, Greece, Romania
Slovakia	300	Czech Rep., Hungary, Poland, Ukraine
Czech Republic	175	Slovakia, Poland, Germany
Poland	175	Russia, Belarus, Ukraine, Slovakia, Czech Rep., Germany
Romania	175	Serbia, Ukraine, Moldova, Hungary, Bulgaria
Japan[c]	–	

* Number of states with ballistic missiles: 26.

a. States that have nuclear weapons.

b. States believed to be trying to build nuclear weapon.

c. States developing space-launch missiles adaptable as long-range ballistic missiles.

d. Iraq's missile capability was supposedly destroyed after the Gulf War.

In an honest way, Boulding approves of Gandhian ideas and their relevance for establishing new order of peace. In this point of view, the world leaders at United Nations have declared the first decade of the twenty-first century as a decade of peace and non-violence. However, for understanding the dynamism of Gandhian techniques, an inquiry on peace and non-violence, is more significant.

According to Gandhiji, peace is the temple of truth and non-violence is the greatest force at the disposal of humankind. Both are two sides of a coin, which are, as noted by him, "mightier than the mightiest weapon of destruction devised by the ingenuity of man. There is no greater fallacy than the belief that aims and purposes are one thing, while methods and tactics are another."[15] Therefore, truth and non-violence are methods, which have to be adopted for achieving lasting peace. In the same vine of argument, Thomas Paine compares the society to peace and government to evil. Peace for him is bestowed with truth and non-violence and governance more often with evil thinking by neglecting the deserving poor for the cause of sate power or prestige. According to Bertrand Russell, education is the key to the new world, which will lead to equitable and non-violent society where human live in harmony with one another and nature.[16] If the people, especially the rulers, realize the truth and non-violence, there would be cycle of non-violence creating more rings all over.

Thus, the dynamic non-violence can encircle the entire life setting starting from individual to global unit. For Gandhiji, love is the element of truth. In other words, love is the ray of light in the universe of truth. Without love, therefore, it is impossible to be a truth or non-violence oriented person as an individual unit or a nation as a collective unit. In this line of logical thinking, Gandhiji proposed plans for world peace appealing to the world leaders immediately after the American bombs thrown on the cities of Hiroshima and Nagasaki in Japan to wipe out the menace of atomic bomb by simply adopting human development approach as their major one not the deterrence. In fact, his ideas expressed during Second World War helped formulate India's policy with regard to general and complete disarmament with series of initiatives by Indian leaders in the UN for nuclear Test Ban Treaty including the successfully ended Comprehensive Test Ban Treaty (CTBT) of the present century.[17] For perfect exposition of understanding in this respect, it is better to note Gandhiji's quotation again. It reads: "Truth in action is *ahimsa*, love. Truth and love, *satya* and *ahimsa*, are like the two sides of a coin. All great religions enjoin the practice of love...non-violence is complete innocence. Complete non-violence is complete absence of ill will against all that lives. Non-violence is innocence in its action form, good will towards all life.[18] It is pure love... Hatred deflects our thinking; endanger the very sense of humanity." Thus, truth, love, peace and non-violence are the pillars of his philosophy without which human development is impossible. These four dynamic concepts of Gandhiji, if truly adopted, would work as nuclei of atom, which would help achieve "thermo nuclear peace" at a larger scale. For achieving it, Gandhiji advocated an important technique known as Satyagraha—insistence on truth.[19]

Satyagraha, as Gandhiji noted, is not an idealistic concept but it is practical and dynamic method to achieve peace. According to him, it has to be implemented in order to achieve the objective of peace in a given condition. He considered this as the only means for obtaining peace. For him, therefore, Satyagraha was everything that can achieve not only local peace but also the international one. Therefore, an internationalist interested in this effort should hold firmly the truth and bravely wage the war of peace against unjust and violent world order.[20] This type of international *Satyagraha* should be, as guided by Gandhiji, based on non-violent order of action including non-violent mass action. Thus, *Satyagraha* is a "cell of action" which is considered by him as a weapon more powerful in the hands of a perfect non-violent soldier.

New Perspective for Nuclear-Free Universe

Peace cannot be achieved without realizing the concepts and techniques of Gandhiji. The present order for achieving peace, as described above, rests on violence, force and power, which create a cycle of violence among nations. It leads, as experienced, to unhealthy competition by spreading violence all over the world. This is explained as follows.[21]

Use of Force (Deterrence)

↑↓

Violence (War or Terrorism)

↑↓

Tensions (Cold War or Proxy War)

↑↓

Armaments (Abuses of S & T)

The principles of Gandhiji on the other hand suggest that 'love' could be adopted as the 'means' for achieving non-violent or 'perfect peace'. According to Gandhiji, peace without love is violence and love without peace is also violence. Therefore, the concept, love is the centre for non-violent action. Without it, human development is not possible.[22] Love can work as a supreme power in the process of human development by creating dynamic cycle of non-violence. According to Gandhiji, peacemaker should build peace army for developing the humanity. It is necessary to quote here the Gandhiji's statement. It reads..."The moral principles on which civilization rests are truth and love. If people everywhere respond to them truthfully, the world will be brought closer together and the darkness of violence which we see around us may be dispelled."[23] In this connection, in 1980s, members of UN General Assembly have suggested that the concept of deterrence may be replaced by the concept of non-violence. In continuation of that, they have also declared, as noted above, this century as century of peace and the first decade of it is devoted for the ideals of Gandhiji. As of the reason, 189 countries have adopted a historic Millennium Declaration at the UN providing a new development agenda for world nations for achieving peace, prosperity and human development in the twenty first century.[24]

For achieving the millennium goal of UN, 'destructive expenditure' should be avoided and all the existing weapons should be abolished in a time bound manner. Similarly, all other weapons should also be curtailed with an aim of attaining general and complete Disarmament in this new millennium.[25] Staggering investment on such weapons should be diverted for human development. It is to be noted that the dollars spent on developing the long range MX missiles (missile experimental) of the US that can reach any part of the world in twenty minutes could have helped eradicate poverty in all the African Countries. The warring capacity of a nation, as guided by the deterrence, should not be a scale for measuring the leadership quality of a nation. Instead, the generosity of helping out deserving countries of the world has to be the scale. In this connection, India's recent help to tsunami-affected Sri Lanka can be noted.[26] The next section deals with the concept of knowledge society, which is closely related to the ideals of non-violence.

Towards Universal Nuclear Non-Proliferation Treaty

Today, there is a widespread awareness all over the world to understand about the concept of knowledge society. Knowledge society means 'information based society' that will enable the world nations develop a universal initiative for attaining peace and prosperity through innovative ways meeting all the challenges in the process of human development. Attaining prosperity not creating cycle of violence as done by deterrence is the order of the day. Such universal peace centric initiative is to achieve an equitable social order by ensuring everyone, the universal accessibility for human prosperity. In this connection, the President of India, His Excellency Dr. A.P.J. Abdul Kalam notes that the twenty first century belongs to universal knowledge society and it has opened up tremendous opportunities for every individual to live in peace irrespective of the geographical area he or she live in.[27] As of the reason, every area of international relation should be augmented with universal 'non-violent knowledge' aiming to establish global knowledge society. Without peace centric universal initiative international peace can never be achieved. India, being a potential actor in the knowledge filed, has already initiated work towards this direction by constituting 'knowledge society task force' headed by the Planning Commission. It will, therefore, participate; rather lead the process of what one calls it as knowledge revolution aiming to attain universal peace order, especially in the field of nuclear disarmament.

As knowledge takes the front seat in the process of human development, its products reach any part of the world with unprecedented speed by the help of the revolutionary information and communication technology (ICT).[28] Thus, the globe becomes village in this modern age what one calls it as 'mind age'. Having highest number of human potential in the knowledge field including a leading number of youth in the world and being one of the best destinies of high-tech, India can play a significant role in building on knowledge society. Therefore, knowledge based democratization of international relation is must, which will help the humanity explore peace and non-violence in the new millennium. Peace and non-violence are by-products of love—the centre of non-violent knowledge. Non-violent knowledge is the one that contributes for peace, prosperity and human development without any discrimination. Hence, a product of science and technology is nothing but a product of love. Because of the dedication of a person who spends time and energy devoted with love of involvement in the process of production, the humanity benefits using it.[29] Without love of knowledge that has no boundary or prejudice human prosperity is impossible.

As of the reason, predisposed way of dealing with international relation through economic and political domination by one power (uni-polar) or two (bi-polar) in this new millennium will never help. Such approach will bring further sorrow to the entire globe creating stumbling blocks in the way of establishing non-violent knowledge society that is pertinent for new world order. In this connection, the former Secretary General of the UN, Boutros Boutros-Ghali expresses that 'war-centric unilateralism' will destroy the positive acts of UN and it will not allow the present globalization process to help the poor countries.[30] As he notes further that the globalization process should democratize the entire system of international relations by considering to establishing new order of peace and universal nuclear disarmament on the basis of non-violent approaches. Therefore, a universal nuclear non-proliferation treaty (UNPT) should be achieved by developing countries in line with the proposal submitted by India in 1986 for nuclear-free universe along with the support of the United Nations. All the nuclear weapon countries should co-operate this effort without minding for their self-centered disarmament approaches. India's expression on universal nuclear disarmament can be taken as a first step towards this direction. A universal disarmament can only help escape the world nations from the danger of nuclear war. For, the UN should sincerely campaign the nations of the world for signing up UNPT with the sole aim of attaining comprehensive nuclear-weapon-free world by 2020.

NOTES AND REFERENCES

1. For good analysis in this respect, *see* Gunvant Shah, *Gandhi for the New Generation* (Ahmedabad: Navajivan Press, 1982).
2. Dan Smith, *The State of War and Peace Atlas* (London: Penguin Publication, 1997) pp.12-16.
3. *Ibid.*
4. Cited in N. Radha Krishnan (ed.) *Gandhian Perspective of Nations Building for World Peace* (New Delhi: Konark Publishers, 1992) p. 142.
5. *Ibid.* p. 141.
6. *See* for more information on poverty, Guy de Mallac, *Remedies to Mass Poverty* (Madurai: Valliammal Institute, 1994) pp. 1-41.
7. Dan Smith, *The State of War and Peace Atlas,* n. 2, p. 14.
8. *Ibid.*
9. Joshua S. Goldstein, *International Relations* (Washington: Pearson, 2004), p. 226.
10. *Ibid.*, p. 237.
11. *See* Edward Haley, David Keithly and Jack Merritt (ed.) *Nuclear Strategy, Arms Control and the Future* (London: West View Press, 1985), pp: 37-54.
12. *Ibid.*
13. *See* Joshua S. Goldstein, *International Relations*, n. 9, p. 246.
14. *See* M.K. Gandhi, *Hindu Swaraj or Home Rule* (Ahmedabad: Navajivan Press, 1990), pp. 18-20.
15. *Ibid.*
16. *See* M.K. Gandhi and Ruskin *Unto the Last* (Ahmedabad: Navajivan Press, 1998), pp. 3-17.
17. *See* Eric Erickson, *Gandhi's Truth: On the Origins of Militant Non-violence* (New Delhi: Norton and Company, 1989), pp. 66-96.
18. *Ibid.*
19. *Ibid.*
20. *Ibid.*
21. *See* M.K. Gandhi and Ruskin, n. 16, pp. 3-17
22. *Ibid.*
23. *Ibid.*
24. *Ibid.*

25. *See UN Weekly News Letter* 26 July, 1 August, 2003, p. 5.
26. *The Hindu* (Chennai), 10 February 2005.
27. *Ibid*.
28. *See University News* (New Delhi), Vol. 41, No. 48, December 01-07, 2003, 19.
29. *See*, Gary Hammel, *Leading the Revolution* (New York: Harvard Business School Press, 2000), pp. 26-30.
30. *Ibid*.

APPENDICES

APPENDIX 1

Antarctica Treaty

Signed at Washington on 1 December, 1959. Entered into force 23 June, 1961 Depositary: US Government

The Government of Argentina, Australia, Belgium, Chile, the French Republic, Japan, New Zealand, Norway, the Union of South Africa, the Union of Soviet Socialist Republic, the United Kingdom of Great Britain and Northern Ireland, and the United States of America,

Recognizing that it is in the interest of all mankind that Antarctica shall continue for ever to be used exclusively for peaceful purpose and shall not become the some or object of international discord:

Acknowledging the substantial contributions to scientific knowledge resulting from international co-operation in scientific investigation in Antarctica:

Convinced that the establishment of a firm foundation for the continuation and development of such co-operation on the basis of freedom of scientific investigation in Antarctica as applied during the International Geophysical Year accords with the interests of science and the progress of all mankind:

Convinced also that a treaty ensuring the use of Antarctica for peaceful purposes only and the continuance of international harmony in Antarctica will further the purposes and principles embodied in the Charter of the United Nations:

Have agreed as follows:

Article I

1. Antarctica shall be used for peaceful purposes only. There shall be prohibited, *inter alia,* any measures of a military bases and fortifications, the carrying out of military maneuvers, as well as the testing of any type of weapons.

2. The present Treaty shall not prevent the use of military personnel of equipment for scientific research or for any other peaceful purpose.

Article II

1. Freedom of scientific investigation in Antarctica and co-operation toward that end, as applied during the International Geophysical Year, shall continue, subject to the provisions of the present Treaty.

Article III

1. In order to promote international co-operation in scientific investigation in Antarctica, as provided for in Article II of the present Treaty, the Contracting Parties agree that, to the greatest extent feasible and practicable:–
   (a) Information regarding plans for scientific programmes in Antarctica shall be exchanged to permit maximum economy and efficiency of operations;
   (b) Scientific personnel shall be exchanged in Antarctica between expeditions and stations;
   (c) Scientific observations and results from Antarctica shall be exchanged and made freely available.
2. In implementing this Article, every encouragement shall be given to the establishment of co-operative working relations with those Specialized Agencies of the United Nations and other international organizations having a scientific or technical interest in Antarctica.

Article IV

1. Nothing contained in the present Treaty shall be interpreted as:–
   (a) A renunciation by any Contracting party of previously asserted rights of or claims to territorial sovereignty in Antarctica;
   (b) A renunciation or diminution by any Contracting party of any basis of claim to territorial sovereignty in Antarctica which it may have whether as a result

of its activities or those of its nationals in Antarctica, or otherwise;

(c) Prejudicing the position of any Contracting Party as regards its recognition or non-recognition of any other state's right of or claim or basis of claim to territorial sovereignty in Antarctica shall be asserted while the present treaty is in force.

Article V

1. Any nuclear explosions in Antarctica and the disposal thereof radioactive waste material shall be prohibited.
2. In the event of the conclusion of international agreements concerning the use of nuclear energy, including nuclear explosions and the disposal of radioactive waste material, to which all of the contracting parties whose representatives are entitled to participate in the meetings provided for under Article IX are parties, the rules established under such agreements shall apply in Antarctica.

Article VI

The provisions of the present treaty shall apply to the area south of 60 south latitude, including all ice shelves, but nothing in the present treaty shall prejudice or in any way affect the rights, or the exercise of the rights, of any state under international law will regard to the high seas within that area.

Article VII

1. In order to promote the objectives and ensure the observance of the provisions of the present treaty, each contracting party whose representatives are entitled to participate in the meetings referred to in Article IX of the Treaty shall have the right to designate observers to carry out any inspection provided for by the present Article. Observers shall be nationals of the contracting parties, which designate them. The names of observers shall be communicated to every other contracting party having

the right to designate observers, and like notice shall be given of the termination of their appointment.

2. Each observer designated in accordance with the provisions of paragraph 1 of this Article shall have complete freedom of access at any time to any or all areas of Antarctica.
3. All areas of Antarctica, including all stations, installations and equipment within those areas, and all ships and aircraft at points of discharging or embarking cargoes or personnel in Antarctica, shall be open at all times to inspection by any observer designated in accordance with paragraph 1 of this Article.
4. Aerial observation may be carried out at any time over any or all areas of Antarctica by any of the contracting parties having the right to designate observers.
5. Each contracting party shall, at the time when the present treaty enters into force for it informs the other contracting parties, and thereafter shall give them notice in advance of:—
   (a) All expeditions to and with Antarctica, on the part of its ships or nationals, and all expeditions to Antarctica organized in or proceeding from its territory;
   (b) All stations in Antarctica occupied by in nationals; and
   (c) Any military personnel or equipment intended to be introduced by it into Antarctica subject to the conditions prescribed in paragraph 2 of Article I of the present Treaty.

Article VIII

1. In order to facilitate the exercise of their functions under the present treaty, and without prejudice to the respective positions of the contracting parties relating to jurisdiction over all other persons in Antarctica, observers designated under paragraph 1 of Article VII and scientific personnel exchanged under sub-paragraph 1 (b) of Article III of the treaty, and members of the staffs accompanying any such persons, shall be subject only to the jurisdiction of the

contracting party of which they are nationals in respect of all acts or omissions occurring while they are in Antarctica for the purpose of exercising their functions.

2. Without prejudice to the provisions of paragraph 1 of this Article, and pending the adopting of measures in pursuance of sub-paragraph 1 (e) of Article IX, the contracting parties concerned in any case of dispute with regard to the exercise of jurisdiction in Antarctica shall immediately consult together with a view to reaching a mutually acceptable solution.

Article IX

1. Representatives of the contracting parties named in the preamble to the present treaty shall meet at the city of Canberra within two months after the date of entry into force of the treaty, and thereafter at suitable intervals and places, for the purpose of exchanging information, consulting together on matters of common interest pertaining to Antarctica and formulating and considering and recommending to their Governments, measures in furtherance of the principles and objectives of the Treaty, including measures regarding:–
   (a) Use of Antarctica for peaceful purposes only;
   (b) Facilitation of scientific research in Antarctica;
   (c) Facilitation of international scientific co-operation in Antarctica;
   (d) Facilitation of the exercise of the rights of inspection provided for in Article VII of the Treaty;
   (e) Questions relating to the exercise of jurisdiction in Antarctica; and
   (f) Preservation and conservation of living resources in Antarctica.
2. Each contracting party which has become a party to the present treaty by accession under Article XIII shall be entitled to appoint representatives to participate in the meetings referred to in Paragraph 1 of the present Article, during such time as that contracting party demonstrates its interest in Antarctica by conducting substantial scientific research activity there, such as the establishment

of a scientific station or the dispatch of a scientific expedition.

3. Reports from the observers referred to in Article VII of the present Treaty shall be transmitted to the representatives of the contracting parties participating in the meetings referred to in paragraph 1 of the present Article.
4. The measures referred to in paragraph 1 of this Article shall become effective when approved by all the Contracting Parties whose representatives were entitled to participate in the meetings held to consider those measures.
5. Any or all of the rights established in the present treaty may be exercised as from the date of entry into force of the Treaty whether or not any measure facilitating the exercise of such rights have been proposed. Considered or approved as provided in this Article.

Article X

Each of the contracting parties undertakes to exert appropriate efforts, consistent with the Charter of the United Nations, to the end that no one engages in any activity in Antarctica contrary to the principles or purposes of the present Treaty.

Article XI

1. If any dispute arises between two or more of the Contracting Parties concerning the interpretation or application of the present Treaty, those Contracting Parties shall consult among themselves with a view to having the dispute resolved by negotiation, inquiry, mediation, conciliation, arbitration, judicial settlement or other peaceful means of their own choice.
2. Any dispute of this character not so resolved shall, with the consent, in each case, of all parties to the dispute, be referred to the international court of justice for settlement but international court shall not absolve parties to the dispute from the responsibility of continuing to seek to resolve it by any of the various peaceful means referred to in paragraph 1 of this Article.

Article XII

1. (a) The present Treaty may be modified or amended at any time by unanimous agreement of the Contracting Parties whose representatives are entitled to participate in the meetings provided for under Article IX. Any such modification or amendment shall enter into force when the depositary government has received notice from all such Contracting Parties that they have ratified it.

   (b) Such modification on amendment shall thereafter enter into force as to any other Contracting Party when notice of ratification by it has been received by the depositary government. Any such Contracting Party from which no notice of ratification is received within a period of two years from the date of entry into force of the modification or amendment in accordance with the provisions of sub-paragraph 1(a) of this Article shall be deemed to have withdrawn from the present Treaty on the date of expiration of such period.

2. (a) If after the expiration of thirty years from the date of entry into force of the present Treaty, any of the Contracting Parties whose representatives are entitled to participate in the meetings provided for under Article IX so requests by a communication addressed to the depositary government, a Conference of all the Contracting Parties shall be held as soon as practicable to review the operation of the Treaty.

   (b) Any modification or amendment to the present Treaty which is approved at such a Conference by a majority of the Contracting Parties there represented, including a majority of those whose representatives are entitled to participate in the meetings provided for under Article IX, shall be communicated to participate in the meetings provided for under Article IX, shall be communicated by the depositary government to all the Contracting Parties immediately after the termination of the Conference and shall enter into force in accordance with the provisions of paragraph 1 of the present Article.

(c) If any such modification or amendment has not entered into force in accordance with the provisions of sub-paragraph 1 (a) of this Article within a period of two years after the date of its communication to all the Contracting Parties, any Contracting Party may at any time after the expiration of that period give notice to the depositary government of its withdrawal from the present Treaty; and such withdrawal shall take effect two years after the receipt of the notice by the depositary government.

Article XIII

1. The present Treaty shall be subject to ratification by the signatory states. It shall be open for accession by any State which is a member of the United Nations, or by any other state which may be invited to accede to the Treaty with the consent of all the Contracting Parties whose representatives are entitled to participate in the meetings provided for under Article IX of the Treaty.
2. Ratification of or accession to the present Treaty shall be affected by each state in accordance with its constitutional processes.
3. Instruments of ratification and instruments accession shall be deposited with the Government of the United States of America, hereby designated as the depositary government.
4. The depositary government shall inform all signatory and acceding states of the date of each deposit of an instrument of ratification or accession, and the date of entry into force of the Treaty and of any modification or amendment thereto.
5. Upon the deposit of instruments of ratification by all the signatory states, the present Treaty shall enter into force for those states and for states which have deposited instruments of accession. Thereafter the Treaty shall enter into force for any acceding state upon the deposit of its instrument of accession.

6. The present Treaty shall be registered by depositary government pursuant to Article 102 of the charter of the United Nations.

Article XIV

The present Treaty, done in the English, French, Russian and Spanish languages, each version being equally authentic, shall be deposited in the archives of the Government of the United States of America, which shall transmit duly certified copies thereof to the governments of the signatory and acceding states.

Source: *UN Treaty Series*, Vol. 402 (United Nations: New York, 1970–2005).

APPENDIX 2

Treaty on Principles Governing the Activities of States in the Exploration and Use of Outer Space, Including the Moon and Other Celestial Bodies

Signed at London, Moscow and Washington on 27 January, 1967. Entered into force on 10 October, 1967 Depositaries: UK, US and Soviet Government.

The States parties to this Treaty, inspired by the great prospects opeing up before mankind as a result of man's entry into Outer Space.

Recognizing the common interest of all mankind in the progress of the exploration and use of outer space for peaceful purposes.

Believing that the exploration and use of Outer Space should be carried on for the benefit of all peoples irrespective of the degree of their economic or scientific development.

Desiring to contribute to broad international co-operation in the scientific as well as the legal aspects of the exploration and use of Outer Space for peaceful purposes.

Believing that such co-operation will contribute to the development of mutual understanding and to the strengthening of friendly relations between states and peoples.

Recalling Resolution 1962 (XVIII), entitled "Declaration of Legal Principles Governing the Activities of States in the Exploration and Use of Outer Space", which was adopted unanimously by the United Nations General Assembly on 13 December, 1963.

Recalling Resolution 1884 (XVIII), calling upon States to refrain from placing in orbit around the earth any object carrying nuclear weapons or any other kinds of weapons of mass destruction or from installing such weapons on celestial bodies, which was adopted unanimously by the United Nations General Assembly on 17 October, 1963.

Taking account of United Nations General Assembly Resolution 110 (11) of 3 November, 1947, which condemned propaganda designed or likely to provoke or encourage any threat to the peace, breach of the peace or act of aggression, and considering that the aforementioned resolution is applicable to Outer Space.

Convinced that a Treaty on Principles Governing the Activities of State in the Exploration and Use of Outer Space. Including the Moon and other Celestial bodies, will further the purposes and principles of the Charter of the United Nations,

Have agreed on the following:

Article I

The exploration and use of Outer Space, including the moon and other celestial bodies, shall be carried out for the benefit and in the interests of all countries, irrespective of their degree of economic or scientific development, and shall be the province of all mankind.

Outer Space, including the moon and other celestial bodies, shall be free for exploration and use by all States without discrimination of any kind, on a basis of equality and in accordance with international law, and there shall be free access to all areas of celestial bodies.

There shall be freedom of scientific investigation in Outer Space, including the moon and other celestial bodies, and States shall facilitate and encourage international co-operation in such investigation.

Article II

Outer Space, including the moon and other celestial bodies, is not subject to national appropriation by claim of sovereignty, by means of use of occupation, or by any other means.

Article III

States parties to the Treaty shall carry on activities in the exploration and use of Outer Space, including the moon and other celestial bodies, in accordance with international law, including the Charter of the United Nations, in the interest of maintaining international peace and security and promoting international co-operation and understanding.

Article IV

States parties to the Treaty undertake not to place in orbit around the earth any object carrying nuclear weapons or any other kinds of weapons of mass destruction, install such weapons on celestial bodies, or station such weapons in Outer Space in any other manner.

The moon and other celestial bodies shall be used by all states parties to the Treaty exclusively for peaceful purposes. The establishment of military bases, installations and fortifications, the testing of any type of weapons and the conduct of military maneuvers on celestial bodies shall be forbidden. The use of military personnel for scientific research or for any other peaceful purposes shall not be prohibited. The use of any equipment or facility necessary for peaceful exploration of the moon and other celestial bodies shall also not be prohibited.

Article V

States Parties to the Treaty shall regard astronauts as envoys of mankind in outer space and shall render to them all possible assistance in the event of accident, distress, or emergency landing on the territory of another state party or on the high seas. When astronauts make such landing, they shall be safely and promptly returned to the state of registry of their space vehicle.

In carrying on activities on Outer Space and on celestial bodies, the astronauts of one State Party shall render all possible assistance to the astronauts of other States Parties.

State Parties to the Treaty shall immediately inform the other States Parties to the Treaty or the Secretary-General of the United Nations of any phenomena they discover in Outer Space, including the moon and other celestial bodies, which could constitute a danger to the life or health of astronauts.

Article VI

States Parties to the Treaty shall bear international responsibility for national activities in Outer Space, including the moon and other celestial bodies, whether such activities are carried on by governmental agencies or by non-governmental entities, and for assuring that national activities are carried out in conformity with the provisions set forth in the present Treaty. The activities of non-governmental entities in Outer Space, including the moon and other celestial bodies, shall require authorization and continuing supervision by the appropriate State Party to the Treaty. When activities are carried on in Outer Space, including the moon and other celestial bodies, by an international organization, responsibility for compliance with this Treaty shall be borne both by the international organization and by the States Parties to the Treaty participating in such organization.

Article VII

Each State Party to the Treaty that launches or procures the launching of an object into Outer Space, including the moon and other celestial bodies, and each State Party from whose territory or facility an object is launched, is internationally liable for damage to another State Party to the Treaty or to its natural or juridical persons by such objects or its component parts on the Earth, in the air space or in Outer Space, including the moon and other celestial bodies.

Article VIII

A State Party to the Treaty on whose registry an object launched into Outer Space is carried shall retain jurisdiction and control over such object, and over any personal thereof, while in Outer Space or on a celestial body. Ownership of objects launched into Outer Space, including objects landed or constructed on a celestial body, and of their component parts, is not affected by their presence in Outer Space or on a celestial body or by their return to the Earth. Such objects or component parts found beyond the limits of the State Party to the Treaty on whose registry they are carried shall be returned to that State Party, which shall, upon request, furnish identifying data prior to their return.

Article IX

In the exploration and use of Outer Space, including the moon and other celestial bodies, States Parties to the Treaty shall be guided by the principle of co-operation and mutual assistance and shall conduct all their activities in Outer Space, including the moon and other celestial bodies, with due regard to the corresponding interests of all other States Parties to the Treaty. States Parties to the Treaty shall pursue studies of Outer Space, including the moon and other celestial bodes, and conduct exploration of them so as to avoid their harmful contamination and also adverse changes in the environment of the Earth resulting from the introduction of extraterrestrial matter and where necessary, shall adopt appropriate measures for this purpose. If a State Party to the Treaty has reason to believe that an activity or experiment planned by it or its nationals in Outer Space, including the moon and other celestial bodies, would cause potentially harmful interference with activities of their States Parties in the peaceful exploration and use of Outer Space, including the moon an other celestial bodies, it shall undertake appropriate international consultations before proceeding with any such activity or experiment. A State Party to the Treaty which has reason to believe that an activity or experiment planned by another State Party in Outer Space, including the moon and other celestial bodies, would cause potentially harmful interference with activities in the peaceful exploration and use of Outer Space, including the moon and other celestial bodies, may request consultations concerning the activity or experiment.

Article X

In order to promote international co-operation in the exploration and use of Outer Space, including the moon and other celestial bodies, in conformity with the purposes of this Treaty, the States Parties to the Treaty shall consider on a basis of equality any request by other States Parties to the Treaty to be afforded an opportunity to observe the flight of space objects launched by these states.

The nature of such an opportunity for observation and the conditions under which it could be afforded shall be determined by agreement between the States concerned.

Article XI

In order to promote international co-operation in the peaceful exploration and use of Outer Space, States Parties to the Treaty conduction activities in Outer Space, including the Moon and other celestial bodies, agree to inform the Secretary-General of the United Nations as well as the public and the international scientific community, to the greatest extent feasible and practicable of the nature, conduct, locations and results of such activities. On receiving the said information, the Secretary-General of the United Nations should be prepared to disseminate it immediately and effectively.

Article XII

All stations, installations, equipment and space vehicles on the moon and other celestial bodies shall be open to representatives of other States Parties to the Treaty on a basis of reciprocity. Such representatives shall give reasonable advance notice of a projected visit, in order that appropriate consultations may be held and that maximum precautions may be taken to assure safety and to avoid interference with normal operations in the facility to be visited.

Article XIII

The provisions of this Treaty shall apply to the activities of States Parties to the Treaty in the exploration and use of Outer Space, including the moon and other celestial bodies, whether such activities are carried on by a single State Party to the Treaty or jointly with other States, including cases where they are carried on within the framework of international inter-governmental organizations.

Any practical question arising in connection with activities carried on by international inter-governmental organizations in the exploration and use of Outer Space, including the moon and other celestial bodies, shall be resolved by the States Parties to the Treaty either with the appropriate international organization or with one or more States members of that international organizations, which are Parties to this Treaty.

Article XIV

1. This Treaty shall be open to all States for signature. Any State which does not sign this Treaty before its entry into

force in accordance with paragraph 3 of this Article may accede to it at any time.

2. This Treaty shall be subject to ratification by signatory States. Instruments of ratification and instruments of accession shall be deposited with the Governments of the United Kingdom of Great Britain and Northern Ireland, the Union of Soviet Socialist Republics and the United States of America, which is hereby, designated the Depositary Governments.
3. This Treaty shall enter into force upon the deposit of instruments of ratification by five governments including the governments designated as Depositary Governments under this Treaty.
4. For States whose instruments of ratification or accession are deposited subsequent to the entry into force of this Treaty, it shall enter into force on the date of the deposit of their instruments of ratification or accession.
5. The Depositary Governments shall promptly inform all signatory and acceding States of the date of each signature, the date of deposit of each instrument of ratification of and accession to this Treaty, the date of its entry into force and other notices.
6. This Treaty shall be registered by the Depositary Governments pursuant to Article 102 of the Charter of the United Nations.

Article XV

Any State Party to the Treaty may propose amendments to this Treaty. Amendments shall enter into force for each State Party to the Treaty accepting the amendments upon their acceptance by a majority of the States Parties to the Treaty and thereafter for each remaining State Party to the Treaty on the date of acceptance by it.

Article XVI

Any State Party to the Treaty may give notice of its withdrawal from the Treaty one year after its entry into force by written notification to the Depositary Governments. Such withdrawal shall take effect one year from the date of receipt of this notification.

Article XVII

This Treaty, of which the English, Russian, French, Spanish and Chinese texts are equally authentic, shall be deposited in the archives of the Depositary Governments. Duly certified copies of this Treaty shall be transmitted by the Depositary Governments to the governments of the signatory and acceding States.

Source: *UN Treaty Series*, Vol. 610 (United Nations: New York, 1971–2005).

APPENDIX 3

Treaty for the Prohibition of Nuclear Weapons in Latin America *(Treaty of Tlatelolco)*

Signed at Mexico, Distrito Federal on 14 February, 1967. Entered into force on 22 April, 1968 Depositary: Mexican Government.

Preamble

In the name of their peoples and faithfully interpreting their desires and aspirations, the Governments of the States which sign the Treaty for the Prohibition of Nuclear Weapons in Latin America.

Desiring to contribute, so far as lies in their power, towards ending the armaments race, especially in the field of nuclear weapons, and towards strengthening a world at peace, based on the sovereign equality of States, mutual respect and good neighbourliness.

Recalling that the United National General Assembly, in its Resolution 808 (IX), adopted unanimously as one of the three points of a co-ordinated programme of disarmament "the total prohibition of the use and manufacture of nuclear weapons and weapons of mass destruction of every type".

Recalling that militarily denuclearized zones are not an end in themselves but rather a means for achieving general and complete disarmament at a later stage.

Recalling United Nations General Assembly Resolution 1911 (XVIII), which established that the measures that should be agreed upon for the denuclearization of Latin America should be taken "in the light of the principles of the charter of the United Nations and of regional agreements".

Recalling United Nations General Assembly Resolution 2028 (XX), which established the principle of an acceptable balance of mutual responsibilities and duties for the nuclear and non-nuclear powers, and Recalling that the Charter of the Organization of American States proclaims that it is an essential purpose of the

Organization to strengthen the peace and security of the hemisphere.

Convinced

That the incalculable destructive power of nuclear weapons has made it imperative that the legal prohibition of war should be strictly observed in practice if the survival of civilization and of mankind itself is to be assured.

That nuclear weapons, whose terrible effects are suffered, indiscriminately and inexorable alike, constitute, through the persistence of the radioactivity they release, an attack on the integrity of the human species and ultimately may even render the whole earth uninhabitable.

That general and complete disarmament under effective international control is a vital matter which all the peoples of the world equally demand.

That the proliferation of nuclear weapons, which seems inevitable unless States, in the exercise of their sovereign rights, impose restrictions on themselves in order to prevent it, would make any agreement on disarmament enormously difficult and would increase the danger of the outbreak of a nuclear conflagration.

That the establishment of militarily denuclearized zones is closely linked with the maintenance of peace and security in the respective regions.

That the military denuclearization of vast geographical zones, adopted by the sovereign decision of the States comprised therein, will exercise a beneficial influence on other regions where similar conditions exist.

That the privileged situation of the signatory States, whose territories are wholly free from nuclear weapons, imposes upon them the inescapable duty of preserving that situation both in their own interests and for the good of mankind.

That the existence of nuclear weapons in any country of Latin America would make it a target for possible nuclear attacks and would inevitably set off, throughout the region, a ruinous race in nuclear weapons which would involve the unjustifiable diversion, for warlike purposes, of the limited resources required for economic and social development.

That the foregoing reasons, together with the traditional peace-loving outlook of Latin America, give rise to an inescapable necessity that nuclear energy should be used in that region exclusively for peaceful purposes, and that the Latin American Countries should use their right to the greatest and most equitable possible access to this new source of energy in order to expedite the economic and social development of their peoples.

Convinced Finally

That the military denuclearization of Latin America being understood to mean the undertaking entered into internationally in this treaty to keep their territories for ever free from nuclear weapons will constitute a measure which will spare their peoples from the squandering of their limited resources on nuclear armaments and will protect them against possible nuclear attacks on their territories and will also constitute a significant contribution towards preventing the proliferation of nuclear weapons and a powerful factor for general and complete disarmament, and

That Latin America, faithful to its tradition of universality, must not only endeavor to banish from its homelands the scourge of a nuclear war, but must also strive to promote the well-being and advancement of its peoples, at the same time co-operating in the fulfillment of the consolidation of a permanent peace based on equal rights, economic fairness and social justice for all, in accordance with the principles and purposes set forth in the Charter of the United Nations and in the Charter of the Organization of American States,

Have agreed as follows:

Article 1. Obligations

1. The contracting Parties hereby undertake to use exclusively for peaceful purposes the nuclear material and facilities which are under their jurisdiction, and to prohibit and prevent in their respective territories:–
   (a) The testing, use, manufacture, production or acquisition by any means whatsoever of any nuclear weapon.

(b) Shall initiate and consider studies designed to facilitate the optimum fulfillment of the aims of this Treaty, without prejudice to the power of the General Secretary independently to carry out similar studies for submission to and consideration by the conference.

(c) Shall be the organ competent to authorize the conclusion of agreements with governments and other international organizations and bodies.

2. The General Conference shall adopt the Agency's budget and fix the scale of financial contributions to be paid by Member States, taking into account the systems and criteria used for the same purpose by the United Nations.
3. The General Conference shall elect its officers for each session and may establish such subsidiary organs as it deems necessary for the performance of its functions.
4. Each member of the agency shall have one vote. The decision of the General Conference shall be taken by a two-third majority of the members present and voting in the case of matters relating to the control system and measures referred to in Article 20, the admission of new members, the election or removal of the General Secretary, adoption of the budget and matters related thereto. Decisions on other matters, as well as procedural questions and also determination of which questions must be decided by a two-third majority, shall be taken by a simple majority of the Members present and voting.
5. The General Conference shall adopt its own rules of procedure.

Article 10. The Council

1. The Council shall be composed of five members of the Agency elected by the General Conference from among the Contracting Parties, due account being taken of equitable geographic distribution.
2. The Members of the Council shall be elected for a term of four years. However, in the first election three will be elected for two years. Outgoing Members may not be re-elected for the following period unless the limited

number of States for which the Treaty is in force so requires.

3. Each Member of the Council shall have one representative.
4. The Council shall be so organized as to be able to function continuously.
5. In addition to the function conferred upon it by this Treaty and to those which may be assigned to it by the General Conference, the Council shall, through the General Secretary, ensure the proper operation of the control system in accordance with the provisions of this Treaty and with the decisions adopted by the General Conference.
6. The Council shall submit an annual report on its work to the General Conference as well as such special reports as it deems necessary or which the General Conference requests of it.
7. The Council shall elect its officers for each session.
8. The decisions of the Council shall be taken by a simple majority of its Members present and voting.
9. The Council shall adopt its own rules of procedure.

Article 11. The Secretariat

1. The Secretariat shall consist of a General Secretary, who shall be the chief administrative officer of the Agency, and/or such staff as the Agency may require. The term of office of the General Secretary shall be four years and he may be re-elected for a single additional term. The General Secretary may not be a national of the country in which the Agency has its headquarters. In case the office of the General Secretary becomes vacant, a new election shall be held to fill the office for the remainder of the term.
2. The staff of the Secretariat shall be appointed by the General Secretary, in accordance with rules laid down by the General Conference.
3. In addition to the functions conferred upon him by this Treaty and to those which may be assigned to him by the General Conference the General Secretary shall ensure,

as provided by Article 10, paragraph 5, the proper operation of the control system established by this Treaty, in accordance with the provision of the Treaty and the decisions taken by the General Conference.

4. The General Secretary shall act in that capacity in all meetings of the General Conference and of the Council and shall make an annual report to both bodies on the work of the Agency and any special reports requested by the General Conference or the Council or which the General Secretary may deem desirable.
5. The General Secretary shall establish the procedures for distributing to all contracting parties information received by the Agency from governmental sources and such information from non-governmental sources as may be of interest to the agency.
6. In the performance of their duties the General Secretary and the staff shall not seek or receive instructions from any government or from any other authorities external to the agency and shall refrain from any action which might reflect on their position as international officials responsible only to the Agency; Subject to their responsibility to the Agency, they shall not disclose any industrial secret or other confidential informations coming to their knowledge by reason of their official duties in the agency.
7. Each of the Contracting Parties undertakes to respect the exclusively international character of the responsibilities of the General Secretary and the staff and not to seek to influence them in the discharge of their responsibilities.

Article 12. Control System

1. For the purposes of verifying compliance with the obligations entered into by the Contracting Parties in accordance with Article, a control system shall be established which shall be put into effect in accordance with the provisions of Articles 13-18 of this Treaty.
2. The control system shall be used in particular for the purpose of verifying:–

(a) That devices, services and facilities intended for peaceful uses of nuclear energy are not used in the testing of manufacture of nuclear weapons;
(b) That none of the activities prohibited in Article 1 of this Treaty is carried out in the territory of the Contracting Parties with nuclear materials or weapons introduced from abroad; and
(c) Those explosions for peaceful purposes are compatible with Article 18 of this Treaty.

Article 13. IAEA Safeguards

Each Contracting Party shall negotiate multilateral or bilateral agreements with the International Atomic Energy Agency for the application of its safeguards to its nuclear activities. Each Contracting Party shall initiate negotiations within a period of 180 days after the date of the deposit of its instrument of ratification of this Treaty. These agreements shall enter into force, for each Party, not later than eighteen months after the date of the initiation of such negotiations except in case of unforeseen circumstances or force majeure.

Article 14. Reports of the Parties

1. The contracting Parties shall submit to the Agency and to the International Atomic Energy Agency, for their information, semi-annual reports stating that no activity prohibited under this Treaty has occurred in their respective territories.
2. The Contracting Parties shall simultaneously transmit to the agency a copy of any report they may submit to the International Atomic Energy Agency which relates to matters that are the subject of this Treaty and to the application of safeguards.
3. The Contracting Parties shall also transmit to the Organization of American States, for its information, any report that may be of interest to it, in accordance with the obligations established by the Inter-American System.

Article 15. Special Reports Requested by the General Secretary

1. With the authorization of the Council, the General Secretary may request any of the Contracting Parties to provide the Agency information regarding any event or circumstance connected with compliance with this Treaty, explaining his reasons. The Contracting Parties undertake to co-operate promptly and fully with the General Secretary.
2. The General Secretary shall inform the Council and the Contracting Parties forth with of such requests and of the respective replies.

Article 16. Special Inspections

1. The International Atomic Energy Agency and the Council established by this Treaty have the power of carrying our special inspections in the following case:
   (a) In the case of the International Atomic Energy Agency, in accordance with the agreements referred to in Article 13 of this Treaty:–
      (i) When so requested the reasons for the request being stated, by any Party which suspects that some activities prohibited by the Treaty have been carried out or are about to be carried out, either in the territory of any other Parties or in any other places on such latter Party's behalf, the Council shall immediately arrange for such an inspection in accordance with Article 10, paragraph 5.
      (ii) When requested by any Party which has been suspected of or charged with having violated this Treaty, the Council shall immediately arrange for the special inspection requested in accordance with Article 10, paragraph 5.

   The above requests will be made to the Council through the General Secretary.
2. The costs and expenses of any special inspection carried out under paragraph 1, sub-paragraph (b), Sections (i) or (ii) of this article shall be borne by the requesting Party or Parties, except where the Council concludes on the

basis of the report on the special inspection that, in view of the circumstances existing in the case, such costs and expenses should be borne by the Agency.

3. The General Conference shall formulate the procedures for the organization and execution of the special inspections carried out in accordance with paragraph 1, sub-paragraph (b), Sections (i) and (ii) of this article.
4. The Contracting Parties undertake to grant the inspectors carrying out such special inspection full and free access to all places and all informations which may be necessary for the performance of their duties and which are directly and intimately connected with the suspicion of violation of this Treaty. If so requested by the authorities of the Contracting Party in whose territory the inspection is carried out, the inspectors designated by the General Conference shall be accompanied by representatives of said authorities, provided that this does not in any way delay or hinder the work of the inspectors.
5. The Council shall immediately transmit to all the Parties, through the General Secretary, a copy of any report resulting from special inspections.
6. Similarly, the Council shall send through the General Secretary to the Secretary-General of the United Nations, for transmission to the United Nations Security Council and General Assembly, and to the Council of the Organization of American States, for its information, a copy of any report resulting from any special inspection carried out in accordance with paragraph 1, sub-paragraph (b), Sections (i) and (ii) of this article.
7. The Council may decide, or any Contracting Party may request, the convening of a special session of the General Conference for the purpose of considering the reports resulting from any special inspection. In such a case, the General Secretary shall take immediate steps to convene the special session requested.
8. The General Conference, convened in special session under this article, may make recommendations to the Contracting Parties and submit reports to the Secretary-General of the United Nations to be transmitted to the United Nations Security Council and the General Assembly.

Article 17. Use of Nuclear Energy for Peaceful Purposes

Nothing in the provisions of this Treaty shall prejudice the rights of the Contracting Parties, in conformity with the Treaty, to use nuclear energy for peaceful purposes, in particular for their economic development and social progress.

Article 18. Explosions for Peaceful Purposes

1. The Contracting Parties may carry out explosions of nuclear devices for peaceful purposes—including explosions which involve devices similar to those used in nuclear weapons or collaborate with third Parties for the same purpose, provided that they do so in accordance with the provisions of this article and the other articles of the Treaty, particularly Articles I and 5.
2. Contracting Parties intending to carry out, or to co-operate in carrying out, such an explosion shall notify the Agency and the International Atomic Energy Agency, as far in advance as the circumstances require, of the date of the explosion and shall at the same time provide the following informations:
   (a) The nature of the nuclear device and the source from which it was obtained;
   (b) The place and purpose of the planned explosion;
   (c) The procedures which will be followed in order to comply with paragraph 3 of this article;
   (d) The expected force of the device; and
   (e) The fullest possible information on any from the explosion or explosions, and measures which will be taken to avoid danger to the population, flora, fauna and territories of any other Party or Parties.
3. The General Secretary and the technical personnel designated by the Council and the International Atomic Energy Agency may observe all the preparations, including the explosion of the device, and shall have unrestricted access to any area in the vicinity of the site of the explosion in order to ascertain whether the device and the procedures followed during the explosion are in conformity with the information supplied under

paragraph 2 of this article and the other provisions of the Treaty.

4. The Contracting parties may accept the collaboration of third parties for the purpose set forth in paragraph 1 of the present article, in accordance with paragraphs 2 and 3 thereof.

Article 19. Relations with Other International Organizations

1. The Agency may conclude such agreements with the International Atomic Energy Agency as are authorized by the General Conference and as it considers likely to facilitate the efficient operation of the Control System established by this Treaty.
2. The Agency may also enter into relations with any international organization or body, especially any which may be established in the future to supervise Disarmament or measures for the control of armaments in any part of the world.
3. The Contracting Parties may, if they see fit, request the advice of the Inter-American Nuclear Energy Commission on all technical matters connected with the application of this Treaty with which the Commission is competent to deal under its Statute.

Article 20. Measures in the Event of Violation of the Treaty

1. The General Conference shall take note of all cases in which, in its opinion, any Contracting Party is not complying fully with its obligations under this Treaty and shall draw the matter to the attention of the Party concerned, making such recommendations as it deems appropriate.
2. If, in its opinion, such non-compliance constitutes a violation of this Treaty which might endanger peace and security, the General Conference shall report thereon simultaneously to the United Nations Security Council and the General Assembly through the Secretary-General of the United Nations, and to the Council of the Organization of American States. The General Conference shall likewise report to the International Atomic Energy

Agency for such purposes as are relevant in accordance with its Statute.

Article 21. United Nations and Organization of American States

None of the provisions of this Treaty shall be construed as impairing the rights and obligations of the Parties under the Charter of the United Nations or, in the case of States Members of the Organization of American States, under existing regional treaties.

Article 22. Privileges and Immunities

1. The Agency shall enjoy in the territory of each of the Contracting Parties such legal capacity and such privileges and immunities as may be necessary for the exercise of its functions and the fulfillment of its purposes.
2. Representatives of the Contracting Parties accredited to the Agency and officials of the Agency shall similarly enjoy such privileges and immunities as are necessary for the performance of their functions.
3. The Agency may conclude agreements with the Contracting Parties with a view to determining the details of the application of paragraphs 1 and 2 of this article.

Article 23. Notification of Other Agreements

Once this Treaty has entered into force, the Secretariat shall be notified immediately of any international agreement concluded by any of the Contracting Parties on matters with which this Treaty is concerned; the Secretariat shall register it and notify the other Contracting Parties.

Article 24. Settlement of Disputes

Unless the Parties concerned agree on another mode of peaceful settlement, any question or dispute concerning the interpretation or application of this Treaty which is not settled shall be referred to the International Court of Justice with the prior consent of the Parties to the controversy.

Article 25. Signature

1. This Treaty shall be open indefinitely for signature by:
   (a) All the Latin American Republics, and
   (b) All other sovereign States situated in their entirety south of latitude 35 north in the western hemisphere; and except as provided in paragraph 2 of this article, all such States which become sovereign, when they have been admitted by the General Conference.
2. The General Conference shall not take any decision regarding the admission of a political entity part or all of whose territory is the subject, prior to the date when this Treaty is opened for signature, of a dispute or claim between an extra-continental country and one or more Latin American States, so long as the dispute has not been settled by peaceful means.

Article 26. Ratification and Deposit

1. This Treaty shall be subject to ratification by signatory States in accordance with their respective constitutional procedures.
2. This Treaty and the instruments of ratification shall be deposited with the Government of the Mexican United States, which is hereby designated the Depositary Government.
3. The Depositary Government shall send certified copies of this Treaty to the Governments of signatory States and shall notify them of the deposit of each instrument of ratification.

Article 27. Reservations

This Treaty shall not be subject to reservations.

Article 28. Entry Into Force

1. Subject to the provisions of paragraph 2 of this article, this Treaty shall enter into force among the States that have ratified it as force among the States that have ratified it as soon as the following requirements have been met:–

(a) Deposit of the instruments of ratification of this Treaty with the Depositary Government by the Governments of the States mentioned in Article 25 which are in existence on the date when this Treaty is opened for signature and which are not affected by the provisions of Article 25, paragraph 2;
(b) Signature and ratification of Additional Protocol I annexed to this Treaty by all extra-continental or continental States having *de jure* or *de facto* international responsibility for territories situated in the Zone of application of the Treaty;
(c) Signature and ratification of the Additional Protocol II annexed to this Treaty by all powers possessing nuclear weapons;
(d) Conclusion of bilateral or multilateral agreements on the application of the Safeguards System of the International Atomic Energy Agency in accordance with Article 13 of this Treaty.

2. All signatory States shall have the imprescriptibly right to waive, wholly or in part, the requirements laid down in the preceding paragraph. They may do so by means of a declaration which shall be annexed to their respective instrument of ratification and which may be formulated at the time of deposit of the instrument or sub-squinty. For those States which exercise this right, this Treaty shall enter into force upon deposit of the declaration, or as soon as those requirements have been met which have not been expressly waived.
3. As soon as this Treaty has entered into force in accordance with the provisions of paragraph 2 for eleven States, the Depositary Government shall convene a preliminary meeting of those States in order that the Agency may be set up and commence its work.
4. After the entry into force of this Treaty for all countries of the Zone, the rise of a new power possessing nuclear weapons shall have the effect of suspending the execution of this Treaty for those countries which have ratified it without waiving requirements of paragraph 1, sub-paragraph (c) of this article, and which request such

suspension; the Treaty shall remain suspended until the new power, on its own initiative or upon request by the General conference, ratifies the annexed Additional Protocol II.

Article 29. Amendments

1. Any Contracting Party may propose amendments to this Treaty and shall submit its proposals to the Council through the General Secretary, who shall transmit them to all the other Contracting Parties and, in addition, to all other signatories in accordance with Article 6. The Council, through the General Secretary, shall immediately following the meeting of signatories convene a special session of the General Conference to examine the proposals made, for the adoption of which a two-thirds majority of the Contracting Parties present and voting shall be required.
2. Amendments adopted shall enter into force as soon as the requirements set forth in Article 28 of this Treaty have been complied with.

Article 30. Duration and Denunciation

1. This Treaty shall be of a permanent nature and shall remain in force indefinitely, but any Party may denounce it by notifying but any Party may denounce it by notifying the General Secretary of the Agency if, in the opinion of the denouncing State, there have arisen or may arise circumstances connected with the content of this Treaty or of the annexed Additional Protocols I and II which affect its supreme interests or the peace and security of one or more Contracting Parties.
2. The denunciation shall take effect three months after the delivery to the General Secretary of the Agency of the notification by the Government of the signatory State concerned. The General Secretary shall immediately communicate such notification to the other Contracting Parties and to the Secretary-General of the United

Nations for the information of the United Nations Security Council and the General Assembly. He shall also communicate it to the Secretary-General of the Organization of American States.

Article 31. Authentic Texts and Registration

This Treaty, of which the Spanish, Chinese, English, French, Portuguese and Russian texts are equally authentic, shall be registered by the Depositary Government up accordance with Article 102 of the United Nations Charter. In Depositary Government shall notify the Secretary-General of the Organization of American States for its information.

Transitional Article

Denunciation of the declaration refereed to in Article 28, paragraph 2, and shall be subject to the same procedures as the denunciation of this Treaty, except that it will take effect on the date of delivery of the respective notification.

Additional Protocol I

The undersigned plenipotentiaries, furnished with full powers by their respective Governments.

Convinced that the Treaty for the prohibition of Nuclear Weapons in Latin America, negotiated and signed in accordance with the recommendations of the General Assembly of the United Nations in Resolution 1911, (XVIII) of 27 November, 1963, represents an important step towards ensuring the non-proliferation of nuclear weapons,

Aware that the non-proliferation of nuclear weapons is not an end in itself but, rather, a means of achieving general and complete disarmament at a later stage, and

Desiring to contribute, so far as lies in their power, towards ending the armaments race, especially in the field of nuclear weapons, and towards strengthening a world at peace, based on mutual respect and sovereign equality of States.

Have agreed as follows:

Article 1

To undertake to apply the statute of de colonization in respect of warlike purposes as defined in Articles 1, 3, 5 and 13 of the Treaty for the Prohibition of Nuclear Weapons in Latin America in territories for which, *de jure* or *de facto*, they are internationally responsible and which lie within the limits of the geographical zone established in that Treaty.

Article 2

The duration of this Protocol shall be the same as that of the Treaty for the Prohibition of Nuclear Weapons in Latin America of which this Protocol is an annex and the provisions regarding ratification and denunciation contained in the Treaty shall be applicable to it.

Article 3

This Protocol shall enter into force, for the States which have ratified it, on the date of the deposit of their respective instruments of ratification.

Additional Protocol II

The undersigned Plenipotentiaries, furnished with full powers by their respective Governments.

Convinced that the Treaty for the Prohibition of Nuclear Weapons in Latin America, negotiated and signed in accordance with the recommendations of the General Assembly of the United Nations in Resolution 1911 (XVII) of 27 November, 1963, represents an important step towards ensuring the non-proliferation of nuclear weapons,

Aware that the non-proliferation of nuclear weapons is not an end in itself but, rather, a means of achieving general and complete disarmament at a later stage, and complete disarmament at a later stage, and

Desiring to contribute, so far as lies in their power, towards ending the armaments race, especially in the field of nuclear weapons, and towards promoting and strengthening a world at peace, based on mutual respect and sovereign equality of States.

Have agreed as follows:

Article 1

The statute of denuclearization of Latin America in respect of warlike purposes, as defined, delimited and set forth in the Treaty for the Prohibition of Nuclear Weapons in Latin America of which this instrument is an annex, shall be fully respected by the parties to this protocol in all its expressed aims and provisions.

Article 2

The Governments represented by the undersigned Plenipotentiaries undertake, therefore, not to contribute in any way to the performance of acts involving a violation of the obligations of article 1 of the Treaty in the territories to which the Treaty applies in accordance with Article 4 thereof.

Article 3

The Governments represented by the undersigned Plenipotentiaries also undertake not to use or threaten to use nuclear weapons against the Contracting Parties of the Treaty for the Prohibition of Nuclear Weapons in Latin America.

Article 4

The duration of this Protocol shall be the same as that of the Treaty for the Prohibition of Nuclear Weapons in Latin America of which this Protocol is an annex, and the definitions of territory and nuclear weapons set forth in Articles 3 and 5 of the Treaty shall be applicable to this Protocol, as well as the provisions regarding ratification, reservations, denunciation, authentic texts and registration contained in Articles 26, 27, 30 and 31 of the Treaty.

Article 5

This Protocol shall enter into force, for the States which have ratified it, on the date of the deposit of their respective instruments of ratification.

Source: *UN Treaty Series*, Vol. 634 onwards (United Nations: New York, 1971–2005).

APPENDIX 4

South Pacific Nuclear-Free-Zone Treaty

The Parties to this Treaty

United in their commitment to a world at peace;

Gravely concerned that the continuing nuclear arms race presents the risk of nuclear war which would have devastating consequences for all people;

Convinced that all countries have an obligation to make every effort to achieve the goal of eliminating nuclear weapons, the terror which they hold for humankind and the threat which they pose to life on earth;

Believing that regional arms control measures can contribute to global efforts to reverse the nuclear arms race and promote the national security of each country in the region and the common security of all;

Determined to ensure, so far as lies within their power, that the bounty and beauty of the land and sea in their region shall remain the heritage of their peoples and their descendants in perpetuity to be enjoyed by all in peace;

Reaffirming the importance of the Treaty on the Non-Proliferation of Nuclear Weapons (NTP) in preventing the proliferation of nuclear weapons and in contributing to world security.

Noting in particular, that Article VII of the NPT recognizes the right of any group of states to conclude regional treaties in order to assure the total absence of nuclear weapons in their respective territories.

Noting that the prohibitions of implantation and emplacement of nuclear weapons on the Sea-bed and the ocean floor and in the sub-soil thereof contained in the Treaty on the Prohibition of the Employment of Nuclear Weapons and Other Weapons of Mass Destruction on the Sea-Bed and the Ocean Floor and in the sub-soil Thereof apply in the South Pacific;

Noting also that the prohibition of testing of nuclear weapons in the atmosphere or under water, including territorial waters or high seas, contained in the Treaty Banning Nuclear Weapon Tests in the Atmosphere, in Outer Space and Under Water applies in the South Pacific;

Determined to keep the region free of environmental pollution by radioactive wastes and other radioactive matter;

Guided by the decision of the Fifteenth South Pacific Forum at Tuvalu that a nuclear free zone should be established in the region at the earliest possible opportunity in accordance with the principles set out in the communiqué of that meeting;

Agreed as follows:

Article 1. Usage of Terms

For the purposes of this Treaty and its Protocols:–

(a) "South Pacific Nuclear-Free-Zone" means the areas described in Annex 1 as illustrated by the map attached to that Annex;

(b) " territory" means internal waters, territorial sea and archipelagos water, the Sea-Bed and sub-soil beneath, the land territory and the airspace above them;

(c) "nuclear explosive device" means any nuclear weapon or other explosive devices capable of releasing nuclear energy, irrespective of the purpose of which it could be used. The term includes such a weapon or device in unassembled; and

Partly assembled forms, but does not include the means of transport or delivery of such a weapon or device if separable from and not an indivisible part of it;

(d) "Stationing" means implantation, emplacement, transportation on land or inland waters, stockpiling, storage, installation and deployment.

Article 2. Application of the Treaty

1. Except where otherwise specified, this Treaty and its Protocols shall apply to territory within the South Pacific Nuclear-Free-Zone.
2. Nothing in this Treaty shall prejudice or in any way affect the rights, or the exercise of the rights, of any State under international law with regard to freedom of the seas.

Article 3. Renunciation of Nuclear Explosive Devices

Each Party undertakes:–

(a) not to manufacture or otherwise acquire, possess or have control over any nuclear explosive device by any means anywhere inside or outside the South Pacific Nuclear-Free-Zone;
(b) not to seek or receive any assistance in the manufacture or acquisition of any nuclear explosive device;
(c) not to take any action to assist or encourage the manufacture or acquisition of any nuclear explosive device by any State.

Article 4. Peaceful Nuclear Activities

Each party undertakes:

(a) not to provide source or special fissionable material, or equipment or material especially designed or prepared for the processing, use or production of special fissionable material for peaceful purposes to:–
    (i) Any non-nuclear-weapon State unless subject to applicable safeguards required by Article III, 1 of the NPT, or
    (ii) Any nuclear-weapon State unless subject to applicable safeguards agreements with the International Atomic Energy Agency (IAEA).

    Any such provision shall be in accordance with strict non-proliferation measures to provide assurance of exclusively peaceful non-explosive use.

(b) To support the continued effectiveness of the international non-proliferation system based on the NPT and the IAEA safeguards system.

Article 5. Prevention of Stationing of Nuclear Explosive Devices

1. Each Party undertakes to prevent in its territory the stationing of any nuclear explosive device.
2. Each Party in the exercise of its sovereign rights remains free to decide for itself whether to allow visits by foreign ships and aircraft to its ports and airfields, transit of its airspace by foreign aircraft and navigation by foreign ships in its territorial sea or archipelagos waters in a manner not covered by the rights of innocent passage, archipelago sea lane passage or transit passage of straits.

Article 6. Prevention of Testing of Nuclear Explosive Devices

Each Party undertakes:

(a) to prevent in its territory the testing of any nuclear explosive device;
(b) not to take any action to assist or encourage the testing of any nuclear explosive device by any State.

Article 7. Prevention of Dumping

1. Each Party undertakes:
   (a) not to dump radioactive wastes and other radioactive matter at sea anywhere within the South Pacific Nuclear-Free-Zone;
   (b) to prevent the dumping of radioactive wastes and other radioactive matter by anyone in its territorial sea;
   (c) not to take any action to assist or encourage the dumping by anyone of radioactive wastes and other radioactive matter at sea anywhere within the South Pacific Nuclear-Free-Zone;
   (d) to support the conclusion as soon as possible of the proposed Convention relating to the protection of the

natural resources and environment of the South Pacific region and its Protocol for the prevention of pollution of the South Pacific region by dumping, with the aim of precluding dumping at sea of radioactive wastes and other radioactive matter by anyone anywhere in the region.

2. Paragraphs 1 (a) and 1 (b) of this Article shall not apply to areas of the South Pacific Nuclear-Free-Zone in respect of which such a Convention and Protocol have entered into force.

Article 8. Control System

1. The Parties hereby establish a control system for the purpose of verifying compliance with their obligations under this Treaty.
2. The control system shall comprise:
   (a) reports and exchange of information as provided for in Article 9;
   (b) consultations as provided for in Article 10 and Annex 4 (1);
   (c) the application to peaceful nuclear a activities of safeguards by the IAEA as provided for in Annex 2;
   (d) a complaints procedure as provided for in Annex 4.

Article 9. Reports and Exchanges of Information

1. Each Party shall report to the Director of the South Pacific Bureau for Economic Co-operation (the Director) as soon as possible any significant event within its jurisdiction affecting the implementation of this Treaty. The Director shall circulate such reports promptly to all Parties.
2. The Parties shall endeavor to keep each other informed on matters arising under or in relation to this Treaty. They may exchange information by communicating it to the Director, who shall circulate it to all Parties.
3. The Director shall report annually to the South Pacific Forum on the status of this Treaty and matters arising under or in relation to it, incorporating reports and communications made under paragraphs 1 and 2 of this

article and matters arising under Articles 8 (2) (d) and 10 and Annex 2 (4).

Article 10. Consultations and Review

Without prejudice to the conduct of consultations among Parties by other means, the Director, at the request of any Party, shall convince a meeting of the Consultative Committee established by Annex 3 for consultation and co-operation on any matter arising in relation to this Treaty or for reviewing its operation.

Article 11. Amendment

The Consultative Committee shall consider proposals for amendment of the provisions of this Treaty proposed by any Party and circulated by the Director to all Parties not less than three months prior to the convening of the Consultative Committee for this purpose. Any proposal agreed upon by consensus by the Consultative Committee shall be communicated to the Director who shall circulate it for acceptance to all Parties. An amendment shall enter into force thirty days after receipt by the depositary of acceptance from all Parties.

Article 12. Signatures and Ratification

1. This Treaty shall be open for signature by any Member of the South Pacific Forum.
2. This Treaty shall be subject to ratification. Instruments of ratification shall be deposited with the Director who is hereby designated depositary of this Treaty and its Protocols.
3. If a Member of the South Pacific Forum whose territory is outside the South Pacific Nuclear-Free-Zone becomes a Party to this Treaty, Annex I shall be deemed to be amended so far as is required to enclose at least the territory of that Party within the boundaries of the South Pacific Nuclear-Free-Zone. The delineation of any area added pursuant to this paragraph shall be approved by the South Pacific Forum.

Article 13. Withdrawals

1. This Treaty is of a permanent nature and shall remain in force indefinitely, provided that in the event of a violation by any Party of a provision of this Treaty essential to the achievement of the objectives of the Treaty or of the spirit of the Treaty, every other Party shall have the right to withdraw from the Treaty.
2. Withdrawal shall be effected by giving notice twelve months in advance to the Director who shall circulate such notice to all other Parties.

Article 14. Reservations

This Treaty shall not be subject to reservations.

Article 15. Entries Into Force

1. This Treaty shall enter into force on the date of deposit of the eighth instrument of ratification.
2. For a signatory which ratifies this Treaty after the date of deposit of the eighth instrument of ratification the Treaty shall enter into force on the date of deposit of its instrument of ratification.

Article 16. Depositary Function

The depositary shall register this Treaty and its Protocols pursuant to Article 102 of the Charter of the United Nations and shall transmit certified copies of the Treaty and its Protocols to all Members of the South Pacific Forum and all States eligible to become Party to the Protocols to the Treaty and shall notify them of signatures and ratifications of the Treaty and its Protocols.

DONE at Rarotonga, this Sixth day of August, One thousand nine hundred and eighty five, in a single original in the English Language.

Annex I: South Pacific Nuclear-Free-Zone

A. The area bounded by a line:–

1. commencing at the point of intersection of the Equator by the maritime boundary between Indonesia and Papua New Guinea;

2. running thence northerly along that maritime boundary to its intersection by the outer limit of the Exclusive Economic Zone of Papua New Guinea;
3. thence generally north-easterly, easterly and south-easterly along that outer limit to its intersection by the Equator;
4. thence east along the Equator to its intersection by the meridian of Longitude 163 degrees East;
5. thence north along that meridian to its intersection by the parallel of Latitude 3 degrees North;
6. thence east along that parallel to its intersection by the meridian of Longitude 171 degrees East;
7. thence north along that meridian to its intersection by the parallel of Latitude 4 degrees North;
8. thence east along that parallel to its intersection by the meridian of Longitude 180 degrees East;
9. thence south along that meridian to its intersection by the Equator;
10. thence east along the Equator to its intersection by the meridian of Longitude 165 degrees West;
11. thence north along that meridian to its intersection by the parallel of Latitude 5 degrees 30 minutes North;
12. thence east along that parallel to its intersection by the meridian of Longitude 154 degrees West;
13. thence south along that meridian to its intersection by the Equator;
14. thence east along the Equator to its intersection by the meridian of Longitude 115 degrees West;
15. thence south along that meridian to its intersection by the parallel of Latitude 60 degrees South;
16. thence west along that parallel to its intersection by the meridian of Longitude 115 degrees East;
17. thence north along that meridian to its southernmost intersection by the outer limit of the territorial sea of Australia;
18. thence generally northerly and easterly along the outer limit of the territorial sea of Australia to its intersection by the meridian of Longitude 136 degrees 45 minutes East;
19. thence north-easterly along the geodesic to the point of

Latitude 10 degrees 50 minutes South, Longitude 139 degrees 12 minutes East;

20. thence north-easterly along the maritime boundary between Indonesia and Papua New Guinea to where it joins the land border between those two countries;
21. thence generally northerly along that land border to where it joins the maritime boundary between Indonesia and Papua New Guineas, on the northern coastline of Papua New Guinea; and
22. thence generally northerly along that boundary to the point of commencement.

B. The areas within the outer limits of the territorial seas of all Australian Islands lying westward of the area described in paragraph A and north of Latitude 60 degrees South, provided that any such areas shall craze to be part of the South Pacific Nuclear-Free-Zone upon receipt by the depositary of written notice from the Government of Australia stating that the areas have become subject to another treaty having an object and purpose substantially the same as that of this Treaty.

Annex 2: IAEA Safeguards

1. The safeguards referred to in Article 8 shall in respect of each Party be applied by the IAEA as set forth in an agreement negotiated and concluded with the IAEA on all sources or special fissionable material in all peaceful nuclear activities within the territory of the Party, under its jurisdiction or carried out under its control anywhere.
2. The agreement referred to in paragraph 1 shall be, or shall be equivalent in its scope and effect to an agreement required in connection with the NPT on the basis of the material reproduced in document INFCIRC/153 (Corrected) of the IAEA. Each Party shall take all appropriate steps to ensure that such an agreement is in force for it not later than eighteen months after the date of entry into force for that Party of this Treaty.
3. For the purposes of this Treaty, the safeguards referred to in paragraph 1 shall have as their purpose the verification of the non-diversion of nuclear material

from peaceful nuclear activities to nuclear explosive devices.

4. Each Party agrees upon the request of any other Party to transmit to that Party and to the Director for the information of all Parties a copy of the overall conclusions of the most recent report by the IAEA on its inspection activities in the territory of the Party concerned and to advise the Director promptly of any subsequent finding of the Board of Governors of the IAEA in relation to those conclusions for the information of all Parties.

Annex 3: Consultative Committee

1. There is hereby established a Consultative Committee which shall be convened by the Director from time to time pursuant to Articles 10 and 11 and Annex 4 (2). The Consultative Committee shall be constituted of representatives of the Parties, each Party being entitled to appoint one representative who may be accompanied by advisers. Unless otherwise agreed, the Consultative Committee shall be chaired at any given meeting by the representative of the Party which last hosted the meeting of Heads of Government of Members of the South Pacific Forum. A quorum shall be constituted by representatives of half the Parties. Subject to the provisions of Article 11, decisions of the Consultative Committee shall be taken by consensus or, failing consensus, by a two-thirds majority of those present and voting. The Consultative Committee shall adopt such other rules of procedure as it sees fit.
2. The costs of the Consultative Committee, including the costs of special inspections pursuant to Annex 4, shall be borne by the South Pacific Bureau for Economic Co-operation. It may seek special funding should this be required.

Annex 4: Complaints Procedure

1. A Party which considers that there are grounds for a complaint that another Party is in breach of its obligations

under this Treaty shall, before bringing such a complaint to the Director, bring the subject matter of the complaint to the attention of the Party complained of and shall allow the latter reasonable opportunity to provide it with an explanation and to resolve the matter.

2. If the matter is not so resolved, the complainant Party may bring the complaint to the Director with a request that the Consultative Committee be convened to consider it. Complaints shall be supported by an account of evidence of breach of obligations known to the complainant Party. Upon receipt of a complaint the Director shall convene the Consultative Committee as quickly as possible to consider it.
3. The Consultative Committee, taking account of efforts made under paragraph 1, shall afford the Party complained of a reasonable opportunity to provide it with an explanation of the matter.
4. If, after considering any explanation given to it by the representatives of the Party complained of the Consultative Committee decides that there is sufficient substance in the complaint to warrant a special inspection in the territory of that Party or elsewhere, the Consultative Committee shall direct that such special inspection be made as quickly as possible by a special inspection team of three suitably qualified special inspectors appointed by the Consultative Committee in consultation with the complained of and complainant Parties, provided that no national of either Party shall serve on the special inspection team. If so requested by the Party complained of the special inspection team shall be accompanied by representatives of that Party. Neither the right of consultation on the appointment of special inspectors, nor the right to accompany special inspectors, shall delay the work of the special inspection team.
5. In making a special inspection, special inspectors shall be subject to the direction only of the Consultative Committee and shall comply with such directives concerning tasks, objectives, confidentiality and procedures as may be decided upon by it. Directives shall take account of the legitimate interests of the Party

complained of in complying with its other international obligations and commitments and shall not duplicate safeguards procedures to be undertaken by the IAEA pursuant to agreements referred to in Annex 2(1). The special inspectors shall discharge their duties with due respect for the laws of the Party complained of.

6. Each Party shall give to special inspectors full and free access to all information and places within its territory which may be relevant to enable the special inspectors to implement the directives given to them by the Consultative Committee.
7. The Party complained of shall take all appropriate steps to facilitate the special inspection, and shall grant to special inspectors privileges and immunities necessary for the performance of their functions, including inviolability for all papers and documents and immunity from arrest, detention and legal process for acts done and words spoken and written, for the purpose of the special inspection.
8. The special inspectors shall report in writing as quickly as possible to the Consultative Committee, outlining their activities, setting out relevant facts and information as ascertained by them, with supporting evidence and documentation as appropriate, and stating their conclusions. The Consultative Committee shall report fully to all Members of the South Pacific Forum, giving its decision as to whether the Party complained of is in breach of its obligations under this Treaty.
9. If the Consultative Committee has decided that the Party complained of is in breach of its obligations under this Treaty, or that the above provisions have not been complied with, or at any time at the request of either the complainant or complained of Party, the Parties shall meet promptly at a meeting of the South Pacific Forum.

APPENDIX 5

Treaty on the Non-Proliferation of Nuclear Weapons

Signed at London, Moscow and Washington on 1 July, 1968
Entered into force on 5 March, 1970
Depositaries: UK, US and Soviet Governments

The States concluding this Treaty hereafter referred to as the "Parties to the Treaty".

Considering the devastation that would be visited upon all mankind by a nuclear war and the consequent need to make every effort to avert the danger of such a war and to take measures to safeguard the security of peoples.

Believing that the proliferation of nuclear weapons would seriously enhance the danger of nuclear war.

In conformity with resolutions of the United Nations General Assembly calling for the conclusion of an agreement on the prevention of wider dissemination of nuclear weapons.

Undertakirg to co-operate in facilitating the application of International Atomic Energy Agency safeguards on peaceful nuclear activities.

Expressing their support for research, development and other efforts to further the application, within the framework of the International Atomic Energy Agency safeguards system of the principle of safeguarding effectively the flow of source and special fissionable materials by use of instruments and other techniques at certain strategic points.

Affirming the principle that the benefits of peaceful applications of nuclear technology, including any technological by-product which may be derived by nuclear-weapon States from the development of nuclear explosive devices, should be available for peaceful purposes to all Parties to the Treaty, whether nuclear-weapon or non-nuclear-weapon States.

Convinced that, in furtherance of this principle, all Parties to the Treaty are entitled to participate in the fullest possible exchange of scientific information for and to contribute alone or in co-operation with other States to the further development of the applications of atomic energy for peaceful purposes.

Declaring their intention to achieve at the earliest possible date the cessation of the nuclear arms race and to undertake effective measures in the direction of nuclear disarmament.

Urging the co-operation of all States in the attainment of this objective.

Recalling the determination expressed by the Parties to the 1963 Treaty banning nuclear weapon tests in the atmosphere, in Outer Space and under water in its Preamble to seek to achieve the discontinuance of all test explosions of nuclear weapons for all times and to continue negotiations to this end.

Desiring to further the easing of international tension and the strengthening of trust between States in order to facilitate the cessation of the manufacture of nuclear weapons, the liquidation of all their existing stockpiles and the elimination from national arsenals of nuclear weapons and the means of their delivery pursuant to a Treaty on general and complete disarmament under strict and effective international control.

Recalling that, in accordance with the Charter of the United Nations, States must refrain in their international relations from the threat or use of force against the territorial integrity or political independence of any State, or in any other manner inconsistent with the Purposes of the United Nations, and that the establishment and maintenance of international peace and security are to be promoted with the least diversion for armaments of the world's human and economic resources.

Have agreed as follows:

Article I

Each nuclear-weapon State Party to the Treaty undertakes not to transfer to any recipient whatsoever nuclear weapons or other nuclear explosive devices or control over such weapons or explosive devices directly, or indirectly and not in any way to assist, encourage, or induce any non-nuclear-weapon State to manufacture or otherwise acquire nuclear weapons or other nuclear explosive devices, or control over such weapons or explosive devices.

Article II

Each non-nuclear-weapon State Party to the Treaty undertakes not to receive the transfer from any transferor whatsoever of nuclear weapons or other nuclear explosive devices or of control over such weapons or explosive devices directly or indirectly; not to manufacture or otherwise acquire nuclear weapons or other nuclear explosive devices and not to seek or receive any assistance in the manufacture of nuclear weapons or other nuclear explosive devices.

Article III

1. Each non-nuclear-weapon State Party to the Treaty undertakes to accept safeguards, as set forth in an agreement to be negotiated and concluded with the International Atomic Energy Agency in accordance with the Statute of the International Atomic Energy Agency and the Agency's safeguards system for the exclusive purpose of verification of the fulfillment of its obligations assumed under this Treaty with a view to preventing diversion of nuclear energy from peaceful uses to nuclear weapons or other nuclear explosive devices. Procedures for the safeguards required by this Article shall be followed with respect to source or special fissionable material whether it is being produced, processed or used in any principal nuclear facility or is outside any such facility. The safeguards required by this Article shall be applied on all sources or special fissionable material in all peaceful nuclear activities within the territory of such State, under its jurisdiction, or carried out under its control anywhere.
2. Each State Party to the Treaty undertakes not to provide: (a) source or special fissionable material, or (b) equipment or material especially designed or prepared for the processing, use or production of special fissionable material to any non-nuclear-weapon State for peaceful purposes, unless the source or special fissionable material shall be subject to the safeguards required by this article.

3. The safeguards required by this article shall be implemented in a manner designed to comply with Article IV of this Treaty and to avoid hampering the economic or technological development of the Parties or international co-operation in the Held of peaceful nuclear activities, including the international exchange of nuclear material and equipment for the processing use or production of nuclear material for peaceful purposes in accordance with the provisions of this article and the principle of safeguarding set forth in the Preamble of the Treaty.
4. Non-nuclear-weapon States Party to the Treaty shall conclude agreements with the International Atomic Energy Agency to meet the requirements of this article either individually or together with other States in accordance with the Statute of the International Atomic Energy Agency. Negotiation of such agreements shall commence within 180 days from the original entry into force of this Treaty. For States depositing their instruments of ratification or accession after the 180 days period, negotiation of such agreements shall commence not later than the date of such deposit. Such agreements shall enter into force not later than eighteen months after the date of initiation of negotiations.

Article IV

1. Nothing in this Treaty shall be interpreted as affecting the inalienable right of all the Parties to the Treaty to develop research, production and use of nuclear energy for peaceful purposes without discrimination and in conformity with Articles I and II of this Treaty.
2. All the Parties to the Treaty undertake to facilitate and have the right to participate in the fullest possible exchange of equipment materials and scientific and technological information for the peaceful uses of nuclear energy. Parties to the Treaty in a position to do so shall also co-operate in contributing alone or together with other States or international organizations to the further development of the applications of nuclear energy for peaceful purposes, especially in the territories of non-nuclear-weapon States

Party to the Treaty, with due consideration for the needs of the developing areas of the world.

Article V

Each Party to the Treaty undertakes to take appropriate measures to ensure that, in accordance with this Treaty under appropriate international observation and through appropriate international procedures, potential benefits from any peaceful applications of nuclear explosions will be made available to non-nuclear-weapon States Party to the Treaty on a non-discriminatory basis and that the charge to such Parties for the explosive devices used will be as low as possible and exclude any charge for research and development. Non-nuclear-weapon States Party to the Treaty shall be able to obtain such benefits, pursuant to a special international agreement or agreements, through an appropriate international body with adequate representation of non-nuclear-weapon States. Negotiations on this subject shall commence as soon as possible after the Treaty enters into force. Non-nuclear-weapon States Party to the Treaty so desiring may also obtain such benefits pursuant to bilateral agreements.

Article VI

Each of the Parties to the Treaty undertakes to pursue negotiations in good faith on effective measures relating to cessation of the nuclear arms race at an early date and to nuclear disarmament, and on a treaty on general and complete disarmament under strict and effective international control.

Article VII

Nothing in this Treaty affects the right of any group of States to conclude regional treaties in order to assure the total absence of nuclear weapons in their respective territories.

Article VIII

1. Any Party to the Treaty may propose amendments to this Treaty. The text of any proposed amendment shall be

submitted to the Depositary Governments which shall circulate it to all Parties to the Treaty. There upon, if requested to do so by one-third or more of the Parties to the Treaty, the Depositary Governments shall convene a conference to which they shall invite all the Parties to the Treaty, to consider such an amendment.

2. Any amendment to this Treaty must be approved by a majority of the votes of all the Parties to the Treaty, including the votes of all nuclear-weapon States Party to the Treaty and all other Parties which, on the date the amendment is circulated, are members of the Board of Governors of the International Atomic Energy Agency. The amendment shall enter into force for each Party that deposits its instrument of ratification of the amendment upon the deposit of such instruments of ratification by a majority of all the Parties, including the instruments of ratification of all nuclear-weapon States Party to the Treaty and all other Parties which, on the date the amendment is circulated are members of the Board of Governors of the International Atomic Energy Agency. Thereafter, it shall enter into force for any other Party upon the deposit of its instrument of ratification of the amendment.
3. Five years after the entry into force of this Treaty, a conference of Parties to the Treaty shall be held in Geneva, Switzerland, in order to review the operation of this Treaty with a view to assuring that the purposes of the Preamble and the provisions of the Treaty are being realized. At intervals of five years thereafter, a majority of the Parties to the Treaty may obtain by submitting a proposal to this effect to the Depositary Governments, the convening of further conferences with the same objective of reviewing the operation of the Treaty.

Article IX

1. This Treaty shall be open to all States for signature. Any State which does not sign the Treaty before its entry into force in accordance with paragraph 3 of this article may accede to it at any time.

2. This Treaty shall be subject to ratification by signatory States. Instruments of ratification and instruments of accession shall be deposited with the Governments of the United Kingdom of Great Britain and Northern Ireland, the Union of Soviet Socialist Republics and the United States of America, which is hereby designated the Depositary Governments.
3. This Treaty shall enter into force after its ratification by the States, the Governments of which are designated Depositaries of the Treaty and forty other States signatory to this Treaty and the deposit of their instruments of ratification. For the purposes of this Treaty, a nuclear-weapon State is one which has manufactured and exploded a nuclear weapon or other nuclear explosive devices prior to 1 January, 1967.
4. For States whose instruments of ratification or accession are deposited subsequent to the entry into force of this Treaty, it shall enter into force on the date of the deposit of their instruments of ratification or accession.
5. The Depositary Governments shall promptly inform all signatory and acceding States of the date of each signature, the date of deposit of each instrument of ratification or of accession, the date of the entry into force of this Treaty and the date of receipt of any request for convening a conference or other notices.
6. This Treaty shall be registered by the Depositary Governments pursuant to Article 102 of the Charter of the United Nations.

Article X

1. Each Party shall in exercising its national sovereignty have the right to withdraw from the Treaty if it decides that extraordinary events, related to the subject matter of this Treaty, have jeopardized the supreme interests of its country. It shall give notice of such withdrawal to all other Parties to the Treaty and to the United Nations Security Council three months in advance. Such notice shall include a statement of the extraordinary events it regards as having jeopardized its supreme interests.

2. Twenty five years after the entry into force of the Treaty in conference shall be convened to decide either the Treaty shall continue in force indefinitely, or shall be extended for an additional fixed period or periods. This decision shall be taken by a majority of the Parties to the Treaty.

Article XI

This Treaty, the English, Russian, French, Spanish and Chinese texts of which are equally authentic, shall be deposited in the archives of the Depositary Governments. Duly certified copies of this Treaty shall be transmitted by the Depositary Governments to the Government of the signatory and acceding States.

Source: *UN Treaty Series*, Vol. 729 onwards (United Nations: New York, 1971–2005).

APPENDIX 6

Treaty on the Prohibition of the Emplacement of Nuclear Weapons and other Weapons of Mass Destruction on the Sea-bed and the Ocean Floor and in the subsoil thereof

Signed at London, Moscow and Washington on II February 1971
Entered into force on 1st May 1972

Depositaries: UK, US and Soviet Governments

The States Parties to this Treaty, Recognizing the common interest of mankind in the progress of the exploration and use of the Sea-bed and the ocean floor for peaceful purposes.

Considering that the prevention of a nuclear arms race on the Sea-Bed and the ocean floor serves the interests of maintaining world peace, reduces international tensions and strengthens friendly relations among States.

Convinced that this Treaty constitutes a step towards the exclusion of the Sea-Bed, the ocean floor and the sub-soil thereof from the arms race.

Convinced that this Treaty constitutes a step towards a treaty on general and complete disarmament under strict and effective international control, and determined to continue negotiations to this end.

Convinced that this Treaty will further the purposes and principles of the Charter of the United Nations, in a manner consistent with the principles of international law and without infringing the freedoms of the high seas.

Have agreed as follows:

Article I

1. The States Parties to this Treaty undertake not to emplant or emplace on the Sea-bed and the ocean floor and in the

subsoil thereof beyond the outer limit of a Sea-bed zone, as defined in Article 11, any nuclear weapon or any other types of weapons of mass destruction as well as structures, launching installations or any other facility specifically designed for storing, testing or using such weapons.

2. The undertakings of paragraph 1 of this article shall also apply to the Sea-bed zone referred to in the same paragraph, except that within such Sea-bed zone, they shall not apply either to the coastal State or to the Sea-bed beneath its territorial waters.
3. The States Parties to this Treaty undertake not to assist, encourage or induce any State to carry out activities referred to in paragraph 1 of this article and not to participate in any other way in such actions.

Article II

For the purpose of this Treaty, the outer limit of the Sea-bed zone referred to in Article I shall be coterminous with the twelve miles outer limit of the zone referred to in Part II of the Convention on the Territorial Sea and the Contiguous Zone, signed at Geneva on April 29, 1958, and shall be measured in accordance with the provisions of Part 1, Section II, of that Convention and in accordance with international law.

Article III

1. In order to promote the objectives, of and insure compliance with the provisions of this Treaty, each State Party to the Treaty shall have the right to verify through observation the activities of other State Parties to the Treaty on the Sea-bed and the ocean floor and in the sub-soil thereof beyond the zone referred to in Article I, provided that observation does not interfere with such activities.
2. If after such observation reasonable doubts remain concerning the fulfillment of the obligations assumed under the Treaty, the State Party having such doubts and the State Party that is responsible for the activities giving

rise to the doubts shall consult with a view to removing the doubts. If the doubts persist, the State Party having such doubts shall notify the other States Parties, and the Parties concerned shall co-operate on such further procedures for verification as may be agreed, including appropriate inspection of objects, structures, installations or other facilities that reasonably may be expected to be of a kind described in Article I. Those Parties in the region of the activities, including any coastal State, and any other Party so requesting, shall be entitled to participate in such consultation and co-operation. After completion of the further procedures for verification, an appropriate report shall be circulated to other Parties by the Party that initiated such procedures.

3. If the State responsible for the activities giving rise to the reasonable doubts is not identifiable by observation of the object, structure, installation or other facilities, the State Party having such doubts shall notify and make appropriate inquiries of States Parties in the region of the activities and of any other State Party. If it is ascertained through these inquiries that a particular State Party is responsible for the activities, that the State Party shall consult and co-operate with other Parties as provided in paragraph 2 of this article. If the identity of the State responsible for the activities cannot be ascertained through these inquiries, then further verification procedures, including inspection, may be undertaken by the inquiring State Party, which shall invite the participation of the Parties in the region of the activities, including any coastal State, and of any other Party desiring to co-operate.

4. If consultation and co-operation pursuant to paragraphs 2 and 3 of this article have not removed the doubts concerning the activities and there remains a serious question concerning fulfillments of the obligations assumed under this Treaty, a State Party may, in accordance with the provisions of the Charter of the United Nations, refer the matter to the Security Council, which may take action in accordance with the Charter.

5. Verification pursuant to this article may be undertaken by any State Party using its own means, or with the full or partial assistance of any other State Party, or through appropriate international procedures within the framework of the United Nations and in accordance with its Charter.
6. Verification activities pursuant to this Treaty shall not interfere with activities of other States Parties and shall be conducted with due regard for rights recognized under international law, including the freedoms of the high seas and the rights of coastal States with respect to the exploration and exploitation of their continental shelves.

Article IV

Nothing in this Treaty shall be interpreted as supporting or prejudicing the position of any State Party with respect to existing international conventions, including the 1958 Convention on the Territorial Sea and the Contiguous Zone, or with respect to fights or claims which such State Party may assert, or with respect to recognition or non-recognition of rights or claims asserted by any other State, related to water of its coasts, including, *inter alia*, territorial seas and contiguous zones, or to the Sea-bed and the ocean floor, including continental shelves.

Article V

The Parties to this Treaty undertake to continue negotiations in goodfaith concerning further measures in the field of disarmament for the prevention of an arms race on the Sea-bed, the ocean floor and the subsoil thereof.

Article VI

Any State Party may propose amendments to this Treaty. Amendments shall enter into force for each State Party accepting the amendments upon their acceptance by a majority of the States Parties to the Treaty and, thereafter, for each remaining State party on the date of acceptance by II.

Article VII

Five years after the entry into force of this Treaty, a conference of Parties to the Treaty Shall be held at Geneva, Switzerland, in order to review the operation of this Treaty with a view to assuring that the purposes of the preamble and the provisions of the Treaty are being realized such review shall take into account any relevant technological development. The review conference shall determine, in accordance with the views of a majority of those Parties attending, whether and when an additional review conference shall be convened.

Article VIII

Each State Party to this Treaty shall in exercising its national sovereignty have the right to withdraw from this Treaty if it decides that extraordinary events related to the subject matter of this Treaty have jeopardized the supreme interests of its country. It shall give notice of such withdrawal to all other States Parties to the Treaty and to the United Nations Security Council three months in advance. Such notice shall include a statement of the extraordinary events it considers to have jeopardized its supreme interests.

Article IX

The provisions of this Treaty shall in no way affect the obligations assumed by States Parties to the Treaty under international instruments establishing zones free from nuclear weapons.

Article X

1. This Treaty shall be open for signature to all States. Any State which does not sign the Treaty before its entry into force in accordance with paragraph 3 of this article may accede to it at any time.
2. This Treaty shall be subject to ratification by signatory States. Instruments of ratification and of accession shall be deposited with the Governments of the United States of America, the United Kingdom of Great Britain,

Northern Ireland and the Union of Soviet Socialist Republics, which is hereby, designated the Depositary Governments.

3. This Treaty shall enter into force after her deposit of instruments of ratification by twenty two Governments, including the Governments designated as Depositary Governments of this Treaty.
4. For States whose instruments of ratification or accession are deposited after the entry into force of this Treaty, it shall enter into force on the date of the deposit of their instruments of ratification or accession.
5. The Depositary Governments shall promptly inform the Governments of all signatory and acceding States of the date of each signature, of the date of deposit of each instrument of ratification or of accession, of the date of the entry into force of this Treaty, and of the receipt of other notices.
6. This Treaty shall be registered by the Depositary Governments pursuant to Article 102 of the Charter of the United Nations.

Article XI

This Treaty, the English, Russian, French, Spanish and Chinese texts of which are equally authentic, shall be deposited in the archives of the Depositary Governments. Duly certified copies of this Treaty shall be transmitted by the Depositary Governments to the Governments of the States signatory and acceding thereto.

Source: *UN Treaty Series*, Vol. 729 onwards (United Nations: New York, 1971-2005).

APPENDIX 7

Nuclear Infrastructures of the United States

Location, Organization and Activity

Antigua

Located within the Latin American Nuclear-Free-Zone, Antigua plays a key role in strategic submarine missile testing programmes.

Naval Facility: former processing station for SOSUS closed in 1982-1984, base to be retained for other purposes o AN/FPQ-14 tracking radar doubles as satellite tracking system, telemetry collection station, command and control, timing and weather systems supporting missile testing from ESMC o Missile Impact Location System (MILS) underwater hydrophone target array 150 miles northeast of the island also supports missile tests from ESMC o satellite communications link to Cape Canaveral, FL.

Australia

Two major strategic facilities are located in Australia, one of two main DSP satellite early warning ground stations at Nurrungar, and a Naval communications facility at North West Cape. Most of the other facilities are related to intelligence collection, space tracking and technology and nuclear test detection. There are also a number of additional minor technical facilities (Adelaide, Amberley, Hobart, Mundaring) involved in seismic research.

Alice Springs	Det 421, AFTAC: nuclear test detection station
Charters Towers	Seismograph detection station operated by the University of Queensland for DARPA
Cocos Islands	Periodic deployment base for nuclear-capable P-3s™

Darwin	Port and airfield used by U.S. forces • B-52 bombers on "Busy Boomerang" and "Glad Customer" operations conduct ocean surveillance from the Darwin airfield • nuclear-capable ships call at the port
Exmouth, North West Cape	Naval Communications Station Harold E. Holt: one of two primary VLF communications stations broadcasting to submarines, operates on 2 million watts power, also used for radio navigation purposes • HF receiver and transmitter for communications with naval forces • FLTSATCOM and DSCS AN/MSC-61 satellite communications station
Lear mouth	AF Solar Observing Optical Network (SOON) observatory • periodic staging base for nuclear-capable P-3s
Narrogin	Seismic detection station operated by Australian Bureau of Mineral Resources and funded by DARPA
Nurrungar	Woomera Air Station: "Joint Defense Space Communications Station," DSP satellite early warning " mission readout station," one of two main stations worldwide (the other is at Buckley ANGB, CO) linked to NORAD via satellite and submarine cable
Pine Gap (Alice Springs)	"Joint Defense Space Research Facility:" main ground station receiving data from reconnaissance and signals intelligence collection satellites
Woodside, Gippsland	OMEGA radio navigation station, operated by the Australian Department of Transportation

Argentina

An OMEGA radio navigation station, operated by the Argentine Navy, is located at Trelew.

Bahamas

Located with the Latin American Nuclear-Free-Zone, the Bahamas plays a key role in submarine training, testing and certification, as well as supporting strategic missile testing from ESMC.

Andros Island	Atlantic Under seas Test and Evaluation Center (ALTEC): deep water range for submarine systems under sea R&D, only permanent underwater noise measuring facility on the east coast of the US, used for Trident submarine certification trials, also key station in the missile submarine security and silencing programmes and sonar testing, ASKOC and SUBROO testing, instrumentation includes a hydrophone acoustic array fixed to a single cable which is buoyed 50 feets below the surface and anchored to the ocean floor, Weapons Range is a 5 by IS mile tracking range used for ASW training and certification against mobile targets
Bassett Cove, GBI	Timing transponder supporting missile testing from ESMC
Carter Cay, GBI	Timing transponder supporting missile testing from ESMC
Deep Creek, Andros Island	Down-range Site 6 of AUTEC
Eleuthera	Naval Facility: processing station for SOSUS, also serves as timing transponder supporting missile testing from ESMC
Fresh Creek, Andros Island	Down-range Site 1 of AUTEC, command and control station
Gibson Cay, Andros Island	Down-range Site 3 of AUTEC with converted Nike Hercules tracking radar
Golding Cay, Andros Island	Down-range Site 4 of AUTEC
Grand Bahama Island (GBI)	Tracking radar, telemetry collection station, command and control station, timing and

	weather systems supporting missile testing from ESMC • Missile Tracking Instrumentation System supporting missile tests from ESMC
Great Stirrup Cay	Timing transponder supporting missile testing from ESMC
High Point Cay, Andros Island	Down-range Site 7 of AUTEC
Marsh Harbour, Great Abaco Island	Timing transponder supporting missile testing from ESMC
Salvador Point, Andros Island	Down-range Site 2 of AUTEC with converted Nike Hercules tracking radar
Treasure Cay, Great Abaco Island	Timing transponder supporting missile testing from ESMC
West End, GBI	Timing transponder supporting missile testing from ESMC

Barbados

The Naval Facility, a former processing station for SOSUS, was closed in 1979.

New Zealand

Black Birch Astronomic Observatory (Blenheim) is a southern hemisphere observatory operated by the US Naval Observatory.

Panama

Located within the Latin American Nuclear-Free-Zone. Panama houses a number of strategic communications and electronics facilities including a Mystic Star and airborne command post receiver at Howard AFB.

Albrook AFS	Global Command and Control System transmitter (receiver at Howard AFB)
Fort Kobbe	(AN/GSC-3!) satellite terminal providing presidential communications support to and from Panama
Fort Randolph	Operating Location BN (OL-BN), AFTAC: nuclear test detection station[118]

Howard AFB	NEACP ground entry point serving the Mystic Star network • Global Command and Control System receiver • 1035th TOS. AFTAC: nuclear test detection station
Semaphore Hill	Long-range radar reporting to the JSS
Summit	Naval Radio Transmitter Facility: I IF communications to naval forces

Puerto Rico

Puerto Rico is a territory of the US located within the Latin American Nuclear-Free-Zone. Authorization has been given, nonetheless, for deployment of 32 nuclear depth bombs to Roosevelt Roads "for wartime ASW operations." In addition, 13 nuclear-related facilities are maintained on the island, including two Mystic Star communications stations. Roosevelt Roads has also been designated as an alternate command center for missile submarines in the Atlantic if continental U.S. bases are destroyed.

Aguada	Naval Radio Facility: LF transmitter kept in non-operating caretaker status since 1974, to be activated to replace closed communications transmitter at Balboa, Panama[129]
Fort Allen, Juana Diaz	Mystic Star transmitter: part of the Presidential and VIP communications network[130]
Cape San Juan Isabella	Future Coast Guard differential Omega radio navigation remote monitoring facility
Muniz ANGB, San Juan IAP	Naval Radio Transmitting Facility: HF and LF transmitters operated under contract, primary links from Puerto Rico to naval forces, Brandywine, MD, and Macdill AFB, FL
Pico del Este	156th Tactical Fighter Group (PRANG): nuclear-capable A-7D
Point Borinquen	Radar and communications site supporting AFWTK, Roosevelt Roads, also serves as JSS radar

Punta Salinas	AF Solar Optical Observing Network (SOON) observatory located at the former SAC Ramey AFB
Punta Tuna	140th Aircraft Control and Warning Squadron (PRANG): air defense radar manned 24-hours
Punta Tuna	Future Coast Guard differential Omega radio navigation facility, coverage in Eastern Caribbean only
Roosevelt Roads	Naval Station: HQ, US Naval Forces Caribbean: command of naval forces in the Caribbean, including nuclear command and control function, contingency headquarters for ballistic missile submarine operations • HQ, Fleet Air Caribbean: command of aircraft, aircraft carrier and ASW operations in the Caribbean • former HQ for Antilles Defense Command, a sub-unified command of Atlantic Command, now replaced by US Forces Caribbean, Key West, FL • Atlantic Fleet Weapons Training Facility (AFWTF): training range consisting of 200,000 square miles of sea areas supporting ship and submarine acceptance trials, ASW operations and test. firings and large scale naval maneuvers • Advanced Underwater Weapons Branch: stand-by nuclear warhead storage site for 32 nuclear depth bombs to be deployed in wartime • periodic nuclear-capable P-3 staging base
Salinas	Mystic Star Control Console and Receiver Facility: part of the Presidential and VIP communications network[131]
Sebana Seca	Naval Radio Receiving Facility: primary receiver for fleet communications entering Puerto Rico and link from Davidsonville, MD and MacDill AFB, FL
Vieques Island	"Inner range" of AFWTF, air-to-ground training range used for aircraft training, "Bullseye Target Two" is designated for practice nuclear bombing

The Former Soviet Union

Cuba

No Soviet nuclear warheads are deployed in Cuba, although the Soviets have developed a number of facilities which are part of the nuclear infrastructure. Two airfields. San Antonio de Los Banos and lose Marti airport, support regular Bear-D reconnaissance and nuclear-capable Bear-F ASW visits to Cuba. The pear-F planes began to operate from Cuba for the first time in 1983. Cienfuegos and Havana are used by Soviet naval forces. Havana and Lourdes house major satellite ground stations and Soviet intelligence gathering facilities. The Lourdes facility probably monitors US missile testing from Cape Canaveral Florida.

France

French Polynesia

Faaa NAS, Tahiti	Escadrille de Servitude 12 : 8 Neptune and Gardian aircraft provide maritime patrol and surveillance services at the Pacific Test Center
Fangataufa	Location of former atmospheric test site, being considered as a second site for possible underground nuclear testing, reported under construction due to sinking of Mururoa Atoll
Mao (Air Base 185)	Section Alouette du Pacifique: 4 Alouette helicopters providing support to the Pacific Test Center
Mururoa Atoll	Centre d'Experimentation du Pacifique (CEP): former atmospheric and current underground nuclear testing at the Pacific Test Center • Escadrille de Servitude 27: 5 Super Frelon helicopters providing airlift support
Papeete, Tahiti (Air Base)	LF radio transmitter operated by the Marine Nationale • Direction Technique des Construction Navales: dockyards for

	overhauling ships assigned to the Pacific Test Center • Escadron de Transport d'Outre-Mer 82 (ETOM 82): airlift supporting nuclear testing

New Caledonia

The Marine National operates an LF transmitter on Noumea-La Tontouta.

Portugal

France operates a number of facilities in the Azores which support missile testing from Landes. A missile tracking station is operated at Flores and Santa Maria airfield supports AMOR aircraft used in tracking and telemetry collection in connection with missile testing.

La Reunion

The Port des Galets Naval base is occasionally visited by French aircraft carriers when deployed to the Indian Ocean. France also operates the Omega Station at Mafate.

Senegal

The Forces Armies Francoises operates an LF radio transmitter at Dakar.

Source: William Arkin and Richard Field house, *Nuclear Battlefield: Global Links in the Arms Race* (Cambridge, M.A., Ballinger, 1985) and SIPRI Year Book 2005.

Bibliography

Primary Sources

Eicht Nations Disarmament Conference Official Records (ENDCOR) 1965, A. 152, 192 and 193.

ENDCOR, Document/240, "Union of Soviet Socialist Republics, Draft Treaty on the Prohibition of the use for Military Purposes of the Sea-bed and ocean floor and the sub-soil There of ", 18 March, 1969.

ENDCOR, PV. 423, 29 July, 1969.

OPANAL, Tenth General Conference Report, S/Information 374, 29 April, 1987.

South Pacific Nuclear-Free-Zone, France, Facts and Figures (Wellington: Embassy of France, June, 1985), pp. 13-16.

UN Comprehensive Study on Nuclear Weapons (New York: UN Press, 1981).

UN Department for Disarmament Affairs (UNDDA), Study on Deterrence (New York: UN Press, 1987).

UN Department of Disarmament Affairs, Report of the Secretary General, The Naval Arms Race (New York: UN, 1986).

United National Disarmament Commission, Official Record (UNDCOR), Supplement No. 18, December 1968.

——, Supplement, January to December 1956.

Document DC/83, Annex 5 (DC/SC.1/41), pp. 41 and 178.

——, Israeli Nuclear Armaments, Document A/36/431, 36th Session, September 18, 1981.

——, 13th Session, Annexes, Agenda item 60, Document A/C.1/ L 219.

——, Fifteenth Session, Annexes, Agenda Items 67, 68, 69 and 73, Document A/4680, Para 17.

United Nations General Assembly Official Records, Eighth Session, 470th Plenary Meeting, 8 December, 1953.

——, 29th Session, Annex, Agenda item 107, Document A/9706.

——, Thirty-first Session, Supplement No.27, A/31/27/Vol. 11, pp. 276-79.

——, Thirty-ninth Session, study on the Question of Antarctica, A/39/583 (Part I), 31 October, 1984.

UN Institute for Disarmament Research (UNIDIR), Satellite Warfare. A Challenge for the International Community (New York: UN, 1987).

United Nations Special Report of the Conference of the Committee on Disarmament (UNSRCCD), Comprehensive study on the Question of Nuclear – Weapon-Free-Zone in all its aspects (New York, UN, 1976).

——, The United Nations and Disarmament, 1945–1985 (New York: UN, 1985).

UN Treaty Series, Vol. 402, No. 6778, p. 72.

US Congress, Congressional Budget Office, Counterforce Issues for the US strategic Nuclear Forces (Washington D.C., GPO, 1978).

——, Planning US General Purpose Forces: The Theatre Nuclear Forces, January 1977, pp. 176-78.

US Department of Defense, Appropriations for 1976 sub-committee on Appropriations (Hearings), House of Representatives, 94th Congress (Washington: US Government Printing office, 1975).

United States Department of State, Documents on Disarmament, Vol. II, 1957-59 (Washington D.C., US Government Printing Office, 1961).

US Senate, Hearings of the Committee on Foreign Relations, 96th Congress, First Session, pp. 1611-1612.

Secondary Sources

Books

Ahmed, A.M., *The Neutrals and Test Ban Negotiations* (New York, 1967).

Arkin, William and Field House, *Nuclear Battlefields: Global Links in the Arms Race* (Cambridge, M.A., Ballinger, 1985).

Asia Yearbook 1985, *South Pacific* (Hong Kong: Far Eastern Economic Review, 1985).

Bader, William, *The United States and the Spread of Nuclear Weapons* (New York: Pegasus, 1968).

Ball, Desmond, *A Suitable Piece of Real Estates: American Installations in Australia* (Sydney: Wale and Iron Monger, 1980), pp. 88-98.

——, (ed.), *The ANZUS Connection* (Sydney: George Allen and Unwin, 1985).

Barnaby, Frank, ed., *Preventing the Spread of Nuclear Weapons* (London: Souvenir Press, 1969).

Beation, Leonard, Must the Bomb Spread: (Harmon's Worth, England: Penguin Books, 1966).

——, and John Maddox, *the Spread of Nuclear Weapons* (London: Chatto and Windus, 1962).

Beck, Peter, *The International Politics of Antarctica* (London: 1980).

Bellany, Ian and Blacker, Coit, eds., *The Nuclear Non-Proliferation Treaty* (London: Frank Cass, 1985).

Birla Institute of Scientific Research, *Economic Research Division, India and the Atom* (New Delhi: Allied Publishers Pvt. Ltd., 1982).

Cultural Department of Embassy of Chile to Singapore, *Chile and the Pacific* (Singapore: Inter-office Services, 1986).

Denborough, Michael, *Australia and Nuclear War* (Sydney: Croom Helm, 1983) pp. 38-54.

Dennis, Jack, ed., *The Nuclear Almanac, Confronting the Atom in War and Peace* (Mass. Addison Wesley Publishing Company, 1984).

Dibb, Paul, "World Political and Strategic Trends: Their Relevance to Australia", in Paul Dibb, ed., Australia's External Relations in the 1980s, *The Interaction of Economic, Political and Strategic Factors* (New York: St. Martin's Press, 1983), pp. 28-43.

Donnelly, Warren, *Pakistan and Nuclear Weapons* (Washington: Congressional Service Publication, 1987).

Dunn, Lewis, *Controlling the Bomb: Nuclear Proliferation in the 1980s* (New Haven, Conn.: Yale Univ. Press, 1982).

——, and Herman Kahn, Trends in Nuclear Proliferation 1975-1995: Projections, *Problems and Policy Options* (New York: Hudson Institute, 1976).

Enthovan, Alain and Smith, Wayne, *How Much is Enough? Shaping the Defense Programme*, 1961-1969 (New York: Harper and Row, 1971).

Epstein, William, *The Last Chance: Nuclear Proliferation and Arms Control* (New York, The Free Press, 1976).

Gelber, Harry, *Nuclear Weapons and Chinese Policy, Adelphi Papers*, No. 99 (London: IISS, 1973).

Gladstone, S., *The Effects of Nuclear Weapons* (Washington: Government Printing Office, 1977).

Goldblat, Jozef, *Arms Control Agreements* (New York: Praeger, 1982).

——, Arms Control Agreements: A Handbook (London: Taylor and Francis, 1983).

Gorbachev, Mikhil, *For a Nuclear Free World* (Moscow: Novosti Press, 1987).

Green Peace International, *The Future of the Antarctica: Background for a Second UN* Debate (Lawes: Green Peace, 1984).

Hang, Rane, ed., *Verification of Arms Control Agreements: The Role of Third Countries* (Geneva: Programme for Strategic and International Security Studies, 1985).

Hastings, Max and Jenkins, Simon, *Battle for the Falklands* (London: Pan Books, 1983).

Hayes, Pater, *American Lake, Nuclear Peril in the Pacific* (New York: Penguin, 1986).

Hewlett, Richard and Duncan Francis, *Nuclear Navy* (Chicago: University of Chicago Press, 1974).

Hurewit, C.J., ed., *Soviet American Rivalry in the Middle East* (New York: Academy of Political Science, 1969).

Jabber, Fuad, *Israèl and Nuclear Weapons: Present Option and Future Strategies* (London: Chatto and Windus, 1971).

Jasani, Bhupendra and Sakata, Toshibomi, eds., *Satellites for Arms Control and Crisis Monitoring* (Oxford: Oxford University Press, 1987).

Kapur, Ashok, *India's Nuclear Option: Atomic Diplomacy and Decision Making* (New Delhi: Praeger, 1976).

Karas, Thomas, *The New High Grounds: Systems and Weapons of Space – Age War* (New York: Simon and Schuster, 1983).

Keohane, Robert and Nye, Joseph, *Power and Interdependence: World Politics in Transition* (Boston: MIT Press, 1977).

Kramish, Arnold, *The Peaceful Atom in Foreign Policy* (New York: Harper and Row, 1963).

Krass, Allan, *Verification: How Much is Enough?* (London: SIPRI, 1985).

Lodgaard, Sverre and Thee, Marek, eds., *Nuclear Disengagement in Europe* (London: Taylor and Francis, 1983).

Madero, Castro, Carlos, "Argentina's Nuclear Energy Programme", *Nuclear Europe* (Bucks), July–August 1983.

Markey and Waller, *Nuclear Peril and Proliferation* (Cambridge: Ballinger Publishers, 1982).

Narks, Anne, ed., *NPT: Paradoxes and Problems* (Washington: The arms control association and the Carnegie endowment for international peace, 1975).

Narwah, Onker and Ann Schulx, eds., *Nuclear Proliferation and the Near Nuclear Countries* (Cambridge, Mass., Ballinger, 1975).

McKnight, Allan, *Atomic Safeguards: A Study in International Verification* (New York: UN International Training and Research, 1971), pp. 1-8.

Moore, John, ed., *Jane's Fighting Ships*, 1981-82 (New York: Collier Books, 1976).

Myer, Stephen, *The Dynamics of Nuclear Proliferation* (London: The University of Chicago Press, 1984).

Payne, Keith, *Laser Weapons in Space Policy and Doctrine* (Boulder: West View Press, 1983).

Pone Man, Daniel, *Nuclear Power in the Developing World* (London: George Allen and Unwin, 1982).

Potter, William, *Nuclear Power and Non-proliferation: An Interdisciplinary Perspective* (Oelgeschlager: Gunn and Hain Publishers, 1982).

Poulose, T.T., *United Nations and Nuclear Proliferation* (New Delhi, B.R. Publishing Corporation, 1988).

Prins, Gwyn, *Defended to Death* (New York: Penguin Books, 1983).

Quester, George, *The Politics of Nuclear Proliferation* (Baltimore: The Johns Hopkins University Press, 1973).

Rais, Rasul, *The Indian Ocean and the Super Powers* (London: Croom Helm, 1986).

Reese, R. Trevor, *Australia, New Zealand and the United States, A Survey of International Relations, 1941-1968* (London: Oxford University Press, 1969).

Report of the Independent Commission on Disarmament and Security Issues, common security: A programme for disarmament (London: Pan Books, 1982).

Robles, Garcia Alfonso, *La Denuclearization de la Americalatina* (Mexico: 1966).

Rochlin, Gene, *Plutonium, Power and Politics* (Berkeley, California: University of California, 1979).

Rosecrance, N.R., *The Dispersion of Nuclear Weapons* (New York: Columbia University Press, 1964).

Seaborg, Glennt, *Kennedy, Khrushchev and the Test Ban* (Berkeley: University of California Press, 1981).

Sinha and Subramaniam, R.R., *Nuclear Pakistan* (New Delhi: Vision Books, 1980).

Smith, Alice, *A Peril and a Hope: The Scientists Movement in America 1945-47* (Chicago: University of Chicago Press, 1965).

Smith, Dan, *South Africa's Nuclear Capability* (London: World campaign against military and nuclear collaboration with South Africa, 1988).

Spector, S. Leonard, *The New Nuclear Nations* (New York: Vintage Books, 1985).

Stares, Paul, *Space and National Security* (Washington: the Brookings Institute, 1987).

Stefanick, Tom, *Strategic Antisubmarine Warfare and Naval Strategy* (Toronto: Lexington Books, 1987).

Stockholm International Peace Research Institute (SIPRI) Year Book, 1984, *World Armaments and Disarmament* (London: Taylor and Francis, 1984).

SIPRI Yearbook, *World Armaments and Disarmament* (London: Taylor and Francis, 1984).

Stockholm paper 6, *The Right to Conduct Nuclear Explosions* (Stockholm, SIPRI, 1975).

Subramanian, K., ed., *India and the Nuclear Challenge* (New Delhi: Lancer International 1986).

Szasz, C. Paul, *The Law and Politics of the International Atomic Energy Agency* (Vienna: IAEA, 1970).

Teller, Edward and Brown, Allen, *The Legacy of Hiroshima* (New York: Doubleday, 1962).

Templeton, Malcolm, "Novelty, Gestures and direction in foreign Policy: Thoughts from the Twentieth Foreign Policy School", in Gold, H., ed., *New Directions in New Zealand Foreign Policy* (Auckland: Benton Ross, 1985).

Treverton, Gregory, "Nuclear Weapons in Europe", *Adelphi Papers, No. 168* (London: Institute for International Strategic Studies (IISS 1981).

Voss, Earl, *Nuclear Ambush: The Test Ban Trap* (Chicago: Regenery Company, 1963). Waltz, N. Kenneth, "The Spread of Nuclear

Weapons: More May be Better", in Schear A. James, ed., Nuclear Weapon Proliferation and Nuclear Risk (London: IISS, 1984).
Wholsetter, Albert, *et al.*, *Moving Toward Life in a Armed Crowd* (Los Angeles: Pan Henriotics, 1975).
——, *The Military Potential of Civilian Nuclear Energy* (Chicago: University of Chicago, 1977).

Articles

Arkin, William, "The nuclear arms race at sea", *Neptune Paper* (Washington), Vol. 1, 1987, pp. 1-15.
——, "Tomahawk: Ominous New Deployment", *Bulletin of Atomic Scientists* (BOAS) (Illinois), Vol. 40, No. 4, 1986, pp.16-22.
Arkin, William and Field House, W. Richard, "Focus on the nuclear infrastructure", *BOAS*, June-July 1985, pp. 11-15.
Audgins, Christie, "NPT Review Conference Off to a Smooth Start as Old Issues Predominate", *Nucleonic Week* (New York), September 5, 1985.
Blix, Hans, "Safeguards and Non-Proliferation, The IAEA Efforts to Counteract the Spread of Nuclear Weapons", *IAEA Bulletin* (Ontario, Concord), Vol. 27, No. 2, summer 1985, pp. 3-8.
Cameron, Allen, "The strategic significance of the pacific islands: a new debate begins", *the Third World Quarterly* (London), Vol. 19, No. 3, fall 1975, pp. 1024-28.
Capable, James, "Is there a naval arms race", *International Relations* (London), Vol. 8, No. 5, May 1986, pp. 455-74.
Carasales, C. Julio, "The future of Tlatelolco 20 years after its signature", *Disarmament* (New York), Vol. XI, No. 1, winter 1987/88, pp. 61-73.
Chaturvedi, Sanjay, "India and the Antarctic treaty system: Realities and prospects", *India Quarterly* (New Delhi), Vol. XLII, No. 4, October–December 1986, pp. 351-80.
Christol, Carl, "International liability for damage caused by space objects", *American Journal for International Law* (Ajil) (Washington), Vol. 74, April, 1980, pp. 346-71.
Cockburn, Milton and Amanda, Buckley, " Pacific Treaty Has Us Worried", *Sydney Morning Herald*, 8 August, 1985, p. 1.
Cohen, Alexander, "Cosmos 954 and the international law of satellite accidents", *Ajil*, Vol. 1984, No. 2, fall 1984, pp. 78-91.

"Communique of the South Pacific forum relating to South Pacific nuclear-free zone treaty, 5-6 august 1985", Disarmament, Vol. VIII, No. 3, winter 1985, pp. 169-70.

Dorrance, John, "Coping with the Soviet Pacific Threat", *Pacific Defense Reporter* (Victoria), July 1983, pp. 27-32.

Fry, Greg, "Towards a South Pacific nuclear free zone", *BOAS* (Illinois), June-July 1985, pp. 16-20.

Fry, Gregory, "Regionalism and international politics of the South Pacific", *Pacific Affairs* (Vancouver), Vol. 54, fall 1981, pp. 455-89.

Garthoff, Raymond, "A Sat-Arms Control: Still Possible", *BOAS*, Vol. 40, No. 7, August/September 1984, pp. 30-36.

——, Banning the bomb in outer space", *International Security*, Vol. 5, No. 3, winter.

Hall, Gus, "For a world without weapons", *Political Affairs* (New York), Vol. 65, No. 3, March 1986, pp. 39-40.

Hass, Ernest, "Why collaborate, Issue-linkage and international regimes", *World Politics* (Princeton), Vol. XXXII, 1979/80, pp. 14-28.

Hocking, Brian and Warhurst, John, "Australia and Britain: Drifting Apart?" *The World Today*, December 1983, pp. 244-45.

Holdren, P. John, "Nuclear power and nuclear weapons: The connection is dangerous", *BOAS*, January, 1983, pp. 40-45.

Jackson, Harold, "Victims of the nuclear colonists", *Manchester Guardian Weekly*, 15 July, 1984, pp. 2-12.

Jones, W. Rodney and Hildreth A. Steven, "Star wars: Down to Earth or Gleem in the sky?", *The Washington Quarterly*, Fall 1984, pp. 16-26.

Kessler, Richard, "Argentina may be scaling down heavy water production plans", Nucleonic Week, May 16, 1985, pp. 13-19.

Kincade, H. William, "Challenges to verification: Old and New", *Arms Control* (Washington), Vol. 3, No. 3, December 1982, pp. 14-30.

Kitney, Geoff, "Us gets tough with Australia over nuclear free zone", *National Times* (Sydney), 25 April, 1986, p. 5.

Kozyrev, V. Andrei, "Outer space and universal security", *Disarmament*, Vol. 10, No. 2, summer 1982, pp. 38-49.

Krauss, Melvyn, "The New Zealand Syndrome Spreads", *The New York Times*, February 17, 1985.

Lilienthal, David, "The atomic energy years 1945–1950", *Journals of David E. Lilienthal* (New York), Vol. 2, 1964, pp. 587-90.

Lini, Walter, "Australia and the South Pacific: A Vanuatu Perspective", *Australian Outlook* (Canberra), No. 38, August 1982, pp. 29-31.

Nahathir, "On Antarctica", *Foreign Affairs Malaysia* (Kuala Lumpur), Vol. 16, No. 1, March 1983, pp. 7-8.

Mcdowell, David, "The Treaty of Rarotonga", *Disarmament,* Vol. XI, No. 1, Winter 1987/88, pp. 93-104.

Mediansky, A.F., "Nuclear-Free Security in the South West Pacific", *Australian Outlook,* No. 39, August 1985, pp. 408-09.

Micallef, Joseph, "A Nuclear Bomb for Libya", *BOAS* August-September 1981, p. 14.

Mihajiovic, Miodray, "Disarmament, Non-Nuclear Weapon States and Security Guarantees", *Review of International Affairs* (Belgrade), Vol. 30, No. 692, February 5, 1979, pp. 26-30.

"New Zealander Assails Us Ship Ban Reaction", *The Sun* (Baltimore), February 27, 1985, pp. 4-6.

New Zealand Nuclear free Zone Committee (NZNFZC), "Nuclear Free", *Journal of NZNFZC* (Wellington), March/April, 1985, pp. 16-18.

Ognibene, Peter, "Living with the Bomb: How Safe is Nuclear Pollution?", *Saturday Review* (Boston), June 24, 1978, pp. 8-12.

Paine, Christopher, "On the Beach: The Rapid Deployment Force and the Nuclear Arms Race", *MERIP Report,* Vol. 13, No. 1, January 1983, pp. 3-11.

Paugh, Micheal, "New Zealand – A Nuclear free Model?" *The World Today,* March 1986, pp. 40-41.

Pike, John, "Anti-satellite weapons and arms control", *Arms Control Today* (Washington), December 1983, pp. 5-7.

Pincus, Walter, "Pacific Experience Shows Difficulty of Cleaning up Radiation", Washington Post, 18 April, 1978.

Redick, R. John, "The Tlatelolco Regime and Non-proliferation in Latin America", *International Organization* (Boston), Vol. 35, No. 1, winter 1981, pp. 103-37.

Robinson, "Soviet Push for Beam Weapons", Aviation week and space technology (New York), Vol. 106, May 2, 1977, p. 16.

Roff, Rabbitt Sue, "New Caledonia: Decolonization and Denuclearization on the Pacific", *Third World Quarterly,* Vol. 8, No. 1, January 1986, pp. 621-38.

Rosenberg, David, "American atomic strategy and the hydrogen bomb decision", *Journal of American History* (New York), Vol. 66, No. 86, 1979, pp. 81-82.

Smith, Gerard and Rathjens, George, "Reassessing Nuclear Non-proliferation Policy", *Foreign Affairs* (New York), spring 1981, pp. 875-94.

Soula, E., "France and the Pacific", *Pacific Monthly*, No. 9, September 1975, pp. 9-16.

Stein, Jonathan, "Anti-Tactical Ballistic Missiles – New Threat to the ABM Treaty", *Arms Control Today*, October 1985, pp. 1-16.

Thakur, Ramesh, "A Dispute of Many Colours: France, New Zealand and the Rainbow Warrior Affair", *The World Today* (London), December 1986, pp. 209-15.

Thakur, Ramesh and Gold, Hyam, "The Antarctic Treaty Regime: Exclusive Preserve or Common Heritage?", *Foreign Affairs Reports* (New York), Vol. XXXXII, Nos. 11 and 12, November-December 1983, pp. 169-86.

Weisgall, M. Jonathan, "Micronesia and the Nuclear Pacific", *School of Advanced Studies (SAIS) Review* (Washington), No. 5, Summer-fall, 1985, pp. 41-56.

Williams, Frederick, "The United States and Non-proliferation", *International Security*, Fall 1978, pp. 18-12.

Wholsetter, Albert, "Spreading the Bomb without Quite Breaking the Rules", *Foreign Policy* (Washington), Winter 1976-77, pp. 36-56.

Zedalis, J. Rex and Wade L. Catherine, "Anti-Satellite Weapons and the Outer Space Treaty of 1967", *California Western International Law Journal* (San Francisco), Vol. 1, No. 8, 1978, pp. 481-90.

Zhivkov, T., "Speech Delivered at the Ceremonial Meeting Dedicated to the 1300th Anniversary of the Foundation of the Bulgarian State", *Sofia Press Agency Release* (Sofia), 20 October, 1981, p. 27.

Newspapers and Periodicals

Atlantic News (Bonn)
Asia Week (London)
Canberra Times
Defense and Foreign Affairs Weekly (New York)

Economist (London)
Hindustan Times (New Delhi)
Indian Express (New Delhi)
International Atomic Energy Agency Bulletin, (Ontario)
Jane's Defence Weekly (London)
National Times (Sydney)
New York Times
Nucleonic Week (New York)
Patriot (New Delhi)
Sun (Baltimore)
Sydney Morning Herald
Times of India (New Delhi)
United Nations Press Release (New York)
Wall Street Journal (New York)
Washington Post
Washington Times

Index